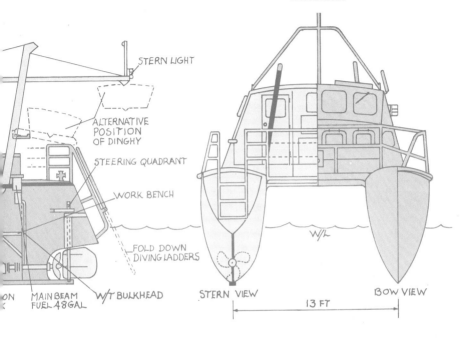

STERN LIGHT

ALTERNATIVE POSITION OF DINGHY

STEERING QUADRANT

WORK BENCH

FOLD DOWN DIVING LADDERS

ON

MAIN BEAM
FUEL 48GAL

W/T BULKHEAD

STERN VIEW

W/L

BOW VIEW

13 FT

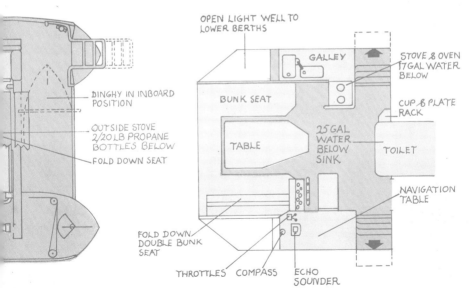

OPEN LIGHT WELL TO LOWER BERTHS

GALLEY

STOVE & OVEN 17GAL WATER BELOW

DINGHY IN INBOARD POSITION

BUNK SEAT

CUP & PLATE RACK

OUTSIDE STOVE 2/20LB PROPANE BOTTLES BELOW

FOLD DOWN SEAT

TABLE

25 GAL WATER BELOW SINK

TOILET

NAVIGATION TABLE

FOLD DOWN DOUBLE BUNK SEAT

THROTTLES   COMPASS

ECHO SOUNDER

Into the Rising Sun

Into the Rising Sun

The Voyage of the *Whai* from New Zealand
to Japan — and Back.

by

R. L. (PETER) SPURDLE

HODDER AND STOUGHTON
AUCKLAND LONDON SYDNEY

For my Mother, Wife and Sisters
on whom I have leant heavily

ISBN 0 340 16605 3

Printed and bound in New Zealand for Hodder and Stoughton Ltd, 52 Cook Street, Auckland, by Wright and Carman Ltd, Trentham.

Contents

The Count

In each of us a mad creature lurks, ready to pop out, say or do the zaniest of things. Whether they embarrass, hurt or amuse, these antics are "aberrations." Well, we had a normal crew with normal aberrations which led, in some instances, to hilarious, unpleasant or even downright dangerous situations.

So let's add another member to our crew—I will call him "the Count". He shall be blamed for the collective or individual misdeeds, the sins of commission or omission that occurred amongst us—in short, our aberrations.

Prologue

The three small islands to our left were curiously uniform in size and I banked the Kittyhawk in a gentle turn towards them. A hundred yards to the right and slightly astern Pirie slid across behind me and over to port. At 200 feet I tightened the turn and, banking steeply, we stared down at the green islets.

We were on a shipping reconnaissance off the west coast of Choiseul Island in the British Solomons. It was 1943 and the Japanese were fighting desperately to hold the New Georgia Group. The three islands had no coral shallows around them but lay on the dark blue of deep water. They were elongated and covered in thick foliage. It was awkward to fly close to them in the narrow bay because of steep hillsides and I kept an eye out for steel cables. Sometimes the wily Japanese slung them between high points to snare the unwary.

There was something definitely wrong and when up-sun of the three islands I saw it. Saw the flash of the sun on glass hidden beneath the leaves.

"Drop tanks! Line astern—go!"

The 90-gallon belly tanks fell tumbling end over end to burst open on the sea. Pirie dropped behind me as I turned away and flew up-sun to position for attack. A wide turn and

"Ninety degrees to port—go!"

We dived almost abreast towards the mystery boats.

"You take the port one."

"Roger."

And in we went in a shallow dive. The .50 calibre machineguns hammered out their deadly hail and tracers spiralled away trailing white smoke to lash the sea to foam or be absorbed in the green foliage. Ricochets could be seen caroming away to skitter across the water in leaping splashes. Leaves and branches were smashed and blown away to reveal the torpedo-boats beneath.

With steep climbing turns to avoid the jungle slopes of Choiseul we flew back down again and again, diving within feet of the sea's surface to flatten out and spray the boats. The sun shone hot into our cockpits and the saliva dried in our mouths with the excitement of the kill. No need for instructions; no need for words. We flew as one. The damn things must sink or burn soon, I thought, and I decided we would fly away for a spell and try and trap any Japs that might attempt salvage.

For some 20 minutes we scouted the coastline for more game and then returned to the attack. Fuel covered the sea in spreading iridescent swirls but there was no sign of life. Japanese gunners were probably shooting at us from under the trees along the shoreline but we couldn't care less in the thrill of the moment. At the first burst of our fire the tracers ignited the fuel and the "islands" burst into flames which ran down and spread across the water. Oily smoke roiled and billowed into the blue sky. It was time to leave—the black column and raging flames would be visible for miles and we were much too near Jap fighter dromes for comfort. We turned towards Kolombangara Island and fled the scene like naughty schoolboys fearful of punishment.

Thirty miles away, looking back over my shoulder by slewing the tail of the Kittyhawk to one side, I could see the tower of smoke like a huge exclamation mark. Kolombangara was dead ahead and in the shallows off the eastern coast Japanese flak gunners liked to bathe. We caught a few in bursts of fire before climbing for the sky and on back to our base on Guadalcanal.

Twenty-two years later I organised the *Windswift* cruise to try and recover some souvenirs of this action and visit again the scenes of youth's high adventure. It was a long journey back to this lonely spot in the Pacific—and long in years. In its fulfilment the whole pattern of my life was changed.

CHAPTER ONE

The Pipe Dream

IT WAS September, 1965. I was at Port Vila in the New Hebrides with the ketch *Windswift*, a crew member, and heartily sick of yachting. The craft I was looking at was something different and Al, the skipper, was telling me how his *Pipe Dream* came into being; how it came to this corner of the mighty Pacific.

Al was tall and gaunt, weathered by the sun and winds of the lonely wastes. His face was lined but at peace. He'd seen a vision, received a message, had been given a path to follow.

The *Pipe Dream* lay becalmed and untidy at its mooring. It was a trimaran of about 35 feet with a mottled hull, mainly white; its mast had the top third bent forward in a graceful curve, strained by some ocean gale. On the aft deck a crude plastic shower stall had been rigged and an ill-assorted trio of small outboards roosted on a cross-rail. Plastic buckets, jerrycans and cardboard cartons were piled about and washing hung limply in the air.

Al looked me straight in the eye and said:

"I was very ill; like to die and in great pain. I prayed to God that if He'd save me I would do anything he asked. Well, I was operated on; it was a very near thing. After a few months I was back at the bench" (he was a worker in an aircraft factory) "and an angel came to see me. The angel asked if I recalled my promise and said he'd come again. You know," Al remarked, "my friends nearby couldn't see or hear the angel and thought I'd flipped."

"Well," Al continued, "a week later he called again and told me what I had to do. 'Oh, no!' said I. 'Oh, yes!' said the angel.

"Of course I had no money—my operation had cleaned me out." (I could see no pun was intended, so listened seriously.) "And to get here required a boat. For weeks I worried and then I dreamed of the answer."

"Well," Al said, "I got these 4 ft diameter sewage pipes, off-cuts from the sanitary department in San Francisco, and joined them. With a ten-ton hydraulic jack I stretched one end, flattening the edges together and welded them to form the bow. At right angles to the bow, the other end was formed into the stern."

It was easy to see how simple the job had been—a gas torch, a jack and a welder. Some clamps, chisels and a sledge-hammer. Cutting two holes in the top of the hull, he'd welded on two short tube sections. These formed turrets or conning towers which, complete with circular hatches, gave access into the main hull. Crudely fitted plastic windows let in light. The two sponsons had been made from smaller pipes. Two feet in diameter and about 20 feet long, these were fastened on either side to the centre hull by three heavy steel joists sitting on steel and rubber pads (to allow a little flexing). The mast was a discarded street-light standard; the tapered steel tube made an ideal "stick".

"The rigging was being thrown in the tide," he said, "but the big-shot who was replacing it gave it to me. It was stainless steel."

Eventually Al had his trimaran, half an hour's tuition in navigation on San Francisco harbour, and was on his way. He didn't tell me what the angel had told him to do, but it took him thousands of miles to an alien way of life and many privations. On this odyssey, calling at Hawaii (by mistake) he met and married a Chinese. I heard later that he married her in both senses of the word, performing the ceremony himself—after all, wasn't he now a preacher and the captain of a boat to boot? And who could challenge the validity of this happy arrangement?

I studied the *Pipe Dream*—it had features I could appreciate. It was strong, simple and safe. When dangerous weather threatened, the crew could reef sail and batten themselves below, pulling the lids of the conning towers shut over them. It could scrape over coral reefs and shoals and never leak a drop. The inside was clean and dry. The whole ship had cost Al less than $500. But best of all was its stability. This was what all boats should have, I thought; this and no leaking seams.

For weeks now the *Windswift* had been rolling along. I'm no sailor and what I think and say about sailing craft would make a yachtie spit. But I don't care—yachties come in three main categories and all are mad!

There's the harbour sailor who sometimes stays out overnight in sheltered bays, sometimes gets caught in a blow and talks about it for the rest of his life. These I can understand—it's a pleasant sport in small quantities. Then there's the more serious buff who goes in for races, deep-sea, long-distance stuff. These people call us "stinkpots", put undersized, underpowered motors in expensive keelers and crack hardy. They scream for tows into harbour or away from lee shores when the wind is too much for them. I don't like competitive sports, bursting blood vessels and all that jazz. The idea of large crews struggling day and night, food and charts and sea water all over the place, broken sleep, wet and weary—ugh!

Thirdly there are the true yachties—nomads, who sail the lonely seas, drifting their lives away, picking up odd jobs in the oddest places. These are fascinating people with fascinating tales to tell. Unfortunately, some of them tell some fascinating tales which make it downright awkward for others following in their wake. Especially if one is hard-up and needs credit or a sympathetic ear.

We had cruised for miles and miles on the *Windswift* in flat calm using the little 2-cylinder Petter diesel. I like the rumble and beat of motors—they lull you to sleep and, as with a loud ticking clock, you get used to the noise and after a few hours don't hear them at all. With a motor vessel there is no need to huddle up, wet and miserable, in an open cockpit: rather a comfortable seat in front of a group of glittering gauges; the radio, the echo-sounder, with compass and charts to hand. This to me is the way to travel.

So I spent a lot of time dreaming my own pipe-dream. I decided on a powered catamaran—two hulls for stability and two motors for reliability. And no sails. Not one.

And so, from four months of frustration and discomfort in the *Windswift* was born the determination to do the trip again, but in my own boat, under power. The *Windswift* was, and is, a grand ketch, seaworthy and sound, but for my purposes and liking, sail was out.

I started construction of *Whai*, the 44-foot steel catamaran which was to take four years of effort and change the whole course of my life. It was built in the open at Wanganui, in the back yard of Production Motor Company. With the help of staff from my firm, two steel cylinders were made. These were of 3/16 inch steel, 25 inches in diameter and 16 feet long, each divided into two 125-gallon fuel and a 40-gallon water tank. These formed the two "keels". Placing them on wooden blocks 13 feet apart, I then built the main body of the boat up from them.

I had no plans—just the length, beam and height I judged sensible and in proportion. The bows and sterns were fabricated by a local firm (we had no rollers nor the necessary art). These were ribbed and welded, then hoisted up against the centre section to complete the hull proper.

It was a lot of work and often the cost and effort seemed too much when the going got rough. I sold my building shares, an insurance policy, increased my overdraft, took highly paid, dangerous jobs in marine salvage, and so on. More and more money was changed to steel in the fierce alchemy of the electric arc. Then there were the two Ford industrial diesels, the Paragon hydraulic gearboxes, an echo-sounder, two stoves and extra water tanks, rubber mattresses and fire extinguishers; instruments, water pumps, navigation lights and deck fittings. There seemed no end to the bits and pieces, but a very definite end to finances. It became obvious much more money was being used than was ever envisaged and that to finish it I would have to go further into debt. I decided the *Whai* could not be a toy but must be used as a tool—it would make an ideal charter boat. After all, it was designed for spearfishing and cruising the open ocean.

This meant approaching the Marine Department to have the *Whai* surveyed. I talked to the local surveyor. He eyed the skeleton of my dreams.

"The department won't like this," he said.

So I drove to Wellington to see his superiors and it went like this . . .

"I wish to have my boat surveyed for charter work."

"Yes, what sort of a boat is it?"

"Oh, a 44-foot steel one."

"Have you the plans with you?"

Long pause. "There are no plans; I'm designing it as I go—I just want to make sure the steel work will be in accordance with regulations."

"No plans!"

"No."

"We will have to have plans." (Oh, hell!)

"Well, can you let me have the necessary steel-work specifications to comply with regulations?"

Fumble-fumble and the presentation of a small booklet.

"Where are you building this boat?"

"In Wanganui."

"Then you'll have to see our resident marine surveyor there."

"I've seen him. He said I'd have to see you people in Wellington."

"Why? Is there something unusual?"

A long pause. A fly buzzed on the window, a blind cord slapped lazily. The confession. The moment of truth.

"It's a catamaran."

By the surveyor's expression I'd used a four-letter word.

"Oh? So it's a catamaran! I'm afraid we can't survey that!"

"Why not?"

"Um—er, well—."

I told a lie.

"I'm too far ahead to stop now. I must finish it. I never im-
agined there'd be any trouble—why, they use them in hundreds
overseas."

"Oh? Where?"

"Ah—er—er." Frantically my memory scrabbled around. "Er,
Hawaii, Noumea—I got my rough dimensions from one I saw
in Noumea."

"How far has it progressed? You shouldn't have started it.
We'd never have allowed it!"

Ah! A weakening.

"Well, it's well on the way. Must have spent £5,000 on it to
date."

A long silence. The fly tried to escape its crystal barrier.

"We've no way to assess it."

"What do you mean?"

"Well, a boat has to be shipshape." (And I'd always thought
that meant being tidy!) "All our calculations are based on
length, beam and depth. How wide is this—er—boat?"

"Over 18 feet."

"Lord!" breathed the chief surveyor. "How much will it
draw?"

"I don't know yet."

"You don't know! You don't know!! Have you no calculations?"

"No, I'm building as I go." Lamely, "I go by the feel of it. . . ."

"Feel of it?" The chief surveyor looked genuinely concerned.
This was something for the book. And the book by which he
lived didn't cover a situation quite like it. The book said this and
that shall be the minimum but I knew it didn't specifically ex-
clude multi-hulls.

The inquisition went on.

"Have you built boats before?"

"Er—partly."

The chief surveyor took comfort. "You realise it'll have to
pass seaworthiness tests, handling and so on?"

I drove home, my mind churning. At least it wasn't the finish;
thank goodness I had got well and truly committed before calling
in Authority. They couldn't very well condemn this out of
hand. Not if it fulfilled their construction requirements. Not if I
cried loud enough and bled all over the place.

And then *THE IDEA* was born. I'd prove the *Whai* was sound—I'd do a big trip in it. More than just a trip to the Islands. Something spectacular; a real deep-sea voyage after which the *Whai* would have to be accepted. Japan. That was it. A trip to Japan and back . . . long chains of islands with only one long hop to Noumea to worry about.

With this excitement fairly lifting me along, the miles flew past. How to finance it? If I made it a share-expenses trip I could get in money now, finish the boat and worry about the travelling costs later. I began calculating the share each crewman would need and put the word out that a trip was planned. I made rough calculations and decided about $800 per crewman was needed. The trip was to take some four and a half months and we would go from Whangarei via Norfolk Island, New Caledonia, the Loyalties, New Hebrides and then to the Solomons. From here the choice of up the west or east coast of New Guinea could be made according to the weather at the time. Through Indonesia and the Philippines, Taiwan and up through the Ryukyu chain of islands to Japan. After New Caledonia, hardly ever more than two days at sea without sighting land. This was a fair cruise—over 14,000 miles (with side journeys) but in my ignorance I based my calculations on a 10-knot cruising speed.

At last she was finished and *Whai* stood massive on her frame waiting for the transporter to carry her to the launching ramp. She'd been lined inside with fibre-glass batts, then covered with ⅛-inch marine-ply panels. The whole of the interior was sprayed with colour fleck paint then lacquered to make washing down easy. Fly spots and scratches, fish scales and squashed mosquitoes don't show—the wear, tear and detritus from the motley crews of years to come.

She has six "cabins" below, three to each hull and in the main cabin, above and across these, there is a double and single bunk. Two more bunks under a canvas canopy on the after deck double as seats during the day. So all told I can sleep 11 in comfort. In the main cabin, starboard side, is a small alcove galley with a neat little gas stove oven and twin sinks. On the other side is the helmsman's fold-down seat, engine gauges, wheel, compass, echo-sounder and radio. Charts and instruments are kept in a large open compartment under the navigation bench near to hand. On either side, short stairways lead to the cabins below. A fold-down table between the main cabin bunks forms the dining bay.

Back of the main cabin, on deck, is the small washroom and

toilet. Wastes are discharged directly between the hulls so there is no danger of flooding bilges, etc. On deck also is the stainless steel tank holding two 20-pound cylinders of propane cooking gas. On each of the transoms is hinged a fold-down ladder for skin-divers to climb aboard. With scuba racks fore and aft, spear-gun holders on the rear platform, the *Whai* is well-equipped for divers. I put an extra two-burner stove on the back for cooking crayfish and other sea foods too aromatic to be cooked inside.

The *Whai* weighs close on 16 tons, but is so rigid that by jacking up one bow she'll rock on the tranverse stern. I designed it this way. With its narrow hulls (4 foot 6 inches beam on the waterline) I expected the craft to ride easily and the water to part and give without too much wracking and twisting strain. The two main beams are made of large rectangular steel tubes 12 inches by 8 inches by $\frac{1}{4}$-inch thick. These are integrally welded into the top of each hull, fore and aft, and double as extra fuel tanks. The third crossmember is of 8-inch by 4-inch tubing and acts as an air duct to the enginerooms. This beam is tied in with the main cabin bulkhead and the two hull bulkheads which separate the cabins from the enginerooms. This bulkhead goes from the main cabin roof to each cabin floor and is pierced only by the heavy engineroom doors, rubber sealed, and the main cabin entrance.

It was an exciting day when the tractor transporter was backed between the hulls and hydraulic jacks lowered the boat on to the creaking chassis. The springs settled and with a cloud of diesel fumes the hybrid monster rolled and swayed pick-a-back from the yard. The gates had been cut down to allow the *Whai's* great breadth to squeeze through, and a traffic car, red light flashing, led the way. With friends on top fending off power and telephone cables we trundled at a frightening pace down to the Castlecliff launching ramp to catch the early tide.

At the ramp we battled with jacks and blocks of wood in a race to remove the transporter before the rising water trapped it. The *Whai* was lowered inch by painful inch on to blocks set on the concrete. Don, the foreman, walked around the bow for more wood and disappeared off the end of the ramp with a splash to flounder in deep water. There were too many sightseers to express ourselves freely, and our muttered curses were covered by the rattling of chains, thumping of wooden blocks and seagulls' cries.

The tide rose, hesitated, and the *Whai* rocked gently, still firmly fixed on the blocks under its stern. We started the motors but the propellors were only partly submerged—at least two feet more to cover. And the tide was over.

We hailed a passing launch and took on a tow. With twin streams of diesel fumes from the exhaust stacks and with the flashing propellors churning the water to foam, the *Whai* ponderously edged forward.

Suddenly, with a dip and a thump, she cleared the blocks and was free. We cast off the tow rope and, thrill of thrills, moved slowly away. Past the yard where her bow and stern sections were made, past the old slimy rockwall and past the rusting *Te Anau* wreck and into the turning basin. Here we tied up alongside a barge for a small ceremony. I cleared a place on the foredeck for my mother. Tiny and frail, but very erect, she released a bottle to swing against the chain guard between the hulls. The champagne foamed, glass tinkled. In a clear voice though tense with emotion she asked for Godspeed and safety for the *Whai* and all who sailed in her.

The ancient prayer, more felt than heard, was blown away over the river and sand dunes. Blown away by the sighing wind and soon forgotten in the call of sea birds and the shuffle of the crowd on the wharf. And suddenly I felt the deck firm and solid beneath my feet. My mother, so very happy for me, came over and we had a quick hug. The *Whai* was truly launched and committed to my care.

My wife pushed her way through the crowd milling about in the cabin. I was feeling a little confused; there was an air of unreality, noise and motion; people, perfect strangers, asked questions. I was trying to concentrate on instruments suddenly alive and with something to tell me.

"There are over 50 people on board! Robbie lost count at 50!"

I only half heard her and was frantic with the pressures of the moment. There was nothing for it but to carry on and complete this, our first cruise. We churned downstream, out between the harbour moles, and the *Whai* lifted to the ocean's swell. I turned her round and brought her back to the wharf.

And cleared everyone off. All but a few who'd worked on her, or worried with me over her, my close friends and family. The *Whai*, for better or for worse, was alive at last and far horizons stretched ahead.

CHAPTER TWO

Norfolk and New Caledonia

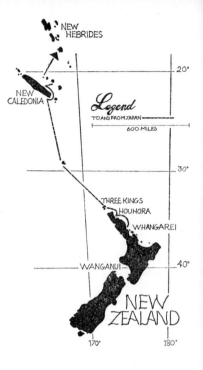

WHEN a yacht leaves New Zealand waters it must be passed safe as to equipment, hull and machinery. The skipper must satisfy the examiners as to his navigating ability and general seamanship. Now the Marine Department doesn't want to be blamed for accidents or incidents at sea or get involved with amateur navigators, small craft and hairy enterprises. So they have struck a bargain with the larger yacht clubs: these provide honorary yacht inspectors to examine boats and crews. However, because of the inordinate number of multi-hulled craft lost at sea over the years (or is it jealousy over their superior speed and comfort?) the conventional yachties have declined to survey multi-hulls.

In self-protection, the multi-hull owners have banded together and formed their own association. It was to this organisation I turned when I wanted the *Whai* surveyed. Because we were a power-only craft they turned it down—propulsion machinery was not their responsibility. I discovered that the Marine Department couldn't decline the hull and machinery examination and between a sympathetic chief surveyor in Whangarei and the good services of the Onerahi Yacht Club's honorary inspectors (for safety equipment) and their navigation examiner, arrangements were made to cope with the *Whai*, but for a time the obstacles put in my way were very real and frustrating.

With some misgivings Oram's yard agreed to pull the boat out of the drink. She wasn't the largest but was certainly the widest they'd handled. Graceful yachts, white and immaculate, edged away as the black *Whai* was winched dripping from the muddy waters. Most of the crew had arrived and we scrubbed the sides, slimy from a short charter season, preparatory to a fresh coat of anti-fouling. The marine inspector pulled on his overalls and started his inspection: fuel tanks, filters, rubber couplings, the universal joints. The kit of spares was laid out—gaskets, injectors, a complete starter motor lent by my friends at Hatea Motors, oil seals, bolts and nuts. Groceries started to arrive, cases of them, and a big medical kit, oils and greases, the thousand and one things necessary on such a long voyage to such out-of-the-way places.

Mike in the engine-room checked tappet clearances; Rafe fitted splash-shields under the main platform. Bill and Cobber helped by Wayne and Callum stripped off the two safety floats, the spear-gun and scuba racks not needed on the trip. The new 12-foot Parkercraft aluminium dinghy arrived and wooden blocks had to be made so it could be stowed athwart the rear platform. This was the Thursday before Easter and we were scheduled to sail on the Saturday.

I just had to pass my navigation—Mike had a smattering but not enough to attempt an actual test. I tried to concentrate and re-read my texts. I worried the life out of Harold Leigh. He was a practical navigator and while his method was not strictly accurate (by mercantile or naval standards) at least he could find his way around. We'd spent many a night both on his *Corsair* and my *Whai*, Harold trying to din into my lazy mind the rudiments of astro-navigation. I modified his system to my liking and had 100 forms printed—I neither trust my memory nor my accuracy and the form, properly filled in, must give the correct answer.

I called on Nigel Knight the yacht club's navigation examiner.

"Oh, so you're Peter Spurdle?"

"Yes." It sounded like a confession.

"Well, take these away and fill them in. No help now, you must do them yourself."

Man, this was something like. I scurried back to the slipway hardly believing my luck.

"I've passed, I've passed," I called, waving the forms in the air.

"What! Already? Congratulations!" The boys were relieved—we'd all been genuinely worried up till then.

I hurried down to the *Corsair* to Harold and we studied the questionnaire together.

"You can do these all right," he said.

"Yes, I'll do them now." Rustle-rustle, scribble-scribble. Doubts—a problem ambiguous. Harold called in Ivan Rolfe, another yachtie, and they argued over the last question. This could be used to my advantage so back to Knight I went.

"Well, here they are—but I can't do the last problem—to me it's ambiguous—how was it intended to read?"

Nigel studied the form. "Um—yes, I see what you mean. This is what was intended."

Sketching rapidly on a scrap of paper. . . . I tried to follow, wearing what I hoped was an intelligent look and with many a "Yes, yes" to cover my stark ignorance. At last it was over. The slightly doubtful examiner, relying on my years to provide commonsense should I become unstuck at sea, signed the navigation clearance.

On the Saturday morning we launched the *Whai*, complete with re-pitched propellors to give it the 10 knots planned. They had been 19-inch diameter by 19-inch pitch but at 2,100 r.p.m. the cruising speed was a bare 8½ knots. The new 21-inch pitch, the experts said, was what was required. Captain Farmer had arrived from Auckland to swing the compasses. We set off down the harbour to the turning basin and after an hour or so a most interesting deviation card was compiled. On 90° heading, as much as 21° East deviation was recorded. This gave me cause to curse the lazy nit who originally adjusted the compass—the crazy deviations that had caused all sorts of doubts on charter work. And he'd milked me of $12 for the job too.

We were motoring up the channel back to town to take on the rest of the supplies, clear the boat and leave for New Caledonia. This was the big moment and as we drove up on a mud-bank with a falling tide, may I be excused if the Captain Bligh in me erupted? Poor Wayne. First time at the wheel and first time up a strange, treacherous channel, he could not be blamed. This time I was nominated "Count," the first of many. By "backing and filling" I managed to reverse off the mud and we arrived later than expected, our schedule all to hell.

We took on fuel and with cheerful yells and high excitement moved out and away from the jetty. It was deep dusk and the lights of Whangarei shone across the darkening water. This was it. We had our fuel and food, our travellers' cheques and our families' best wishes. What more could we want?

The key to the sealed grog locker, of course.

The Customs man had done his job and was the last to say "bon voyage". We drank a toast to him and all authority now left behind as we slipped down the channel, past the flashing beacons, past the port installations and the twinkling lights of Onerahi. I was very tired and looked forward to an early night—the boys could take her up the coast—it was all plain sailing with lighthouses to mark the way, a silvery night and adventure ahead.

I rammed her on Snake Bank. "Count" again and in my own harbour. Some of the crew were a little thoughtful as we pulled off by the light of my red face and churned on towards the open sea. It was about ten at night as we passed the oil refinery at Marsden Point. The *Whai* glowed in the glare from the big waste-gas flame and somehow, in that eerie flickering light, all our hopes of high adventure were underlined and we sang and shouted with the joy of living.

It was 28 March, 1970, 11 minutes past 10 off Busby Head. We had 960 miles of open ocean to Noumea. I slept until dawn, which found us entering the Bay of Islands. I wanted to pick up a chart of the north of New Zealand—how this one had been missed was a mystery. We could see the Royal Yacht *Britannia* gleaming in the sunlight. Gay with bunting, she lay at anchor, a small flotilla of fisheries inspection vessels slowly cirling to keep off inquisitive small craft. A policeman on a patrol boat shouted at us to keep clear. I'm an ardent Royalist and felt hurt. I'd not disturb the Queen for anything. We toasted her in break-fast coffee laced with brandy and set off for the Cavalli Islands up the coast.

At the Cavallis Rafe and Cobber dived for scallops, but got only three. Thirty-eight gallons of fuel used so far—1.9 miles per gallon. The *Whai* was very heavy in the water. She had almost three tons of fuel on board but I decided to take on more: to top up at Houhora. Here we bought 63 gallons. Fuel at Whangarei had cost about 17 cents a gallon, at Houhora it was 23, the cheapest we would get from now on.

The seas roughened up a bit and the wind freshened from the north. To his great disgust Mike was seasick and as we checked the lashings and stowage of gear he was ragged unmercifully. North Cape and Cape Reinga slid behind us and the Three Kings Islands climbed slowly out of the haze. I was dubious about these waters, for strong currents swirl and cold mists form while you watch, even on a brilliant blue day. Here lies the wreck of the *Elingamite* and the teeming gulls whirl down from great crags and call to the drowned seamen. We anchored near a rock, and Wayne and Cobber slipped over the side to dive in the clear waters. Crayfish for supper and an octopus, too.

In darkness we set off on the long hop to Norfolk Island, navigation check-point and the duty-free shops where we hoped to get cameras, spearguns and other adult toys. This was also to be the proof of fuel economy and cruising speed. We began to combat heavy winds and rising seas. We'd been warned to expect rough water for about the first 300 miles out from North Cape, and here it was. Luckily the wind was on our starboard stern quarter and the waves helped us on in great surges.

Two nights out, the howling gale was stripping paint from the tripod mast when we rose on the top of the 25-foot swells. We learned to ignore the creaming white tops and keep our eyes towards the bow. Life was much more reassuring. To look aft was frightening as breaking seas overtook us. The albatrosses got the wind up and deserted us; we were alone.

The radio chattered of a cyclone. As we climbed each wave we could see the marching whitecaps heaving and breaking from horizon to horizon; the gale howled and flung spume against us, stinging and hard as thrown gravel. The sky had clouded over the day we left New Zealand's coast and there were no opportunities for sun shots. I allowed 2° to starboard to compensate for drift in the heavy seas and wind. I was worried—my untried navigation was shaky enough—and we had to proceed on dead reckoning only. No sun for two more days, and more by instinct and the "feel" of the boat's progress through the endless rollers I readjusted our course to only 1° compensation for drift.

We lost touch with Whangarei radio and Lou's friendly voice faded and became indistinct. Port Charles came booming in and the powerful Auckland radio kept an encouraging link with home.

I estimated we should arrive off Norfolk at about 1.15 a.m. on the 3rd. Sure enough, about 4.30 in the afternoon of the 2nd Cobber, with his wonderful eyesight, spotted Phillip Island, Norfolk's small neighbour, on the horizon, a momentary glimpse between heavy rain squalls. I was delighted and crowed and strutted about. Everyone else was surprised and delighted, too, but for different reasons. We pushed on through the squalls until about 7 p.m. when it got dark and we hove-to awaiting dawn. The wind died and the seas eased to a slow swell. The rain drifted away and the stars came out and there, fair and square in what had been our track, was a yacht drifting without lights or lookout.

Someone glanced over the stern and in the glow of the deck lights a shark swam by. In a moment we were all on deck making up shark lines. Using tinned sausage for bait we soon had a six-foot bronze whaler thrashing on the deck. It was very late before the sport palled and we went below. Two sharks landed and two more shot with rifle fire.

At early dawn pretty little Norfolk terns escorted us around the island, past the craggy cliffs and tall pine groves, as we looked for a landing spot. Norfolk has no safe all-weather wharf facilities and yachts must anchor off shore as weather permits. Ball Bay seemed the calmest and a road could be seen winding up through the trees. A runabout came along and friendly locals ferried the crew ashore. I stayed on board to check the motors and steering gear. There were fuel tanks to dip, the fuel consumption to calculate; this worked out at over two miles per gallon, so we had plenty in hand. Our speed, however, seemed to be disappointing, but there had been so many changes in throttle settings during the rough weather that only a guess could be made.

The afternoon wore on. The boys should have been back long ago, and at last two of them struggled down the steep slopes with the water jerry-cans. They had hired a "mini-moke" and leaving the *Whai* I rowed ashore. Norfolk is a fun place with dozens of duty-free shops and clubs. I bought an expensive Bulova Acutron wrist-watch for navigation to replace my underwater watch which had packed up. This unexpected expense was just one of many that cropped up and caused much worry before the journey was over. Fearful for the *Whai's* safety I was run back to Ball Bay while the others carried on to whoop it up ashore, promising an early return. There were problems—the weather could shift and Ball Bay become untenable. As the evening wore on I became increasingly upset and at last, furious, I went to my bunk and at about 11 p.m. heard calls for the dinghy.

To hell with them! Let them sober up on the beach! I felt bloody-minded and disappointed in their taking advantage of me. The yells grew louder and I turned off the cabin light and went on deck. They were flashing a car's lights at the *Whai*, and cursing and arguing among themselves. I enjoyed the moment and then, relenting, climbed in the dinghy to row ashore, only to meet Mike swimming towards me. He'd started off tight but a foot full of sea urchin spines and the lonely naked swim had sobered him.

We up-anchored and took off at 8 a.m. with blue skies and big following seas. Everyone was cheerful, sore heads and all. Even Mike stoically suffered the probing for urchin spines in his heel, which really was a mess. Ball Bay with the abandoned rental moke left on the beach merged into the hills. The *Whai* heaved and surged in the quartering rush of the seas.

Next day, the 5th, we closed down both motors and drifted quietly on the heaving seas to siphon the drummed fuel into the main tanks. On deck in the sun, a little later, and a screeching howl from below. Mike and I stared at each other for a horrified moment, then rushed madly to the throttles and shut down Big Stinky. Oh Gawd, what was that? We opened the engine-room door—everything looked O.K., no mangled steel or broken castings. Try it again, Mike. Another scream and from the gearbox of all things. The one I had overhauled. How bloody lovely. One day out of Norfolk, over 300 miles to go and the journey just begun.

It sounded like a stripped gear and we had no spares of this nature. Then I did something for which I'll forever be ashamed—rigged a "Kon-Tiki" sail, using the boathook lashed to the mast to spread a square of light canvas. We made up a "chip" log and gauged our speed at 5 knots and carried on, calculating to arrive off Noumea in the dark of the 7th. The powerful Armadee light to starboard and the glow of Noumea to port should make a safe landfall. The reefs off New Caledonia are not to be taken carelessly as numerous wrecks have proved.

Each day at 9.30 in the morning and about 3 in the afternoon I got out the sextant and clambered on to the cabin roof. Wedged against the tripod mast I'd get sun shots with Wayne taking the times. Down below I'd clear the mess table and chew pencils for inspiration, struggling with my notion of navigation.

At about 11 p.m. on the 7th we sighted the glow of Noumea, edged our way closer up the coast and hove to for the remaining hours of darkness. I decided on the Dumbea Passage as easier on one-motor entry with the wind and current on our starboard beam. The shameful sail was disassembled and hidden away for good and we anchored off Nge Island, inside the reef, to swim, freshen up and tidy the *Whai*. For Wayne and Cobber this was their first coral water dive.

We motored past the French naval base and into the Cercle Nautique's yacht basin, our yellow quarantine flag dangling from the radio aerial. The big Danforth rattled out into the mud. We'd made it—the crossing of the longest stretch of open sea we expected to encounter.

A Customs officer came on board.

"Parlez-vous Francais?"

"Un petit peu." And that was that. He couldn't speak English and my French could get me wine, women and song only. But no clearance. We gazed forlornly at each other. This was stupid. We had photos taken wearing each other's hats; we drank coffee laced with whisky; we sealed the grog locker. Partly-emptied bottles were disguised as kerosene, cooking oil, anything but alcohol, and full bottles were hidden in bunks for parties yet to come. The officer departed shaking his head and waving uncompleted documents.

An urbane policeman arrived, cool, and departed dishevelled, with all the firearms. This annoyed Cobber no end—his beloved guns rattling around in the back of a police van. He even had to count and record each round of ammunition for every weapon. We had power-heads for shark killing, but didn't declare these or their shells. Enough was enough and we rowed ashore to the cool showers and bar in the clubhouse. And to phone New Zealand for a new driving flange—a lock tab had broken off and a nut unwound, allowing the flange to float on its splines. These had been literally "machined" out clean as a whistle and so there was no drive between gearbox and propellor shaft. It was some "Count's" carelessness and I didn't mince my words.

It was much harder to find suitable invective when the wrong part arrived some days later. I was in a filthy mood. A Customs official had been particularly French and uncooperative. I'd walked for miles collecting signatures, clearances, bits of paper to release the spares so urgently needed and now this cretin said he didn't speak English. But I knew he did. So, with a smile on my face and a little bow, I explained exactly what he was and what he could do with his paper. He was in the awkward position of not being able to retract his "No Engleesh" and so, glaring furiously, he shoved the parcel over and I departed.

That night Rafe and I went to meet the three married couples flying over from New Zealand to join us for a fortnight's cruise around the coast. I was still smarting with rage and disgust over the wrong part and wasn't much concerned when Rafe decided on a haircut in a poky little Vietnamese salon. There are lots of these relics of French Indo-China in Noumea. Rafe's hair was mod and long and straggled over his collar; it was an affront to a square like me. When the barber said to Rafe, "Quelle mode desirez-vous, monsieur?" Rafe looked at me for help. I saw my chance and murmured, "Je suis son père," and, pointing to my short back and sides said, "Comme ca."

The barber clipped away and, soothed by the evening meal and grog, the unfortunate Rafe relaxed further into the chair. Ten minutes later he realised all was not as it should be and asked for a mirror.

"Christ! Look at my bloody hair! Look what he's done to me!" Tears started. I scarcely believed my eyes. Poor Rafe was genuinely upset, but in my opinion much improved.

"You'll find it much cooler in the tropics," I said to soothe him.

"You bastard," he swore. "I'll never forgive you." And with that we went off to meet the airways bus.

The next day the cruise ship *Iberia* arrived in port and hordes of perspiring camera-carrying tourists streamed along the quay to sample Noumea's fun and games. Still feeling bloody-minded and attired in what could be a local tradesman's grubby clothes, I amused myself by muttering audibly "Bloody English tourists! Bloody English tourists" as I threaded my way through the startled groups. This must have been really on the nose—most of them were Aussies!

Rafe was at the jetty chatting with some of the *Iberia's* English crew: he had an amazing facility for striking up casual friendships.

"There's a buffet lunch on board; Des here says we could go out on the boats and just queue up!"

It seemed a grand idea. With 1,500 passengers coming and going, who'd notice our little infiltration? We passed the word around and in twos and threes our crew went out to the *Iberia*, past the officers on watch, through the fancy lounges and breasted the buffet tables loaded with fantastic goodies. Poor Mike, in the 105° engineroom of the *Iberia*, was using a ship's lathe to machine the driving-flange to suit our gearbox. While we gorged ourselves in air-conditioned luxury Mike slaved below, but that night I shouted him a special meal ashore, so he didn't do too badly. I'd like to have included the cruise ship's chief engineer, but one must stop when winning.

Now we were eleven. There were, in addition to Mike, Cobber, Wayne and Rafe, the three couples from the Wanganui Underwater Club: Del and Jim Rutherfurd, Bev and John Short and Linda and Bob Mallasch, all keen divers but mostly new-comers to tropic waters. Full of enthusiasm we took off at the crack of dawn to tour the East Coast and motored down through the islands to the Woodin Passage and on around the south end of New Caledonia to the Havannah Passage. There were the lonely reefs and lighthouses seen on the *Windswift* cruise. It was a grand feeling to be on my own boat and calling the shots. That night we put into Yaté, a little harbour at the entrance to a dark and silent river. We kidded the girls about crocodiles and funnily enough no-one went swimming here. I think we frightened ourselves with our own silly nonsense.

The winds were lousy—strong and persistent. Each day we went diving but mostly in clouded water and a short chop. Not the brilliant clear blue the travel brochures blurb about. We slept at anchor in lonely sheltered bays at night and each day fished the exposed reefs where the blue of the deep waters ran up the channels and guts into the coral massif. We explored native clearings for pawpaws and bananas and bought chickens and fresh bread from isolated settlements. At Thio, a mining town, we bought cheap food at the company commissariat—no-one questioned our right and that night we had a marvellous thrash in a dockside bistro. My last recollections were being unable to eat a spaghetti dish. Later they told me some clown had upended a glass plate over my meal spread out on the table and I couldn't understand why my fork wouldn't pick up the food.

Next day we learned a lesson never to be forgotten. In New Zealand waters a favourite sport is "shoal-jumping." This is motoring quietly ahead of shoaling fish and jumping in front of them. The diver is soon surrounded by thousands of feeding fish, their eyes staring and their mouths gulping at the tiny krill fleeing in panic. This way the fighting kingfish, our favourite gamefish, are taken as they cut through the shoal to investigate us.

A shoal of bonito splashed and leaped towards the anchored *Whai* and with yells of glee we jumped into the water and swam towards the teeming horde. Out of the foam and misty surface water bonito darted, flashing silver bullets, their speed and quick-changing directions a challenge to our skill. Five of us were directly in the path of the oncoming mass when up from the gloom below five sharks flicked into view, turning and zooming towards us. It was obvious a feeding frenzy was on and we back-pedalled, facing the sharks but swimming backwards. This is awkward and slow and poor Del was left behind. We clambered aboard and puffed for a while, not proud of ourselves and each with a different excuse to offer her.

The days passed, swimming and fishing, with plenty of wine at night and good food. We shared the cooking, dishes and turns at the wheel, and after ten days returned to Noumea. One last meal and party ashore and the three couples flew back, back to winter in New Zealand, leaving us to carry on, an all-male crew. We picked up Bill and Callum, the other crew members for Japan, and John Lindsay (a carpenter on his way to a job in Rabaul), who was a good diver and coming with us for the diving.

Back through the Woodin Passage and out into the open ocean. I set course for the Loyalties, our first port of call to be Shepenhe village on Lifou Island. Lifou rose from the sea—first a haze on the horizon, then palms could be seen growing, as it were, out of the glittering water. There was no wind and just a gentle swell. We could see a lonely little church high on a wooded bluff, the Madonna's arms reaching for the sky. On the foreshore hundreds of natives were milling about—it looked like a fishing competition—what else?

There was a Customs officer here I knew, and an old friend, the director of the Royal London Society seminary to meet, so I started to shave. As I lathered up I remembered the reef off the village and hopped out to see if it were visible. Sure enough the ragged tops of coral broke the glassy surface of the bay. All six of the crew were on deck, with the Count at the wheel. I didn't recognise him in his disguise as an ordinary crew member and went back to my shave. Suddenly the *Whai* heaved up on the port side, higher and higher, until I thought we'd roll over. Shouts and confusion. Full of rage I rushed out and there we were, the port hull high and dry on the reef and the Count red-faced and stammering at the wheel.

Six hours later, when we floated off, I turned the *Whai* out to sea.

"Aren't we going ashore?"

"YOU'VE BLOODY WELL BEEN ASHORE!"

I set course for Cape Rossel, the north tip of Uvea, next island in the group.

Seven of them—all looking at women on the beach. In a way it was my fault: we'd done much the same on the *Windswift* in Espiritu Santo and I should have anticipated it.

We arrived early in the dawn light of the 29th, the low-lying island flat and grey. We edged past the creaming surf and ragged cliffs and as the sun painted the coco palms, the reef and the sea came to life in greens and blues. Flying fish hurtled from the depths and sailed away. It was hot and calm and we were going spear-fishing. The eighteen-year-old in me laughed and flexed with delight—we were going fishin'. Happiness is clear water, a powerful speargun and good diving buddies. We anchored 50 yards off Turtle Island and slipped overboard.

The water here is about 78 degrees and teems with fish. Big barracuda arrive, gaze coldly and move off. Turtles browse among dead coral branches, worrying at some tidbit hidden in the spiny rubble. Little coloured fish flick in and out of the coral forests and big blue and green parrotfish gnaw for the succulent polyps, the broken fragments of their limestone houses falling to the bottom. Disturbed, the parrotfishes swim away, pectoral fins sculling in quick jerks and trailing clouds of coral debris pouring out of their rear-ends, for all the world like a topdressing plane in action. Crinoids wave their fronds, some glittering green, others black and gold or dusky red; giant clams breathe quietly on the bottom, their serrated jaws open to the slow current.

And always the shark, that nuisance of the sea. Sneaky, stupid, inquisitive, slow or lightning fast; as unpredictable as Jersey bulls and eternally hunting. More nonsense is written about the shark than any other sea creature. Mike and I were used to them as we had seen hundreds at Minerva Reef, had swum amongst them and killed quite a few with power-heads and conventional spears. You learn to disregard them yet not to entirely ignore them. They are predictable inasmuch as if you see them first your chances of trouble are almost nil—providing you don't do something stupid—like splashing around or making sudden movements, or shooting fish or teasing them.

We were lazing back on the *Whai* when a small blue runabout arrived. A gendarme stood up, stern faced, and two black policemen sat grinning in the cockpit.

"Bon jour," I called. "Parlez-vous Anglais?" Always best to get in first with a smile. We were 15 miles from the police post but, all over the world, there was the well-developed nose for free grog.

"A leetle. Where from are you? What are you doing?"

"We are New Zealanders on our way to Japan."

"I must see passports."

With a bump they drew alongside and we started to fill in the everlasting forms. We all had a beer and one of the native police was induced to show us where to find crayfish. With borrowed goggles and flippers he led the way and soon we knew on what type of shoreline the Melanesians find the elusive tropic delicacy.

The day well spent, we set off for Wasaudie and the little "hotel" in which I had had trouble when on the *Windswift*. Some of the boys rowed ashore to book a meal for later on when it was dark enough for me to approach.

The Indian proprietor served bowls of soup—he stopped abruptly when he saw me.

"I've seen you before!"

"Ah yes, five years ago. We've come again, your food is so good."

Flattered and forgetting, the little man flashed his gold fillings and I breathed again. A dusky young woman wearing an apron looked out from the kitchen. A prettier one than last time—he certainly had deserved better luck with his kitchen staff.

We left early for Beautemps-Beaupré—the loveliest of all the Loyalties. We headed straight out across Uvea's big lagoon and through the gap between Anemata and Ronde Islets—30-odd miles to go. Beautemps is about one mile long by half a mile wide. Perhaps 30 feet high and covered with dense jungle and fringed with pandanus and coconut palms. Here are sharks galore, turtles, splashing mullet and giant salmonee. Here coral niggerheads stand up from the white sand in encrusted tiers, showing brown from the surface against the viridian and azure sea. Hundreds of soot-black flying fox (or fruit bats) flapped and screeched against the blue sky—these were newcomers—there were none five years earlier.

We rowed ashore. "Come with me—leave the others," I whispered to Mike. It was mean but everyone was happy, examining the strangely new things along the beach and the jungle's sombre fringe. Mike, however, didn't follow—he was carried away by the immediate host of photogenic material, the hermit crabs in their thousands, the huge spiders hanging on tennis-court nets strung across shady draughty gaps. Big hornets, their red legs dangling and ready to grab a careless fly, gave us cause to shiver even in the sun's hot glare.

I knew another beach, to windward, where flotsam and jetsam was stranded. Here Jack Nightingall, skipper of the *Windswift*, had found a beautiful Japanese float; here Mark had found a perfect chambered nautilus shell, so hard to come by. There could be only one or two floats, I reasoned, and certainly not enough for all. Sure enough there was a float, and a small, broken, native canoe; a hundred nautilus shells, all imperfect, and dozens of carapaces from the porcelain crayfish.

On this evening the numbers of sharks encountered spoilt the spearfishing. With regret we left the lonely isle. Many years ago it was inhabited—the little cemetery with crude wooden crosses is being smothered by the creeping spinifex and prickly bushes, but in my mind I'll always see the dark jungle and sunken waterholes, the scuttling coconut crabs, blue and grey, in the roots and shadows. I'll feel again the beating sun and hear the surf pounding on the outer reef. Beautemps!

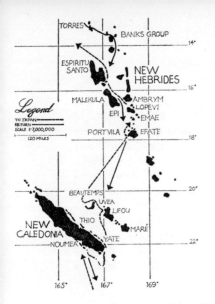

CHAPTER THREE

The Solomons:
Debris of a War

I DON'T know where the hell we are. I haven't the faintest clue.

We should have seen Efate, first of the New Hebrides Islands, an hour earlier. Back to the chart, to the lying figures and bewilderment. It was evening and I dared not continue—too few lighthouses and too many reefs. Dark overtook us with no land in sight. We hove-to for the night.

About 12.30 a.m. a ship came up fast off our stern. We fired up the donkeys and headed towards her. I hoped to stop her and establish our position. We shot off a green flare and the ship slowed down, blinked a searchlight at us, then altered course and hared off. Now what the devil was that about? I don't know what a green flare signifies but using a red signal might have been a bit drastic. I decided to follow—it seemed as likely a direction as any, and in the dawn's grey light there it was—Efate. We rolled past Devil Point and into the deep bay of Port Vila, capital of the New Hebrides.

Vila is a quaint place built on a tree-covered hillside overlooking the big bay with Irriki Island, home of the British resident commissioner, standing a quarter of a mile off the foreshore. Part French, part British, the New Hebrides are conjointly mismanaged by what is called a condominium, better known locally as the Pandemonium. Here you can be arrested by police in pairs, one of each nationality just for luck.

We motored slowly between the harbour marker buoys and over the shallows, to anchor off an old friend's place. As the pick rattled down, the Discombe kids erupted from their waterside home, clapping their hands and screaming with excitement. It had been two years since Reece, Jean and the girls had stayed with us and seen the *Whai's* skeletal beginnings in Wanganui. We had a dreadful thrash ashore at Rossi's Hotel and next day a verbal dressing-down from Jean for the bad language used as crew-members fell off the gangplank into the water. Two of the worst offenders put themselves to work cleaning her car in contrite self-punishment.

Reece Discombe is an Island character. Not one of the old school of rum-soaked hard cases—Reece doesn't drink or smoke —but a very much with-it modern. He has photographed for *National Geographic* and *Paris Match* and discovered many wrecks, the most famous being the *Astrolabe* and *Boussele* of Comte La Perouse, the great French navigator and explorer, who made an ill-fated expedition of discovery in 1788, and foundered on Vanikoro Island in the Santa Cruz Group. For his exploits Reece was made an officer of the Ordre National du Merite (the civilian equivalent of the Legion of Honour) and rewarded with some 160,000 francs from the French Government. He has dived for salvage from all manner of wrecks and is an authority on early local history and underwater photography, being one of the first to use Cousteau's aqualung in the Southern Hemisphere.

"All you bloody yachties are the same." (Reece talking.) "Bludgers!"

And bludge we did. What are friends for, particularly one with a motor garage, tools and transport? Especially one with a doll wife who can really cook and who made us so very welcome?

Reece took us diving—we wanted to find the wreck of a Sunderland flying boat sunk in the bay. It had torn out its bottom on the jagged coral while taking off for Santos. This we couldn't locate. But Callum recovered the ship's bell off the long-lost *Resolution*, a trading ketch, sunk in 1946.

On the 7th we left Vila with shaking hands and aching heads. On board we had a great, ugly gas heater to be delivered to the Rollands on Emae Island, about 50 miles north of Efate, from their son in Vila. This elderly French couple were charming but the evening of their days was rapidly turning sour. The old man's physical strength had gone and the natives were getting restless. In the early days a swift boot or an iron fist kept them in line, but now rot had set in—a Court case against some of the tribe's young men for cattle-stealing had been thrown out and now the old man's authority was all gone, stock were being butchered and no work done. We were to find this sort of unrest right up through Melanesia.

The wind, about 10 knots, was behind us and the seas became flecked with little white crests as we motored on past Epi Island and past Lopevi the volcano. Lopevi smoked and sooty grit drifted over us as we skirted the lava and ash slides along its rugged coast. Trees, bleached white by the poisonous gases, stood lone and stark on the slopes. We went past Paama Island lying hot and hazy, the day growing stifling as the wind dropped. These islands are sombre and silent. Dull green jungle covers their slopes and blue smoke drifts thinly through the leaves marking lonely villages. There is a secretive brooding air, a watchfulness, as if from under the trees dark eyes see again the violent scenes of yesterday—the blackbirders, the massacres, the burning boats.

On one of the islands, in the deep valleys far from the sea, human heads can still be bought and the devil gods of ancient times live again at night when Christian veneer cracks and gives way. The isolated natives of today are shy and keep to themselves in their outlying villages. Leading to one village of some 200 souls we found a track through the bush. Here and there it had been paved with river stones—adulterers are punished by being given so many yards to cover. What a great idea. We could have a four-lane highway from Auckland to Bluff in no time at no expense to the taxpayer.

In the larger towns where the white man sells liquor and movie violence, the natives are becoming arrogant and pushy. They don't need higher education to resent bitterly the difference between their dollar a day to pay and the selling of their time at a dollar an hour. Or two or three, as I found when I had to pay for work done on the *Whai*.

Ambrym Island, with its five volcanoes, rose out of the sea and we followed its western coast up to Craig Bay. We anchored at sundown. We'd had some excitement catching tuna from shoals working the outer reefs. We lost one to a shark which flashed through the melee and took it cleanly off the hook.

The boys rowed ashore taking a tuna as a present for the mission tucked among the coconut palms. Rafe, silly clown, gave the fish to the first adult native he saw and empty-handed we asked the priest for fresh water for our tanks and for any bread he could let us have. He was a very small chap, about 5 feet, gentle and kind. He had lived some 35 years in a simple hut all alone and about 150 blacks were his only companions. Now and again the *Hip Chow* a small copra boat called; now and again his bishop, or a medical team on inspection. We drew 15 gallons of water from the church well. This was the first time we'd had "holy water" on board and it went well with the evening's sundowners.

Navigation in these waters is simple in a power boat. You just decide on the hour of arrival and work backward to set your hour of departure to make it come true. This particular night I took a stupid chance for it was pitch black with no moon and a narrow entrance. We crept in to Luganville, on Espiritu Santo, past reefs glowing with eerie phosphorescent fire while lights from natives' huts and the lonely beacons of kerosene lamps in planters' windows drifted past. We got out the spotlight and in its powerful beam garfish and mullet jumped and skittered over the ebony water.

We were relieved and pleased to tie up alongside the trader *Konanda* against the wharf and savoured the smell of dried copra, hanging sweet and tangy. It was about ten p.m. and the bars of Luganville were still open. John, Mike, Rafe and I went walkabout to try the local brew and the others decided to wait for daylight. First was Carmen's Bar. The last time I'd been there it had been shut—closed because of a killing; now it was going full bore, the juke boxes howling and the natives, all men, dancing together or leaning stupified against the bar. Some cold beers and off to the Tahitian Club a few doors along. The friendly one-legged parrot of my earlier visit had died and the decor had changed. To the others it was fun, but to me the clinking of glasses, the pop and hiss of opening beer-cans brought back other memories.

It was hot and dusty—a thousand trucks and jeeps drove past bumper to bumper. As a Yank said, "The whole world and his brother" were just motoring around in a cloud of dust, and I was trying to get drunk. It was '43 and Espiritu Santo, a French possession, was the staging post for the American thrust against the Japanese who were consolidating in the Solomons further north. We were flying Kittyhawks off a strip at Turtle Bay. Most of them had one or more instruments u/s (unserviceable). The previous night one of my best friends had crashed and died in the sea—and with blood in my eye I had entered the instrument-bashers' workshop. Here they were—repairing watches, encapsulating coins in plastic and making wrist straps and cigarette lighters from aircraft aluminium for sale to the souvenir-crazy Americans. Enraged, I spoke out:

"Last night one of our best pilots was killed. I believe he hadn't enough instruments for night flying and here you bastards are, repairing Yanks' watches. You bloody useless parasites!"

In the startled silence I turned and left, shaking with rage.

Next day the C.O. asked me to apologise! That would be the day! No, I can't forget Santos and drowning my bitterness and sorrow along the same dusty street.

"Oh yes," said Bucketmouth. "The *Coolidge* is about half a mile down the channel, just off the rubbish-dump. I've dived on it often."

We listened carefully—this was to be one of the big dives of the trip; one I'd looked forward to for years. Reece had dived here and the Gallagher brothers from New Zealand. The *President Coolidge* was a fully-laden 33,000-ton liner converted to a troopship. A U.S. boat, she'd hit some of their own mines and had sunk in the channel not a mile from Luganville. Two buoys mark the liner's grave.

An oil slick stained the greenish sea and escaped fuel stank in the still air. We dragged a grapnel to catch on the wreck's hull, put on our scuba gear and in pairs climbed down the ladders over *Whai's* sterns. Ducking under the oil film, Bill, Callum and I finned down and at about 30 feet passed through the thermocline and into the cooler waters of the deep. There it was. Huge beyond belief. She lay partly on her side. We could see about 100 feet along her deck with the bulk of the big ship vanishing into the green, misty distance. Small mortar bombs and 50-calibre ammunition lay scattered across the coral-encrusted plates and sand. Big salmonee and groper lazed past stanchions and beams, and huge silver and green caranx circled the flak nests with their rusty guns pointing at crazy angles. A long ragged gash split the starboard side near the bow. The *Coolidge* lay with her forecastle about 70 feet beneath the surface. Black oil seeped from cracks and floated away up to the surface in twisting gobbets, to spread and spread in an iridescent film. Even after 27 years she still bled, with thousands of tons of fuel oil yet to escape.

On we swam, down past the bridge, with its gaping ports, past the empty davits and wreckage of ventilators and yet more gun mountings. The rotting ropes and rusting cables of escape nets still hung limply from the upper decks. At over 200 feet the huge stern lay exposed, the shattered propellor hubs shorn bare by explosives of the massive bronze blades. These had been salvaged just the previous week by an Australian and New Zealand team operating from the *Pacific Seal*, a 60-foot salvage boat.

Next day we cruised to where the *Seal* was working on the wreck of the *U.S.S. Tucker*, a destroyer also sunk by the har-

bour protection mines, so carefully laid and so carelessly mis-
charted. Or vice versa. There she was, spread out over the bottom in tangled masses of twisted metal. Stainless steel bulkhead
doors lay about and the big turbines were split open like melons
with the blades clustered like seeds around the rusting cores.

The *Tucker* lay in about 70 feet of water on the almost clear
patch of sand. A strong current flowed. The descent was made
hand over hand down a buoy rope and then over the corroded
decks and through gaping steel caves. Small dead fish lay scattered in the chambers of the ruptured hull—casualties of the
blasting for copper and bronze.

John Lindsay was enchanted by the carefree existence of these
jaunty divers and left us here—the carpentry job in Rabaul
easily exchanged for $80 per week and all the diving he could
take. We were sorry to leave him behind, a good diver and
companion. Last seen he was chatting up the pretty island girl
who lived aboard, cook and skivvy for the rough-and-ready
crew.

We had about 900 miles to motor to Honiara, capital of the
Solomons. I decided to go direct to the southern tip of San
Cristobal Island and then up through the group to Guadal-

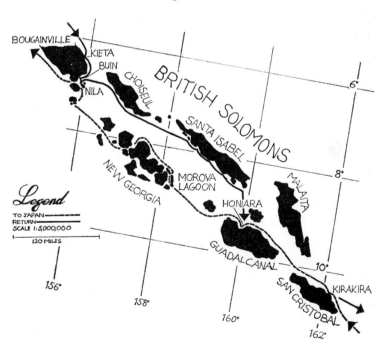

canal. We could dive at the Santa Cruz and Banks Islands on our return journey. The *Whai's* cruising speed was established at a flat 7 knots—a serious blow to our schedule and the cause of many changes of plan. But the fuel economy was excellent; the two 67 h.p. Fords were pushing us along, all 16 tons of us, at about 2½ miles per gallon. This worked out at under 3 gallons per hour total for both these rugged little engines.

The *Whai* gently rocked over the lonely sea. It was stifling hot; the heat seemed to suck all oxygen out of the air. We took it in turns to climb down the stern ladders and get towed along in the wake, the bubbling water tugging lustily at us and the roar of the compressed bow waves rumbling down between the hulls.

I was having trouble sleeping, was tired out and feeling queazy. How marvellous. At home a chap could buy grog, get stoned every night, rot his liver out and be a charge on the State. Yet I couldn't buy sleeping pills of any useful strength for our medical kit. It had been an extraordinary amount of trouble to secure morphia in case of gross injury with unbearable pain. Sure it had to be the 13th and Cobber very sick; scratching and itching all over, eyes sore and forehead puffy. I got out the "Ship Captain's" medical book—the book with the morbidly fascinating coloured pictures of foolish seamen's horrid bits and pieces.

"Well, Cobber, I think you've got heat exhaustion and we'll have to wrap you in a sheet and throw buckets of water over you! Pump up a lilo and put it on the rear seat. It doesn't matter if it gets wet, and you'll be cool there."

Cobber scratched and scratched; his palms, the soles of his feet, and around his torso.

"God! It's almost bloody unbearable," he groaned. Cobber was tough. For him to complain like this it must be serious. I asked Mike to get his symptoms from the beginning and I studied the radio form for calling medical assistance. Mike came into the cabin with a paper for my information. It read:

Medical Bulletin No. 1—13.5.70

Place: ? 13 degrees South 165 deg. East—to be taken with a salt
   tablet.
Vessel: Yes.
Speed: No.
Patient: Cobber, not very.
Symptoms: Complained of a headache on Sunday morning—this
   was isolated from any other complaint at the time. On Tues-

day he complained of itching when on watch; at 5 a.m. he became more distressed. There is a slight swelling of the lips and a puffiness of the face. The area of irritation seems to follow a pattern accompanied by a red rash and small weals up and down the body, legs and arms.

Treatment: 12.5.70. There was a prayer meeting on the rear deck at midnight. 1300 hours 13.5.70: he was given a mild saline solution to drink and sponged down in fresh water after which he was wrapped in a wet sheet.

Prognosis: The outlook is extremely bleak and he may be scratched from the human race. At least he appears to be trying to.

Captain: Spurdle the Terrible.

Date of Burial: ?

Position of Burial: ?

M. Robertshawe, M.D., V.D.

We tried all night on every band on the radio but got no answer and with Cobber shivering and scratching we called into the little settlement of Kirakira on the south-east coast of San Cristobal. This is a Government station and beautifully laid out. The resident doctor was a very pleasant Scot and quickly took charge of our patient.

"No, I haven't been with a woman. Sure I'm sure!" Cobber laughed wryly. At last it was decided he had an allergy and I personally think he must have received a jellyfish sting while hanging over the stern because he was the only one affected like this during the entire trip. With Cobber pumped full of medicines and armed with a chit for the general hospital in Honiara, we took off.

Honiara turned out to be a delightful spot. Lord knows how much the British Government is pouring into these islands. Aussies cynically say the assistance will go on "until the geological survey is completed" and if nothing valuable is found then the natives will be granted self-government. In town the grass verges along the tree-shaded roads were all shorn close by machete-swinging natives and sign-boards mark the ebb and flow of the battles so bitterly fought by the Americans and Japanese. This was the turning point in the drive south by the enemy.

We hired a taxi and drove out to what had been Fighter Two, an airstrip the New Zealand fighter squadrons had flown from. It was being turned into a golf course but standing on the sun-scorched grass I heard again the roar of powerful engines, saw again the coral dust swirling in the air around taxi-ing planes, saw again the flash of sun from shining wings and canopies as the squadrons wheeled above the feathery palms, before setting off on their rendezvous with death. The motors' drone and the dust cloud turned into a truck, a concrete mixer and a construction gang. The spell was broken.

"Have you been with a woman?" Lady Doctor at the hospital talking.

"No," said Cobber. (He was speaking the truth.)

"Are you sure you haven't been with a woman?"

"Yes," said Cobber, quite expecting the next thing to be a "short-arm" inspection.

What had he got if it wasn't an allergy? The doctor, mistaking Cobber's embarrassment for evasion, chanced her luck and repeated the question for the third time. Redfaced and furious, Cobber answered in the only way left to him.

"NO, I HAVEN'T HAD A BLOODY WOMAN!"

When he came back to the boat we were all very thoughtful. We had seen Cobber's distress, his puffed face, red and white weals and knew of the low corpuscle count. It was enough to turn a man off sex, if this sort of thing could happen.

In Honiara, too, Bill and Cobber got a small chart of the Pacific and calculated that we were weeks behind schedule. Our policy had to change from dawdling along, amusing ourselves; we really had to press on. We refuelled; 200 gallons; took on water, fresh vegetables, groceries and went to the Hotel Mendana for the Friday night smorgasbord and barbecue. A fabulous meal—all we could eat for $1.50!

It was as hot as Hades and we took salt tablets and hung over the *Whai's* sterns for relief. The weather was fantastic, day after day of flat calm. Nights we inflated lilos and slept on deck, on the cabin roof, even on the net between the bows. As we slipped through the still waters leaving a trail of phosphorescence behind, the constellations slowly changed and the Southern Cross dipped under the horizon. We sailed up through the famous "Slot" past the Russell Group and entered beautiful Morova Lagoon at the southern end of the New Georgia Group. This is a huge area dotted with islands, reefs and sand bars.

With our large-scale charts and the reflections of the clouds on the water, I found I couldn't navigate with safety. Slowly we edged over to the seaward islands for a dive. The spearfishing was disappointing but there were shoals of small tuna and bonito.

At dusk we were met by a small aluminium dinghy leaping in the slight jobble. The boatman was Chinese and drenched with spray. He shouted at us to follow as there were dangerous reefs ahead. Gratefully we kept in his wake and were led through a winding passage to moor against a copra trader alongside a rickety wharf. It was the site of a timber mill of all things— native hardwoods were being sawn in a primitive set-up. The elderly Australian couple who managed the enterprise had a charming home with wide verandahs on which they entertained us to a rice meal cooked by our Chinese friend. Next day we dived in the deep Lumalina channel. There were big fish but the swift current made the going hard. The *Whai* swung to and fro, and I feared she'd drag her anchor. We set off up the coast. We motored all that day and night with stiff winds also pushing us along.

In the early morning the bulk of Kolombangara lay dead ahead and we skirted close under its jungle-covered slopes. White cockatoos with pale yellow crests flew screaming at our approach. On our way up the Kula Gulf the mists and clouds slowly cleared to expose towering mountains. There were the shallows where Japanese gunners used to bathe. Kahili Aerodrome, a secondary target, used to be on the flat ground ahead of us. The channel dividing Arundel Island on our left from Kolombangara narrowed and we were gliding along in flat calm water with bushclad shores pressing in on either side.

I wanted to see Kahili from the ground—a dozen times I had escorted American bombers that diverted to scatter and waste their loads around Kahili in preference to the dangerous 'dromes on Bougainville. I managed to get a lift up to the big Unilever timber mill and from there to the old airfield. The ground was churned with bomb craters, filled with scummy water, and rusting Japanese trucks festooned with creepers lay hidden under the dense net of jungle. The mill manager told me he had relocated the overgrown airfield only by survey and confirmed that it had been used as an emergency strip by the Japanese. There were a few plane wrecks, but the remarkable jungle growth and boggy ground made exploring almost impossible.

We anchored in a small, sheltered bay off Vella Lavella Island and were welcomed by the natives, who crowded around, all white teeth and shiny black skins. Not only were we a great novelty but probably one of the first groups of New Zealanders to visit them since our men drove out the Japs in '43. At 10 o'clock that night we left for Mono Island in the Treasuries. Here again we got a great welcome and were taken to the airstrip on Stirling Island where, in the gloom of dense jungle, smashed American aircraft were piled. A Lightning fighter lay spread-eagled across the fuselages of two Dauntless divebombers, while the gun turret from a B25 was crushed beneath. Rusting machineguns in groups were still locked together in the remains of their turrets. Over all was an eerie rustling stillness.

Nila next! We'd been instructed at Honiara that this was the port of departure and here we had to "sign out" of the British Solomons. We found a little jetty in front of a grassy compound; it was obviously a large church settlement and a nun came down to greet us. I asked if there were any war relics around and very diffidently she said there were a few planes. A few! We were taken to at least a dozen on the edge of the village—the fuselages of small float biplanes. There was lots of horsing around filming one another climbing in and out of the cockpits and acting "honourable pilots committing hara-kiri!" to the glee of the mission kids. We found out there were four-engined bombers and a complete floatplane sunk in the channel—almost too good to be true.

That night two of the sisters and a couple of "volunteer service abroad" tradesmen came on board for a small social. We were dumbfounded at the amount of Scotch tucked away by the nuns. Nevertheless we learned great respect for them, these selfless women who give over their whole lives to practical Christianity.

During the voyage our crew had had many arguments over the influence of the various churches in the islands. All manner of whites—traders, businessmen, plantation-owners—had aired their views and there was a wide divergence of opinion. I think the sight of big, and I mean really big, churches of different denominations vying for souls from the same small village upset us most. How confused the natives must be.

If the use of church money in the past was misguided the funds of today are spent on worthwhile practical services—hospitals, schooling, visiting teachers and medical teams.

That night Billy came and stood shyly in the shadows on the wharf. He was small, aged, and bony, crowned with a shock of frizzy hair and in his arms he cradled an ancient 12-gauge shot-gun battered and rusty. One of the sisters saw him and so we found a guide for crocodile hunts. His method was simple and direct—to cruise along the narrow channels and shallow mangrove reaches in a canoe. With a powerful torch he would sweep the shores and crocodile eyes reflected the torch's glare in glittering sparks of light.

Billy was without batteries. Could we help him? In a trice the 12-foot dinghy was launched and the little Seagull fuelled up. Bill, Callum and Cobber grabbed rifles and, with Billy sitting astride the bow, they were off into the darkness. The outboard's puttering died away and the party was over. Next day, the nuns promised, a guide would be found to show us the naval guns mounted on the hill at the back of the mission. This had been a Japanese fortress and flying-boat base with thousands of supporting troops. The village's excellent Jap-built water-supply was piped down from the hills. It was the only useful legacy from the war.

We heard the croc. party come banging on board groaning and cursing the pesky outboard. They'd gone for miles up a winding creek and the motor had packed up. Long before they had paddled half the distance back the torch batteries were exhausted and mostly by "Braille" they'd fumbled their way home. Billy was downhearted and wandered off to his hut in disgust. A crocodile skin would have meant a lot of trade tobacco, more shotgun ammunition and batteries for his beloved transistor radio.

Daylight woke us in two aching groups—one with heads, the other with muscles. On the wharf a crowd of Melanesians milled about—it was too early for school or work and here in the *Whai* the outside world had materialised. There were ladders to climb and a net to bounce on. There were portholes to peer in and strange rites like shaving and white man's cooking to watch. A grizzled native introduced himself as our new guide and off we went, sandals on, hats and cameras. Kids of all sizes and shades hopped and skipped and jumped around us.

As we walked single file through the tall kunai grass and across a clearing our guide pointed out the crater where two days before a mission gardener had lit a fire. A bomb, or more likely an old shell, had exploded and he was lucky to escape with his life and not just loss of hearing. Scattered up the tree-covered slopes of the low promontory above the village we saw the debris of war. An old helmet rusted wafer-thin, the remains of a rifle, several shells with the copper driving-bands grooved as if they'd been shot at the hillside and become exposed with the passage of years. Under a jacaranda tree the blackened remains of a truck lay—its gaping doors and windshield frame supporting webs which glittered with dew. Coloured spiders, big as mice, hung on strengthened pads of web. The undergrowth grew thick and the native boys laid about them with flashing cane knives.

"Snakes?"

"Yes, Masta."

"Big ones?"

"Yes. Black fella all buggered up along bite!"

The top of the ridge was honeycombed with trenches and pockmarked with craters. The first gun located was a 4-inch naval rifle with a heavy steel cupola to protect the gunners. Rusting 44-gallon drums full of coral sand formed the revetments and command posts. Storage shelters invited exploration but the fear of spiders and centipedes and other crawling horrors kept us out. We saw about five large guns, including a multi-barrelled anti-aircraft cannon.

Back at the *Whai*, sweaty and tired, we got our gear ready for diving on the sunken aircraft.

"It's just off this pier," and Sister Francisca, "and the four-engined plane about 200 yards down off that little hut."

Cameras and spear-guns, snorkels and masks, flippers and knives—the kids on the wharf were enthralled. In two minutes we located our first Jap plane—a small, low-winged monoplane complete with floats, sitting on clean bottom sand in about 25 feet of water. The Red Sun of Japan painted on the wings and fuselage was still clearly visible. The starboard float had been twisted under the fuselage and the propellor was missing. Otherwise the reconnaissance plane was almost complete. This must be the rare model a wealthy Canadian hoped to recover. One of the nuns had shown us photos of a Zero fighter salvaged from hereabouts by this businessman-adventurer. He had actually taken it back home and by cannibalising the wrecks of a dozen old planes, had got it flying.

Mike eased himself into the cockpit. We took a few photos of each other swimming around the encrusted sides. Then off to find the big plane. We swam over the crumbling chassis of trucks complete with heavy winches now covered in pretty corals. Lion fish with their gorgeous plumed fins and deadly poisonous spines hung motionless in their caves of useless metal. We drifted over clear sand and skirted the coral reef edge. Looming out of the blue surface haze ahead was a large brown shape stretching down into the deepest water below. It was an aircraft wing—terrific. It must have had a wingspan of 100 feet or more. One outer motor and wingtip had broken off but the main bulk of the plane was complete. The fuselage looked huge, magnified by the water. It was a flying-boat sitting on the bottom at about 30 feet. We found that we could stand on the broken end of the wing with our head and shoulders clear of the water.

We explored the wreck for an hour. There was so much to see and do—the twin joysticks were locked solid by corrosion but the seats and rudder-pedals were there and it was an eerie feeling to sit at the useless controls and look through the windscreen's empty frame. Brown surgeon and little striped zebra fish circled in the main cabin and a beautiful little spotted stingray rose from its bed in the mud on the bombardier's seat to glide down and out through a jagged rip. Looking through the navigator's port I could see the two starboard motors with the streamlined struts supporting their great weight. We left the old carcase dragging along all sorts of useless souvenirs.

On the *Whai* we found the local Customs officer, a Melanesian, perspiring in his official clothes. He was completely confused when he found the grog locker broached and the seals broken. This was not allowed but no one had told him what to do in such an event. He wouldn't have a drink and he wouldn't leave— just stood there on the after-deck in lonely perplexity pursing his lips and muttering. Wearying of the delay, I started the motors and he was galvanized to action. He signed the clearance papers and we were off—off to New Guinea.

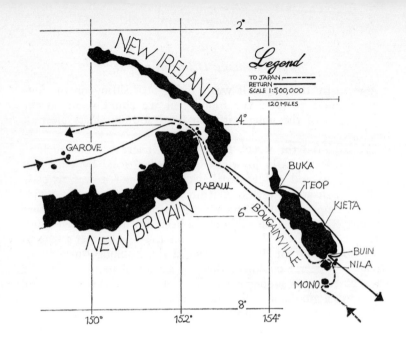

CHAPTER FOUR

To the Heart of Micronesia

THE WEATHER was glorious as we churned down the Nila
Channel and out across the bay towards Balalae Island. Balalae
was one of the main Japanese aerodromes in the Solomons. The
nuns of Nila told us that there were Betty bombers and lots of
trucks scattered in the jungle, but we were to beware of ticks—
bush typhus was possible. We slipped between coral niggerheads
into the green and blue shallows of a little bay to anchor on a
sandy patch 100 yards off the palm-lined shore. It was a dreamy,
languid place, no wind, no sound of surf. Just the rustle of palm
fronds and the cooing of bush doves.

There were a number of trails leading into the bush and after
several false starts we found one that looked as if it could go
somewhere. In the shadows it was stifling, the humidity enervat-
ing. There was no movement other than motes dancing down
stray sunbeams that managed to filter past a hundred branches.
An occasional butterfly flitted among the hanging vines and
spiders, still and watchful, rode their swaying webs, strung between "cutty grass" and supplejack. We felt like whispering in
the silence of this lonesome place. Only doves called mournfully
to each other and the leaf-strewn soil squelched around our
sandals and between our toes.

We struggled on for hours. We found the rusting wrecks of dozens of trucks, a mobile crane, two road-rollers. We found thousands of neatly-stacked Japanese beer bottles and a few badly dented belly tanks, but of Betty bombers there was no sign. Huge craters pockmarked the jungle floor—the big 1,000-pound bomb holes contrasting with the smaller 500-pound craters. Some were filled with green-scummed water and the twisted trunks of fallen palms lay in rotting hurdles over which we scrambled. Every now and again someone would be bitten by an ant—huge red devils with pincers like hot needles.

We came on bunkers, black and forbidding, and at long last the airstrip proper. It was recognizable by the wide aisle of smaller trees growing up since the war. After 25 years or more the hungry, searching roots had succeeded in breaking down the crushed coral surface of the airstrip and the stunted trees competed with saw-tooth grass and vines for a place in the sun.

We were glad to stumble back to the little bay with its clean sand, open sky and clear waters.

I had intended to go up the east coast of Bougainville Island and then over to the New Britain, but a wind came up from the east and we retraced our route past Nila and up the west coast to be clear of land before dark.

At the eastern end of the Gazelle Peninsula, Rabaul is reached through a winding bay with old volcanoes rearing out of the deep water. We motored past Vulcan, the new volcano which rose from the sea between the wars, skirted wharves and docks and the waterfront drive, to drop anchor off the yacht club. This was our first taste of Australian "colonization" and we were impressed with the bustle and boom atmosphere.

Rabaul is fascinating—tree-lined streets and quaint shops in an arc around the bay, with towering hills as a backdrop. The Customs people enraged me by demanding about $2.50 port dues. These were to cover all the Australian territories and were good for three months. Muttering, I paid out—the first and only place where any charge had been made. The boys took in the town and I took in the fuel injectors for service. The service shop took me in; a gross overcharge. The refuelling and provisioning were quickly carried out. The cruise ship *Oriana* had come into port and thousands of tourists had sent the prices sky-high and over-crowded the bars.

We were pleased to wash the mud from our anchor and take off on the long hop across to Wewak on the northern coast of New Guinea. It was 23 May. We were only 200 miles south of the Equator and the days and nights were getting hotter and hotter. A lot of our time was spent lying in the sun improving our suntans, reading books, yarning and lazing the days away. We amused ourselves trying to shoot flying fish with the shotgun. I had borrowed a couple of automatic pistols from a friend in the islands further south and we practised shooting at coconuts floating by and at paper targets thrown overboard. I think we were subconsciously preparing ourselves for the Filipino pirates. Overhead two bo's'n birds circled, trailing long tails like whips, making the day tense with their harsh cries.

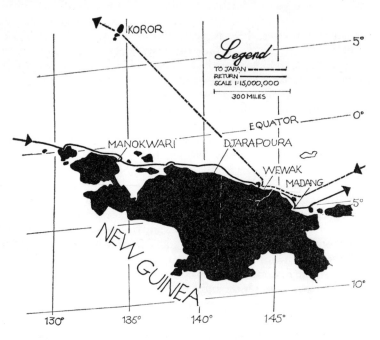

13.45 on the 24th: with a scream the fresh water pump on Little Stinky, the port engine, packed up. We carried on with Big Stinky until the other motor cooled enough to replace the faulty unit. The Fords never gave a moment's worry—just the ancillary gear that I had attached to them. We had a hell of a time with the water-circulating pumps. The suppliers said they wouldn't stand water over 175 degrees but I thought I knew better and it cost me much blood, sweat and tears.

Great confusion on the 25th. Where were we? The steering had been getting pretty sloppy—several times I had caught the Count reading at the wheel. A whole string of Counts had me bobbing up out of my cabin when the telltale compass warned me the helmsman was wandering off course. Tempers were fairly short. I got everyone on deck and we studied the charts, checked times and courses. "She'll be right" and "near enough is good enough" had taken us miles out of our way. We had sighted land 12 hours before it was due, but at last I established our landfall as the island of Karkar instead of Manam as aimed for. Soon we were cruising up the coast past flat mangrove swamp ground—the delta of the mighty Sepik River.

Whole trees floated by and the water turned brown—not by degrees but in a discoloured wall pressed up against the deep blue of the ocean. Fish shoaled along the demarcation line of fresh and salt water. Seagulls perching on coconuts appeared to be standing on the water.

On the 26th we arrived at Wewak just on dusk. The entrance to the wharf was a dreadful little channel between two buoys 25 yards apart and moored in about six feet of water, possibly less. We dropped the Danforth into the mud and eel-grass and as the *Whai* came to a stop she went aground to sit happily on her tails on an even keel.

We had spent three days at sea and couldn't get ashore quickly enough. A native told us where the nearest bar was and so up the hill we went to the motel Sepik, whose Dutch host entertained us right royally with a splendid meal of curried prawns. It was a late late night.

"Ahoy—permission to come on board."
"Sure—goodday to you."
"I'm Paddy Taylor, skipper of the *Princess Pirie* over there. I hear you've divers on board."
"Yes, that's right—we're all divers."
"I wonder if you'd do a salvage job for me? The stupid bastards dropped some cylinders of gas overboard and the hospital urgently needs them. I'll pay you for it! Give you fifty bucks."
I needed the cash and the deal was made. Bill, Cobber and Rafe got their gear, we all piled into Paddy's launch, and set off to the *Princess Pirie*. She was old and worn and had a badly hogged back. Paddy showed me an old print of the original Maori maiden after whom the ship was named. Paddy and I shared a bottle of Scotch while the divers found and hauled the cylinders of nitrous oxide on board. My new friend gave me some much-needed charts and an old *Pacific Pilot*.

"Come back to the *Whai* and have some of ours." Another bottle of Scotch, some rum, some brandy. And then my movements became indistinct. I remember a fearful argument with the Dutchman—what about?—who knows? I remember scuttling away from the motel around and over fences and hiding in drainage ditches while a police Landrover cruised about trying to find me. I remember the uniforms and spotlights. I remember the long swim back to the *Whai* holding my clothes over my head with one hand to keep them dry.

Next morning no one would speak to me. I couldn't find my clothes—just wet underpants lying on the deck. A native paddled out in a dugout and introduced me to my clothes, neatly folded on the dockside. The money! The 40-odd dollars left from the salvage job! It was all there and gratefully I gave the honest fellow a couple of dollars. About as much as he'd earn in a week.

"Well, what did I *do*?" I entreated.

"We don't want to speak about it," said Wayne.

"What do you mean? What happened?"

"I think you ought to forget about it," said Mike.

"Forget it? I don't even know what I'm trying to remember! Why didn't you jokers look after me?"

"What! After Thio? You've got to be joking!" said Cobber.

"All right! I can't go ashore so we may as well shove off!"

I was being childish, but with my aching head I couldn't think of anything better to say. It was a long, lonely day but in the dark of evening I rowed ashore with Mike and we caught a lift to the Windjammer Hotel. The proprietor was strangely cool to me but his wife, a pretty Chinese, laughingly patted me on the head and asked me how I felt. I was nonplussed. As far as I knew I'd never seen either of them before.

A New Zealander, Ross Anderson, introduced himself; he took me to meet his Chinese brother-in-law and talk salvage. They knew of an unworked Japanese cruiser lying in the channel between Kairiru and Mushu Islands over on the horizon. We promised to see them about it on the way back from Japan. There seemed to be a myriad things to do up here in the islands—shell collecting, salvage work, butterfly collecting (illegal), inter-island passenger ferrying, charter fishing parties, and so on.

Back at the *Whai* a runabout came alongside with visitors and we met the crew of the *Mia Mia*, a luxury yacht anchored a few miles around the bay. Jeff Hunter, the owner, agreed to help me with star shots—a branch of navigation I'd not tackled, if I cared to visit his boat. Both Mike and I had developed horrid tropic ulcers from cuts or bites suffered on Balalae Island and Ross took us to Wewak Hospital for treatment.

The *Mia Mia* lay like a white swan among the ugly duckling

At Beautemps in the Loyalty Group

Octopus for tea!

Wayne strokes the
porpoises

Bill and Cobber at Mono Island

traders and canoes. On board were an American couple, Bill and Mona Isley, who were heading for Mona's home in Koror, Palau Island, in the Carolines.

"How are you going to the Philippines? By West Irian? If you do you might be in bad trouble," said Jeff. "An American yacht the *Foxtrot* is being held at Djarapoura naval base and the Indonesians won't let her go. There's another one there too, I believe."

We'd read the warning letter from Fox, owner of *Foxtrot*, pinned to the yacht club noticeboard in Rabaul. It worried me as we had no visas for Indonesian territory. I thought we could get them more easily when closer to the border. I thought the Aussies would have it all wrapped up. But the Aussies knew practically nothing of their neighbours except that natives were being shot and a rebellious tribe in the Berau district were being bombed into submission.

"Well, I don't know," I said. "It seems I'll have to chance a long hop up the coast to Zamboanga or out to the Carolines and across to Tacloban City, but I don't fancy either much."

"I'd go to Palau if I were you," said Jeff. "How about you taking Bill and Mona here; you could refuel at Koror okay."

And so it was decided—the 850-mile open ocean hop to a small island group. No hope of help if anything went wrong, but at least we wouldn't be imprisoned or held to ransom as could happen in Indonesian waters.

Wayne and Callum left us in Wewak to fly home. Neither really took to sea life though ardent skindivers and I think their lady-loves called more eloquently than the adventures ahead.

Mike and I checked and greased everything in sight. We replaced the second water pump and reconditioned the spare unit. We adjusted steering cables, put in a fresh echo-sounder roll, lashed on an extra drum of fuel. Mona and Bill moved on board, we heaved up the anchor and sailed off over the horizon.

Then began the most glorious five days' cruise of the trip. Calm seas and cloudless skies. No wind—just a huge blue lake of flat glass. The first day out we came on a Japanese fishing boat laying out a "long-line". Stretching as far as the eye could see was a line of bamboo marker poles standing upright with their gay flags hanging limp. The Japanese disappeared over the horizon paying out the 14-mile string of baited hooks.

The boys suggested we grab some of the beautiful glass floats and when I demurred (I had visions of having my head cut off) Cobber said, "Hell! Twenty-five years ago you were shooting them! Now you won't even pinch their bloody buoys!"

We crossed the Equator that night and had a special grog-up to celebrate—it was the first time into the Northern Hemisphere for Mike and Cobber.

Boredom and heat. The *Whai* surged on. The sea and sky merged imperceptibly into each other and only at evening and dawn could we discern the horizon. I had trouble with my sun shots. Poor Mona felt the heat and the gentle slow movement of the boat upset her. Bill, however, thrived and regaled us with tales of Vietnam. We slept on deck, lying on rubber air mattresses scattered all over the boat. It was easy to prepare meals as the big cat was as steady as a liner. In the evenings the cook of the day passed food through the top hatch and we sat under the stars eating and yarning, with a stiff sundowner to finish off the day. Practically every night it rained, driving the crew, cursing, below to the stifling cabins, but the rain had its good effect, providing plenty of fresh water caught in the dinghy for showers and the washing of clothes.

Navigation began to worry me. It was such a long way. Suppose a storm developed and land was blotted out at a crucial moment by driving rain? The fact that we had a girl on board began to prey on my mind. It was a great responsibility and however confident I was of my system, grave doubts recurred and would not let me be. I calculated we would sight land at 11.30 the next morning and the day dawned fresh and bright. In the distance cumulus clouds towered high reflecting a white path along our track. Later, it began to rain and everyone was on the foredeck, laughing and soaping themselves, rinsing in the cool downpour. I was sweating with tension as according to my figures Babelthuap, biggest of the Palau group should appear within the hour. The clouds could be a good sign and indicate land. I crossed my fingers.

The rain cleared for a glorious crystal moment and there, figured against the rain wall, was a white fishing boat, its bow wave rippling out in a broad V. Mona cried out and waved. The craft altered course and headed our way. Mona knew the boat—an Okinawan on contract to the local fish-freezing company. We were close to port and as our boats rocked in each other's wake, the clouds lifted and the Palau Islands were dead ahead. It was 11.20 and no peacock felt prouder and no peasant more humble than I. It was fine to accept the congratulations of the crew, but alone in my cabin I admit to a prayer of thanks.

"Get away! Get away! You must get 50 feet away!" The fat policeman in his tight blue shirt and dirty black pants waved his arms furiously; at any moment he'd pull his gun, I thought. The huge sign on the wharf shed read "The Port of Palau, Heart of Micronesian Charm". After that jazz this reception was ridiculous. Two cars shot along the wharf in a cloud of dust and out tumbled Mona's parents and three of her girlfriends.

After minutes of consultation with another policeman, our fat friend allowed us to move alongside and the port doctor came on board followed by the two coppers, Mona's parents and the three girls carrying a cardboard box. There was great confusion, with kisses, and "Have you any contagious diseases on board?", bright flower leis being slung around necks, handshaking and filling in of forms. The main cabin was crowded and the overflow spilled out on to the after-deck. On the wharf wide-eyed Palaunese kids watched the frangipani leis being taken from the box and festooned about us. Mona's mother hung on me a "special one for the captain" of large red and squashy flowers, and like most Kiwis I felt gauche and self-conscious. When the port formalities were completed we were to be allowed ashore, but first we cast off from the wharf and motored to an anchorage near a small shipping office that boasted an all-night security guard.

Mona and Bill went home to a quiet evening, but the rest of us hired a cab and roared away in high good humour to sample Koror's night life. There were (among others) the Virginian, Pelilu, Mac's Cafe, the Cave In and Boom Boom. To us the place was jumping—there were construction battalion (Cee-Bee) soldiers, civilians, tourists, and last, but not the quietest, the warriors off the *Whai*.

The women tended to be stocky, with good figures and hot devouring eyes—yummy was the consensus of opinion. These people of Micronesia appear to be a cross between Malay and Polynesian types—with perhaps a touch of Asian.

"Sure," said a huge Yank, "they spend all their time hopping in and out of bed." We could well believe it—the large brown eyes, silky black hair, lovely figures and a wiggling walk that would bring a stone idol to life. But sometimes the vision was spoilt by the stained teeth and bright scarlet tongue of the betel-nut chewer.

I was introduced to the chief administrator, a Palaun of about forty.

"Have you permission to come to our islands?" was the greeting.

"No. Is it necessary?"

"You'd better see me in the morning."

Well, we were staying only two days and so I'd forget it. If I didn't show up on the morrow he'd ask for me the next day, but we'd be gone. Through a bit of jiggery-pokery in Wewak I had wangled a clearance for Tacloban City in the Philippines as well as for Koror, so if I wasn't cleared by the Palaunese, what the hell! I could still go to Tacloban without further formality.

As we drove to the Owens' home we noticed the makeshift air of Koror town. Bob Owen told us how, when the Caroline Islands had been retaken, American policy was to eradicate Japanese influence. Tangibles like concrete roads and the bigger buildings were destroyed, ripped up and not replaced. This crazy policy has resulted in quagmires when it rains. This and the Caucasian domination may account for the male Palauns' chip-on-the-shoulder attitude.

Bob Owen is a scientist, entomologist to the Government. He is also an ex-U.S. Air Force pilot of B26's in North Africa and Italy. Tall, stooped and with a lined, pensive face, Bob could really cut loose after hours and was hard to keep up with. During work hours he showed us his salt-water crocodiles (live), his beetles (dead), his pet monkey (head only, preserved in formalin) and, out of hours, how to play in Palau. Hira, his wife, was blonde and pretty like Mona. They entertained us with a feast of Chinese food and then off we went to the Pelilu Club social.

A drunk Kiwi construction engineer sat at our table. He was employed by an American firm at Guam and was in Koror for a break. He had become so Americanized that he forgot he was born a New Zealander and no novelty to us. He taunted Cobber over something or other and kept asking him to hit him. We were in company and enjoying ourselves but at long last, fed up, Cobber obliged. The clobbered Kiwi sat there practically paralysed. His eyes watered and blinked but I don't think he saw or heard us. All we heard was Cobber cursing. He'd broken a knuckle and rammed it halfway into his fist, which upset his skindiving for a month but not his ego.

There were many Japanese tourists at Koror, mostly ex-servicemen or parents of lost sons revisiting the old battlefields. Also businessmen, readying for takeovers if and when the Americans leave. Like MacArthur, they will return—and be welcomed.

Our own welcome was running out. I'd received word my presence was required by the Administration. There had been a holdup over refuelling, as I had to get a chit for the release of diesel from the Director of Shipping. And so I was forced to go along quietly and get fleeced of port dues, tax-on-entry dues and another for clearance. At last we were free and after an admonishment, "Do not return without permission," I gathered up the gang and off we went on a spearfishing expedition with three young American Peace Corps volunteers as guides.

The fishing was poor, we were buzzed by several sharks and the water was cloudy with nothing edible to shoot. The brilliant day and the flat calm were magnificent, however, and we motored past the "Stone" Islands growing out of the lagoon like mushrooms. Unfortunate would be the swimmer trying to land on one of these—the limestone bases are cut away by the sea's action and overhang the water like verandahs. It would be impossible to climb out, and eventually, exhausted, the swimmer would drown, even though touching and looking at dry land.

We only just cleared the island's great girdle of reefs before dusk, heading for Tacloban City, 700-odd miles away. In the morning we started to come on huge floating logs. As far as the eye could see were these drifting trees, their stark roots and gnarled branches reaching for the sky. Seagulls perched on them, flying off with harsh cries of annoyance as we drew abreast. One of the trees looked for all the world like a dinghy with four black figures huddled in it. I altered course, just in case, and in doing so came on an extraordinary sight.

Something big and black was splashing and worrying at a log, shaking it and making it roll in the water.

"They're sharks!"

There was a mad scramble for guns and cameras. Sure enough several sharks were charging the slimy hulk, biting pieces out of it. I cut the motors and we drifted silently. Were they sharpening their teeth or chewing off the goose-neck barnacles which covered the submerged parts? Bill pointed into the water.

"Hell! Don't fall overboard! There are dozens of 'em. Look at that!"

We peered over the rails. There were dozens of sharks all right and some of them quite large.

"I want to shoot one!" shouted Bill. "I'll get my power-head!"

"Hell, you can't swim there," I said. "You wouldn't last a minute!"

"I'll stay on the ladder—it'll be okay!"

And Bill was off gathering up mask, goggles and gun. Mike started to assemble his under-water movie camera in frantic haste, and the rest watched the silent ballet of twisting dark shapes below. Bill lowered the ladder and slowly climbed down, bending double to peer under the surface.

"Look out, Bill!" He scrambled up the ladder in fright. We roared with laughter.

"Go on, we were only kidding." And down he went again, gun at the ready.

"Shoot! Shoot!" The spear zipped away. The powerhead hit the big fish but failed to explode. I was upset because the powerheads had been designed by me to kill on impact.

"Uh, forgot the safety-catch," mumbled Bill and loaded again. The sharks circled silently, coming closer and closer to examine the stainless steel ladders shining in the water.

Another shot, and the safety still on, and another, this time to pull up short through not enough free line run out.

"For God's sake, Bill, calm down, calm down!" And with the fourth shot he planted a 10-footer high on the back. There was a muffled thud, a cloud of bubbles. The shark heaved, paused, and then slid down out of sight into the deeps. The explosion attracted more sharks. Mike climbed down the port ladder to film the action.

Bill hit another and then it was over—the sharks were too cocky and the ladders too exposed to be safe. We amused ourselves with the rifles, potting at the odd dorsal that broke water. We tried another log for fish, and shoals of little shimmering sardines wriggled away from the safety of its tangled roots to the dubious shelter between the cat's hulls. A grey remora, long and sleek, drifted over towards us; then its host, a pointy-nosed blue shark with cold black eyes, came to investigate.

We were very thoughtful. I had made the rule that anyone going outside at night for any reason whatever had to check out and back with the helmsman. After the sharks, everyone was much more conscientious; falling overboard would be highly dangerous in these waters.

Mike and I were still having trouble with leg ulcers and were taking pills which seemed to be reducing them. But the heat and perspiration didn't help. Rafe was having trouble with a bad gash on his knee caused through falling into a ten-foot ditch on Palau. Bill had never really adjusted to sea travel and felt ill each time we put to sea. What with Cobber having violent stomach upsets after every good meal ashore, in one way or another our first-aid kit had quite a workout.

A gentle wind blew on our port side from the south and the miles slid by day after day. Just in front of each bow, small bonito started to gather, keeping a few feet ahead. Now and again big turtles were seen sunning themselves and flying fish, startled by our approach, shattered the surface into shards of flying crystal as they soared away from us over the sea. At night our wake could be seen for half a mile, glowing and throbbing with eerie life. Each dawn and dusk, just as the sun touched the horizon, tuna and bonito would leap in graceful arcs as they broke surface chasing little fish.

7 June: We were drawing near landfall—I expected to see Dinagat Island about dusk on the 8th. I found that the Count had placed the portable radio near the compass. Good grief! How long had it been there? It could have been there since Palau and if so, how far were we off course? Or were we? I took away the radio with its twin magnetic speakers but could detect no correcting swing of the compass needle. Keeping fingers crossed we carried on—according to my sun shots everything was O.K.

A super-tanker appeared. First, a grey haze of diesel smoke then two thin yellow masts, then the high superstructure rose over the sea's edge and then the huge hull. It crossed half a mile in front of us and as we rocked in its wake the beat of its powerful motor could be felt as well as heard. The thrill of "channel" fever affected us all and we were excited at the thought of the Philippines so close. Dinagat, blue-grey on the horizon, slowly grew larger and by nightfall the lonesome beam of Desolation Point lighthouse was astern.

We entered Leyte Gulf and the lights on Leyte and Samar Islands blinked distant on either side as the coastlines slowly closed. Tacloban lay ahead somewhere in the velvet darkness; there was no moon and a high thin cloud dimmed all but the brightest of the constellations. The scent of luxuriant plant life filled the air. I went to my bunk and took a sleeping-pill. Navigation was all over—by morning's light we should be well up the gulf with a few hours' cruising to bring us to port. I'd left written instructions to call me half an hour before dawn.

"Pete! Wake up, wake up!" Rafe was shaking my shoulder. Stupefied from the drugged sleep, I was brought back to the here and now by the urgent whisper.

"Wha's wrong? What's up?"

Rafe was very excited. "I think there are pirates! They're all round us!"

I grabbed an automatic and rushed up on deck.

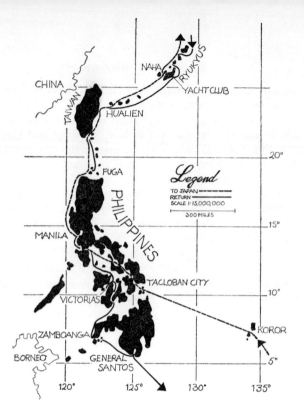

CHAPTER FIVE

Roundabout to Manila

"WHERE? Where?" The darkness pressed all around. *Whai* was cruising on one motor as we needed only 5 knots to arrive a few miles offshore at dawn. I started the other donkey so it would warm up and give us extra speed should we need it. Cobber sat up from his lilo.

"What's up?"

"Rafe thinks there are pirates!"

"Whacko!" shouted Cobber. He leapt to his feet and was off down below to collect his armoury.

Ahead and to port four mysterious lights were twinkling.

"I don't think they'd show any lights," I muttered, but switched off our own navigation lights just in case. In complete darkness we surged on, the only lights in the whole sphere of blackness the four glimmers now sliding past about a quarter of a mile away, and the ripple of phosphorescence in our wake. Suddenly another light, way up ahead, and then two more to starboard. We were now ringed by lights shedding golden tracks towards us. More and more of the strange lights flickered into life—some flaring to brightness instantly and others to gutter and go out, only to be relit. We counted 46 lights strung like a necklace around the *Whai* and I dared not carry on without showing our steaming lights.

"What the hell's going on?" Mike up from his bed, blinking and peering.

"Don't know—never seen anything like it. There must be a hundred boats out there."

We bandied ideas around until wearying of the spectacle, the crew drifted off, putting away their weapons and settling down again to sleep.

I was due on the wheel in about an hour so stayed on with Rafe to help if needed. As I brewed cocoa the strange lights slipped by but never close enough to see what was underneath. The lights ahead seemed to stay just as far away, an illusion but very real and unnerving.

To port I saw the green starboard and yellow masthead light of a small vessel travelling parallel with our course. The stranger was going almost exactly at our speed and an increase of 25 r.p.m. pulled us close in behind. In the greying dawn its outline slowly became more distinct. Our involuntary guide threaded in and out of the maze of lamps and at last we could make out their meaning. Dozens of vintas, small trimarans, lay on the oily waters with lamps slung low between their outriggers. The fishermen pulled up curiously shaped nets, trapping little surface fish attracted to the lights. Now and again really big "tris" with half a dozen crew lay silently drifting, the smoke from small cooking fires wreathing their tall masts. Then the sun rose hot and golden over the hills of Samar and all mystery was gone. We were trailing along in the wake of a dirty little tub covered with bamboo bales and with a ragged crew who came aft, looked at us, relieved themselves, spat and went forward again.

Tacloban City sprawled ahead, brown, white and grey. The coconut palms and thick bush behind accentuated the drab waterfront. This was the city made famous by General Mac-Arthur, who waded ashore at this spot to fulfil his promise, "I will return!"

The coasts drew closer and closer, narrowing the channel between the two islands. A tide set must have been flowing towards us because large rafts of water hyacinths floated past, matted green leaves and buoyancy bulbs with pale mauve flowers. Small trees, coconut fronds and husks, all manner of flotsam drifted about. Big fish traps and holding pens built from great bamboo poles were stuck into the muddy bottom or tethered to anchors. On catwalks around the pens small shacks perched, giving shelter to the watchmen cooking their morning meal over little charcoal fires.

I slowed the *Whai* and idled her past the main wharf. We saw the harbour offices with flags drooping in the sun. Our own yellow quarantine flag flapped idly with the draught of our passage. Back and forth alongside the docks we cruised—no officials, no one to guide us and so, getting tired of hanging about, I drew her alongside. The boys threw up the mooring ropes to the Filipinos clustering the dusty concrete wharf.

There were dozens and dozens of them, all grinning and staring at us. "Hi Joe! Hi Joe! Hi Joe!" Waving and calling to us, it was to be this way of greeting throughout the Philippines. Wherever we went we were mobbed by adults and kids alike chanting the wartime greeting for the American liberators. Our shorts were a novelty, all the men and boys wore skintight long pants. We were to find that women laughed and stroked our furry arms, were amazed at hairy chests and legs.

"I won't be long—better wait on board. Keep an eye on things and don't allow anyone to get on unless in uniform." With this admonishment I clambered on to the wharf helped by a dozen eager hands. A tricycle taxi, fantastically frail, pushed through the crowd.

I had only U.S. dollars and, taking a chance, crawled into the tiny interior. Completely oblivious of the press of bodies, the driver gave it the gun, scattering people in all directions.

The driver spoke a little English and with many a wrong turning we arrived outside a large white building, with a blue anchor in bas-relief above the door. On the steps two officials stood talking. They were dressed in mufti but their badge of office clearly denoted authority in the shape of chromium-plated .44 Colts tucked into hip pockets.

"Can you help me?" I opened. "I want to see the immigration and health authorities." A long thoughtful stare. "Come with us." And so up the stairs and into a shabby second-storey office.

"So you're off a boat? Where from?"

"We're from New Zealand. We've just got in from the Palau Islands."

Incredulous looks.

"What are you doing here; how long are you staying?"

"Well, we're on our way to Manila and then Japan. We want fuel, water, vegetables and meat."

"H'm." The Chief of Immigration looked me over, sizing up the shabby sandals, well-worn shorts and sports shirt. The expensive underwater watch. A private cruise. H'm.

"It will cost you $62 harbour dues."

"What! Hell, we've never paid dues before! Not even in French New Caledonia—and they're tough! We're only a little boat!"

"How big are you?"

"Only 40 feet." The cat had its tail bobbed a trifle.

"H'm. Well, I'll consider it. In the meanwhile you're free to go ashore."

"Thank you very much. Would you care to look over my boat? And have a drink?" They looked at each other, patted me on the shoulder and we went off the best of buddies.

The crowd above the *Whai* was even thicker—we were a real novelty. We found that unemployed were everywhere, lounging around with nothing to do except gawk at and amuse themselves with whatever was free. We had to learn to ignore the curious, but to watch our valuables. Desperate poverty is so rife in the Philippines, who can condemn the man who seizes his chance with your watch or camera and loses himself in the crowd? No Social Security, no handouts, no one to turn to. Get money to eat or die—it's as simple as that. But get it.

We opened the grog locker and demolished a bottle of Scotch. The heat was appalling and even the Filipinos began to wilt. With cheery excuses they left us to the joys of Tacloban City. Clutching cameras, we pushed our way through the throng. We met our first jeepnies—wartime jeeps transformed by many hours of work, chrome and ornaments into the gaudiest of taxis. Some had their chassis lengthened and long seats were placed in the back on either side facing each other. Dusty tassels dangled from the canopied roofs and religious medallions and transfers almost covered the windscreens. We were to find the Filipinos needed all the help they could get with their crowded roads and reckless driving. I don't know whether the pictures of Jesus' Bleeding Heart helped, but the framed prayer "Help us, O Lord" was a comfort.

Grinning from ear to ear the driver took us to the bank to change travellers' cheques into pesos and centavos. Now armed with that joy of joys, spending money, we roared off, scattering chickens and kids every which way—we were "off to market to buy a fat pig, home again, home again, dancing a jig!" Well, anyway we went to the market. This covered two acres or more and was divided into sections—here fruit and vegetables in endless variety and abundance, here fish of all sizes, colours, shapes and smells. The meat section made us shudder—hunks of raw flesh too horrible to guess the origin. Whole small pigs roasted brown, crackling split and glazed with coconut milk, vied with chicken legs tied in bunches. The clawed feet only I mean.

Out in the sun, shallow ditches oozed slimy filth, stinking and fermenting. Discarded leaves and husks, bits of offal, fish scales and rotten fruit in piles attracted hordes of fat black flies. Mosquitoes danced in the shadows and in a little side alley we found an old man crouched over an open fire, slowly turning and basting a pig. The colour and sounds, the movement and swirl of thousands of people milling about. Kids pushed up to us to gaze wide-eyed at our fair skins and unusual clothes. Cameras worth a year's salary were touched in awe but particularly interesting studies were almost impossible to film, with so many "actors" pushing to preen in the foreground.

Mike and Bill, both over 6ft. 2in., towered over these small, lightly boned people. A pretty girl at a fruit stall jumped on a crate and looked Mike in the eyes. Giggling she pointed out to her friends that still didn't top him. She said "Tom Jones" and everyone laughed. Mike was to get sick to death of "Tom Jones" being called out to him. And as Tom Jones is only about 5ft. 6in. it must have been the muttonchop whiskers and the dark good looks which motivated them.

Bill and Cobber started to bargain for pineapples—they bought over a dozen scungy looking things for 8 centavos each after much hard bargaining. I was mad because I'd spent a dollar on four beauties and now we had far too many.

"Oh, we'll eat them ourselves—not to worry."

Darkness fell with the setting sun. We never really got used to the sudden change from daylight to dark in the tropics. No twilight hours at all. Back at the boat I met a smiling smoothie.

"You want water? Food? Fuel?"

"Yes. Where's the water hydrant?"

"No hydrant—I sell water for the port. I can get you food cheap, too."

It became an argument which I quickly lost and had to recover my new acquaintance's goodwill or we'd go without.

Of all the rackets I came across during the trip, this cheerful chap had the best: for 3 percent of his take, paid in the form of "protection money", he had the sole rights to sell fresh water to all the ships that came to Tacloban. I believe he had the fuel bunkering tied up, too. He invited me to meet his wife and see his home—probably one of the best in Tacloban City.

His wife was truly beautiful. Probably next closest to his heart was a tired old diesel engine which thumped and banged away drawing water from under his backyard to fill the water trucks plying to and from the wharves. I was introduced to his "cousin" who would act as our guide to the city's night spots. This character turned out to be a shameless "commission man". On everything we bought, in every bar and club we visited, this pest took his percentage. At first it was a mystery, then an amusement and in the end a damned bore to have him scuttle ahead of us into shops to mutter with the proprietor. We heard the arguments but didn't cotton on to what was happening. In the end he went too far and "arranged" women for the entire crew off his own bat. When they were ignored he got very angry and claimed he was out of pocket.

"Hard luck!" said Bill.

"Use them yourself," said Mike, and full of expensive watered-down "whisky" we staggered back to the Cat.

Cobber was grumpy as he'd had the last watch and missed most of the fun. So when the importunate cousin came down to try again for his expenses, it was a delight to hear Cobber's:

"Go away you scavenging bastard! Don't you come on this boat or I'll bloody well drop you! I mean it!"

The morning was hot and bright. We hired a jeepnie to tour the town. We didn't want to see the city itself—it was sprawling and rundown—we wanted to see the slum area near the market and explore the villages lining the bayside. We found the slums and shanty towns of the Caingñin—the squatters who build from discarded roofing iron, hammered-out tin cans, old packing cases and even bits of cardboard on frames of scrap wood. These crude shelters, huddled together, form a scene so dreadful it is difficult to describe.

We'd seen the primitive palm-frond and cane shacks of Melanesia but this was different—this was a ghastly travesty of living. No building bylaws, no sewage, no water, no property rights—just a jumble of rickety, dirty hovels propping each other up. The lucky ones stood on decaying piles over tidal water which stank and bubbled. They at least had no disposal problems for their garbage or sewage.

But in this dreadful mess beauty bloomed in heart-rending glimpses of what-could-be. Little gamin faces with enormous dark eyes—the little doll children playing in scabrous doorways. And, just here and there, a pot plant ablaze with tropic colour hung from sagging rafters to put to shame the peeling posters or chipped enamel signs.

This was our introduction to the huge problem which is the Philippines. A country rich in people, minerals, soil and climate. A country so torn with inequalities of wealth and position, with such abuses of power and lack of employment as to baffle a hundred Solomons.

In all the teeming thousands of Tacloban we didn't see another white face—it was strangely unnerving in a way—we really were strangers in a foreign land. But we found little trouble in being understood—there was always someone who spoke English and was ready to help. The Filipinos are extremely friendly and we liked them, villains and all. We were amused by the hundreds of little Sarisari stores—mostly make-shift affairs—just open-fronted stalls perhaps 15ft. long. It seems these are the height of attainable ambition for many Filipinos—they are little shops in which small luxuries are sold—Coca Cola, cigarettes, biscuits, cooked corncobs, etc. At night kerosene lamps hanging from their eaves cast an inviting glow, adding a kind of sleazy glamour to what in harsh daylight was just another little dump.

The Immigration Chief was a boat enthusiast and the gift of a book on Hartley designs really pleased him. We got our clearance for Manila from the bemused official and all port dues were waived. With lots of "Hi Joe's!" and a cloud of carbon from the exhausts we cast off to get through the narrow waterway dividing Leyte from Samar in daylight.

As the sun rose higher wild ducks, startled, exploded off the water in panic. Blue herons flapped by and shining beetles droned across our path to distant shores. We motored past a little islet of red clay, bare but for a clump of tall kunai grass on top. Curious white objects stuck on stakes drew my attention. Through the binoculars three human skulls grinned and shimmered in the heat.

It took all day to complete the passage past village after village, their fleets of tiny fishing trimarans floating like stained and tattered waterlilies from shore to shore. It was dusk when we left the entrance lights and headed out into Carigara Bay and towards the Samar Sea. With Daram Island to starboard and Biliran to port, the *Whai* pushed through the jobble towards Maripipi. There were lots of islands but few lighthouses to mark the way.

I had no idea what sort of currents to expect, no idea of their speed or direction, so we steered by dead reckoning mid-channel between the scattered land masses. Until now I had done no regular tricks at the wheel, but the darkening skies and dozens of islands and reefs now made it necessary for me to be constantly on watch, to check and recheck our position and to plot new courses. Heat lightning, even more constant than that over New Guinea, flickered and flashed in brilliant bursts above the mountains and high ground of the islands. One could almost navigate by it—in fact, the eerie display of sudden golden light often confirmed the presence of land.

Past Santo Nino, Camandag and Almagro; past Togapula and on, with Masbate to port and Ticao to starboard. Names to excite the imagination. We passed Baqui Point Light in the hot darkness; just the diesels' chuntering and the hiss and slap of our bow waves to mark our passage. Some of the few lighthouses were red, not white, and confused me, as my charts were not as up to date as they should have been. We were well into the Sibuyan Sea with Burias Island ahead, at dawn. We skirted Burias by heading between Mariocuque and the larger Mindoro, home of the dreaded headhunters. In olden days it was a brave or foolhardy crew that sailed these waters. Even now the high mountain and thick jungle slopes seemed forbidding. We passed many small trimaran dugouts with ragged fishermen handlining for fish. They stared at us, sitting perfectly still, impassive, until their frail craft rocked in our wake. Then they grabbed tins and baled. We avoided them after we saw how low their freeboard was and how their trimarans wouldn't roll with the waves but slopped water.

The sea among the islands was cloudy and greenish with plankton and river run-off, making underwater visibility too poor for skindiving. At this stage we hadn't learned of the tremendous fishing pressure by net, poison and explosives. We hadn't learned that right up through the Philippines, Ryukyus and Japan, whole areas of coastline are now marine deserts stripped of reef fishes.

Clouds, heavy and dull, trailed rain curtains across our path to hide the island panorama. A hasty confirmation of our position and course had to be made before the wet wall enclosed us. Then we were in a sphere of grey, the little whitecaps smoothed off to an oily swell, and I put on an extra lookout. Now and again the rain would lift a little and our circle of vision increase to a hundred yards or so. The lead-coloured water reflected light in a pale sheen and it was impossible to anticipate shoaling water by colour changes. Every ten minutes or so we switched on the echo-sounder but the deeps were too great to register.

Coral waters are always dicey—from depths of hundreds of feet the bottom can shoot up to the surface in a matter of yards. Coral even grows outward in shelves to overhang these cliffs. The best guide to depth is the sea's shading from deep blue to pale green. Coral near to the surface, say within two or three feet, shows brown, but in the half light of dawn and dusk the colours can't be seen.

Evening again and the rainwashed air was clear and cool. Verde Island ahead and beyond it Maricaban, vaguely green in the pallid sunset. We were getting exotic music on the radio—tomorrow we'd be in Manila. There was plenty of fresh water for washing clothes and we had all soaped ourselves and rinsed off in the rain. Surplus water ran out the dinghy drain hole to stream into the bubbling wake. Bottles of gin and vodka were brought out, and a pineapple from under the front seat.

"It's gone bad! The ruddy thing's all spongy!" Bill cursed and got another. And another.

"Should have got the best—those cheap ones are pretty expensive, eh?" I crowed.

Dawn. Rain again and no sight of land—I'd taken a westerly course to clear Cape Santiago by some miles, and it was time to turn inshore to establish our true position. The rain hissed down to splatter the sea in a million interlocking rings; it splashed in little dancing pearls.

"Land!" shouted Mike. "Dead ahead about a hundred yards!"

"Quick! Hard aport, Bill!" Slowly the cat came about.

"Reverse her!" The *Whai* trembled and rumbled as the swirling water churned and backed along the port hull. The great grey cliff receded into the rain.

We motored quietly, the echo-sounder humming and clicking and three of us peering into the wet. Out of the rain curtain, a darkness to starboard loomed—land. But where were we? The water was deep, over two hundred feet. There were no waves just a low sucking surge which climbed, paused, and ran back off the cliff's base in little cascades.

We took it in turns to stand on the starboard bow to guide with hand signals. Even in the muggy air we got chilled in the cool downpour and the draught from our slow progress. After many false alarms I fixed our position as off Fuego and it was now too late to arrive in Manila by daylight. Our slow edging in the mist and rain from headland to headland plus a southern set of current, had delayed us too long. It didn't warrant entering a strange and busy harbour and being forced to hang about the bay waiting for daylight.

The author, who flew against the Japanese in the war, now appears as "Kamikaze Pete"

Roasting pigs in an alley in Tacloban City, Philippines

Passing the Filipino
trimaran

The Filipino "jeep-
nie" gaudily transfor-
med from a wartime
jeep into a taxi

Dawn found us still puttering past craggy cliffs and little bays. Coconut and banana palms, patches of cleared land and stands of thick bush lined the shore, with occasional huts half hidden in the jungle. Limit Point was astern and Big Manila Bay ahead. We couldn't see the far shoreline and I had to set a compass course in the general direction of the city. Passing lights became cargo boats, liners and fishing craft. The lights of shore dimmed out and smoke, blue and filmy, rose to dress the new day.

With both motors working hard the *Whai* seemed to rush along. We were all excited by the prospects ahead—a really big city—so much to see and do.

I had no idea where the local yacht club could be—or, in fact, if there was one. We headed towards a series of tall silver structures on the starboard shore.

"What the heck are those?" I asked, handing Bill the binoculars.

He studied the shining triangles and long low shapes.

"Dunno. Are they oil tanks?"

"Let's have a look." And Mike had a turn. "They're airplanes! Hell, there must be 20 of them—they're huge!"

Sure enough there they were—giant military cargo planes on an airstrip not much above sea level and right at the edge of the bay. My charts showed nothing to indicate an airfield at this point but we headed across in case there was a jetty where we could tie up and get the score about local harbour procedure and layout.

"There's a yacht—head towards it!" and off we went to hail down a smart 40-footer flying a Filipino burgee.

"Follow my tender," shouted the owner. "He's going to the yacht club."

The yacht club marina was protected by a concrete wall in front and on one side, and on the other by a wharf. Alongside the wharf a dark blue-grey Philippine Navy landing-craft was moored. Also two unkempt and rust-streaked junk-like fishing boats. They were confiscated Okinawans caught poaching in local waters. A sleek launch also lay alongside, its superstructure riddled and pocked by bullets: a cigarette smuggler caught down the coast.

We pulled alongside the club's jetty. A shipwright working on a small keeler led me to the office and the Customs, Immigration and Health authorities were notified. We were given a mooring amongst glittering immaculate white yachts and big power cruisers. The *Whai* settled down with a puff of smoke and a last rumble. She deserved a rest.

We waited and waited and waited. Three hours or more went by and at last I could stand it no longer. Club launches plied back and forth, picking up and delivering crew. They seemed to be summoned by the ringing of ships' bells, hooters, yells or loud whistles. I tried my luck with a piercing two-finger whistle and sure enough a launch headed our way.

In the clubhouse our officials were having rum and Cokes. Wiping the crumbs of a toasted sandwich from his moustache, the port doctor said:

"We'll be with you in a minute. You shouldn't come ashore, you know."

Chastened I returned to the *Whai* to endure another hour. It was a very cheerful group that eventually came on board to inspect our grog locker and papers.

"Have you any drugs?"

"Only some morphia in case of injury." And this was sealed up.

"You seem to have a lot of spirits?"

"Yes, we've a long trip ahead of us."

"Would you sell me a bottle?" This from the Customs!

"No, I can't do that, but you can have a bottle of gin."

"And one for me, too?" Immigration this time.

"Sorry, I can't spare any more—share your friend's bottle."

A long pause, long faces. Then they were all smiles again and with much backslapping and handshaking, off they went to the clubhouse. We changed into our best and whistled up a tender. In the club the trio of officials held their glasses on high in a silent toast to the crew of the *Whai* now breasting the bar. We met the club's hostess, a beautiful girl who asked us to wait for the vice-president and meanwhile to enjoy the hospitality of the club.

"Hope he's a long time coming," said Cobber, getting on the outside of a cold beer.

A waiter came to me, a bunch of chits in his hand.

"Please sign, Mr Captain, sir, for food and drinks."

"What food? What drinks?"

"The Customs and Immigration, Captain."

"I didn't authorise any food or drink—let's see them."

And there it was—30-odd pesos' worth, about $8 eaten and drunk on my account by our three friends. I looked around, but they were gone.

The club secretary drew me aside:

"Don't rock the boat, Peter. They could make it very tough for everyone. If we didn't go along with them they could insist on examining all visitors in the roadstead instead of here in the marina—you could wait at anchor for days. Forget it. Have another drink."

And that was that.

Manila Yacht Club is fabulous. Although weak in numbers by our standards (the membership is about 400) and the total number of keelers and power yachts only about four or five dozen, there is a permanent staff of over two dozen: chefs, barmen, waiters, shipwrights, clerks and boatmen. The whole complex is protected by armed guards, on duty 24 hours a day. The meals are excellent and very cheap, the drinks tall and cold. It was an earthly paradise and we wallowed in the unaccustomed luxury of showers and exotic cooking.

At the club bar we had met a lonely American anxious to "show us the town". We started off with the "Ugly American": a typical clip joint—a dozen tables and half a dozen "hostesses". Behind the bar a suave, dapper type metered out tiny but expensive drinks. Black-haired, olive-skinned Filipino girls came up and slid their little arms around us or stroked our necks— the price of their attention the purchase of fruit drinks at spirit rates.

We tried another and another club—the difference was only in decor; each had its signs exhorting patrons to hand in their "firearms and other deadly weapons," each had its little flock of harpies brought to instant life on our entrance. Harpies is too harsh a name—there was something pathetic about these unfortunates cadging drinks on commission.

"So you're the New Zealanders! I'm Judy Wagner. Welcome to Manila!"

Judy was tall and blonde.

"My husband should be along soon; let's have a drink on him! Ramon! Over here!"

We were introduced to more club members, expatriates of many lands: there were the Gots, Lola and José, both Spanish Basques; Dr Foster, an American dentist and his wife. His wife said, "I haven't cooked a meal or made a bed for 21 years—why should I want to go back to the States?" Vadim Bailovsky, a pale elderly man, a stateless White Russian with an extraordinary life story. Often when we needed transport his air-conditioned limousine and his chauffeur were at our disposal. Then there was George Woods, an ex-U.S. Army colonel who had been in the fighting at Munda airstrip in the Solomons during my tour of duty there and was now a director of the world's largest sugar refinery.

Jackson Wagner, a geologist, arrived tense and uptight from a flight back from Negros Island in a light plane. He unwound and, mellowed with whisky sours, invited the crew to his home for dinner. By this time everyone was extremely cheerful and we piled into the Wagner cars to take off with a roar. Mike, Bill and I were in Judy's car. We soon sobered up. The evening traffic was pouring along Roxas Boulevarde. Jeepnies and taxis jockeyed for the lead in reckless bursts of speed, but they couldn't match Judy's élan and complete disregard for the rules of the road. Much subdued we tottered out on arrival; it had been an experience we didn't intend to repeat.

"Where the devil did you get to, Jackson? Is that car of yours playing up again?" And Judy sailed off to supervise the meal, a fantastic meal—Indonesian style, course after excellent course.

I insisted that we relieve our hosts of the long drive back to the Club.

"What did you want to do that for?" cried Rafe. "It cost us over three pesos each!"

"Well, hell, I wasn't going to ride with Judy again!"

"Nor me!" said Mike.

"Or me!" echoed Bill.

Next day was Sunday, the day for cockfighting. Judy and Jackson collected us for the drive through Manila's countryside to our first cockfight. Mike, Bill and I chose Jackson's car and climbed in. Rafe, an atheist, should be all right with Judy as she was escorted by her favourite priest, Father Clark, a youngish Irish-American. The Devil looks after his own, it is said, so I figured that with both sides working for her Judy would make it there and back safely.

Before we had even left the city proper the Caingñin's dreadful shacks appeared on waste ground and even vacant city lots like a nightmare fungus. On either side of a railway line stretched an unbroken mass of hovels, crowding the shining rails dangerously close.

Manila sprawls for miles around the bay and inland, the low rolling hills are fenced off, secluded sanctuaries for the wealthy. We drove through one of these enclaves. At checkpoints armed guards in smart uniforms eyed us suspiciously—they were hired by the residents of the select suburbs to keep out undesirables. Most of the beautiful homes were enclosed behind high brick or stone walls, often topped with broken glass. Most had their own private guards day and night, and savage dogs, too. It was a grim indication of the tremendous gulf between the "haves" and "have-nots" in this strange country.

We passed a big Mercedes with all its windows silvered like mirrors. It was quite impossible to see if anyone was inside.

"That's a great idea!" said Bill who loves cars. "No glare—it really must keep the sun out!"

"Keeps the bullets out!" muttered Jackson. "They're quite common—stops assassins!"

Rice paddy fields became more and more numerous and brick and concrete buildings gave way to unpainted wooden homes bleached grey from sun and rain. Glass windows were replaced by the latticed capis-shell screens, unique and attractive. These are windows, palely translucent, made in little squares, each "pane" half of a thin-walled seashell. All manner of lampshades, screens and ornaments are made from the capis, but as windows they are most picturesque. Water buffalo lumbered along the grassy verges, heavy and solid with huge widespread horns. Children straddled the beasts to guide them with thumping sticks and shrill cries.

We came to an ancient Spanish church, one of the oldest in the Philippines, and the presbytery where Father Clark offici-ated. Out came ice and drinks. Judy unpacked the bulging hampers and we had a picnic lunch on a verandah overlooking a valley green with coffee bushes and paddy fields.

By two o'clock we were well away again and only the timely arrival of one of Father Clark's flock reminded us of the cock-fighting. We were to find the alcohol a help in stomaching this gruesome sport.

Cockfighting is probably the most popular entertainment in the Philippines. Gamblers come from all over Latin America, Mexico, Spain and the Southern States of America to wager on the fighting birds. We were surprised at the size of the crowd packing the barnlike arena—and this only a relatively small "meet" in the insignificant village of Morong. We watched the fitting of spurs to the roosters' left legs. They are, in fact, grace-fully curved knives of polished steel, sharp as a scalpel. From boxes of several dozen, different in the attaching lugs only, a wicked weapon would be selected to fit precisely each particular bird. They were then painstakingly bound on by specialists. In the last bindings fine wire was embedded so a lucky stroke couldn't cut free the spur and so disarm an otherwise able com-batant.

There were other experts too; they were equipped with probes and forceps, lint and lotions to help the valuable victors, if possible, to fight again another day. In a small enclosure, separated from the main hall, owners paraded their birds for would-be punters to size them up. In the centre of the hall a square of earth and sawdust was raised about three feet. It was approximately 20 feet square and surrounded by wire mesh to a height of some eight feet. "Bleachers" lined the building in tiers and wildly gesticulating bookies called and calculated their odds. No tote—no tickets—just bets honoured by word of mouth and woe betide a welsher—his life would be as short as that of the bird he bet on.

Mike and I approached one of the officials (he had an automatic bulging his hip pocket) and he was most helpful, describing with huge enjoyment the rules of the sport. We asked if we could get inside the cockpit for photography and in a trice were hoisted on to the top of the big cage to prepare our cameras.

"Be careful! Keep clear of the birds—they could injure you!"

Two birds cradled in their owners' arms were brought in and were allowed to peck at each other's combs, first one and then the other. When thoroughly aroused—and the betting concluded—they were released to rush at each other. There was a brief skirmish, a fluttering and leaping—the flash of spurs and, unbelievably, one lay dead in the dust. Our new friend had told us this could happen, but it was obvious the fight was secondary to the betting. Another pair of shining birds was brought in to play their grisly part. This time the battle lasted longer—too long for us as we watched one bird tripping on its own entrails released by a wicked slash.

Its fighting strength ebbed away, but not its rage and will to fight. Even when the victor jumped on the collapsed bundle of feathers to crow and flap in triumph, the loser pecked feebly at its opponent's yellow-scaled legs.

We escaped into the open, into fresh air and sunlight. Our escort gathered us up and got us into a jeepnie.

On the way back to Manila we drove past the magnificent cultural complex and the new Makati office centre of handsome glass and concrete towers. What a land of contrasts. Paddy fields and buffalo—boulevards and limousines. Long-haired little beauties in chic clothes and high heels tapping past paunchy guards lounging in office foyers with pump shotguns in hand.

Next day there was to be a special parade of film and T.V. stars, popular band groups, etc. Mike and I got off to an early start. Jeepnies from out of town lined the boulevards and avenues in hundreds. There was a festive air and great jets trailing their brown highways over the city added zest to the spectacle. We walked for miles to reach Rizal Place, a huge plaza of ornamental gardens, reflecting pools and fountains, dominated by the monument to Dr Rizal, martyr in the cause of freedom.

"Hey, just look at that! It's like a black sea—all the black heads!" I exclaimed. The countless thousands pressing close together made a carpet of dark hair right across the square.

"I'd like to squeeze some of 'em!" muttered Mike, eyeing an olive-skinned vision nearby.

We clambered on top of a concrete plinth and the full scene was exposed—gone the sea of black hair, now the splash of gay frocks gave colour to the moving masses.

Mike and I never did see the parade. There were over a quarter of a million people milling in the area and we just couldn't force a passage.

"Telephone for you, Captain!" How I loved that title!

A rich feminine voice. "My name is Monique; a friend and I understand you are going to Indonesia and wondered if we could come along. We could help with costs and cooking."

"Sorry, but we're going up to Japan. I don't expect to be in Indonesia for at least six weeks."

A long pause. "Well, could we come and see you?"

"Sure. I'll be either in the club or out on my boat the *Whai* for the rest of the day."

Monique and Robbie presented themselves. We sat on the verandah drinking rum and cokes and got acquainted. First good point—they obviously didn't object to drink. First bad point—both smoked. Apart from Bev Short and Mona Isley, the *Whai* had been free of butts and ash-spreaders as none of the men smoked at all. Monique was dark and plump, wore glasses and had all the confidence and push in the world. Robbie was petite. They were both single, 24, and old school chums. Monique had come out to the Philippines as a Peace Corps volunteer and Robbie, a trained nurse, joined her later. They were working their way around the world and were now prepared to come to Japan and back, providing we'd take them on to Indonesia on our return voyage.

"What will it cost?" asked Monique.

"Well, if you two are prepared to do all the cooking and help with the dishes, it'll cost you $30 a week each."

"U.S. or Australian?" Quick Monique.

"U.S." And the two had a hasty consultation. "It's more than we expected." Monique again.

"Well, it's pretty cheap—food, drinks and accommodation, plus the travel! Can you better that any other way? But you must realise that the boys have to agree unanimously about this—we decided before we left home there'd be no women crew on board."

That night I put it to the vote—the boys were sick of cooking and I needed the extra cash.

"No more cooking!" chortled Cobber.

"Women!" breathed the Count.

"There'll be none of that!" I warned.

And so it was decided. The two girls moved on board to introduce us to a more civilised existence. I organised visas for Taiwan, National China, bought extra food and arranged for refuelling.

I had found out early in the voyage that duty-free fuel could be bought. "Where do I go for the diesel?" I asked the Shell rep.

"We'll bring it to you!" was the reply. "Tomorrow at ten we'll send a tanker around." Sure enough a tanker arrived. In my innocence I had expected a tanker-truck to pump fuel into us while alongside the wharf. But this was a real tanker—old, rusting and low in the water. A hose came aboard and we were in business.

"That's not quite the thing to do!" said Ernesto. "We have pumps."

"Yes, but I can't afford your prices! This way it's duty free—saves me 3 or 4 cents a gallon and every little counts!"

Loaded with fresh fruit and vegetables and with plenty of San Miguel beer down below, we assured our many club friends that, like MacArthur, "we would return!"

"Watch out for typhoons! Don't take chances! And remember what I said about pirates!" shouted the owner of a fleet of tugs. He had confirmed stories I'd heard and added his own facts.

"None of my tugs come into Manila Bay at night," he had said.

"You're joking!"

"No, I'm dead serious, Peter—we've had crews come in stripped completely naked—the whole boat gone over like a vacuum cleaner. We used to use nylon tows but the pirates would cut the rope to the last barge in a heavy sea and the tug daren't turn back. Now we use wire hawsers."

"Why don't you arm the crews?"

"What! Against machine-guns and hand grenades? No, we can't expect our men to risk their lives."

"Whenever I'm out in my yacht," said the owner of the *Green Beret*, "I always fire off a few rounds if I see a strange craft approaching. It shows we're armed and alert."

And to these cheery words of warning we departed in broad daylight and with our armament close to hand.

I wanted to see over Corregidor Island and its famous fortifications, but the urge to clear out into open sea before nightfall was too strong and we motored past between its rugged cliffs and the reefs off Cochinos Point. We were now in the South China Sea and cruising along Luzon's rough coastline, past Subic Bay and the lighthouse on Palauig Point flashing in the dusk. The next two days took us to Lingayen Gulf and on up the coast to Cape Bojeador and into the Babuyan Channel. It was dark when we coasted into the narrow passage between Fuga (Refuge) and the smaller Barit Island. There was a 40-foot motorboat anchored off the white sand beach of Fuga, and on board an open cooking fire cast red light on the figures moving around it. A woman on board laughed, so I took a chance on our neighbours and, dropping anchor nearby, came to rest.

When we awoke the strange craft had gone and we were alone on gin-clear waters. Fish glided from coral cave to branching stag-horn forest. Patches of clean sand showed the marks where our anchor chain had dragged in arcs and loops. On shore a man's lone figure sat on a log staring out at us. He was a white man and waved to us when he saw us come on deck to launch the dinghy.

"My name's Lenny. Welcome to Fuga Island. Where are you from?"

And so we met a mystery man—suposedly writing a book on Fuga and its ancient Spanish history. He might be an author, but he was much more—an expert on small arms and certainly a soldier of fortune. He introduced us to Miguel—the Filipino straw boss of Fuga—and to Johnny, a fat youth, one of three armed guards. Johnny was detailed to keep an eye on us. I had the funny feeling that Lenny wasn't free to talk openly; he paid a curious deference to Miguel.

"Is there anything to see on Fuga?"

Lenny kicked at a piece of driftwood and looked towards the homestead.

"Well, there are a few Japanese caves and an old Spanish church."

"Any good diving around here?"

"There's the wreck of a Spanish tax-gathering boat sunk about 1890."

"How deep? Is there much to see?" This was more like it!

"It's in about 20 feet—not much left and very scattered. It's an old steamer."

"Let's go!" we cried.

"I'll have to ask Miguel if it's O.K."

"Surely he won't mind? He doesn't own the seabed, or even the island!"

"Ah, you don't understand. I'll ask him." Off he went. While we waited we drew water from a well and filled the ship's tanks, a slow job needing half a dozen trips out and back in the dinghy humping the heavy containers.

"Sorry, fellas—no go. Miguel doesn't want you to dive." There was an awkward silence.

"What does he like to drink?" I asked.

"Whisky; when he can get it."

"Come over to the *Whai* and we'll get a bottle."

With the grog and a pile of old magazines, Lenny left to butter up the boss.

"Tell Miguel we'll call on our way back to dive on the wreck! And we'd like to see the caves and old church too!" I shouted after him.

"O.K., stick round, Peter. I've a lot of books I've finished with —I'll get them for you."

Lenny came back with a curious collection—his taste was catholic and again I got the impression of a man fairly bursting to talk with fellow Caucasians and yet not free to do so.

We waved goodbye and set off into the Luzon straits.

CHAPTER SIX

Chinese Naval Engagement

"Now just keep your course. It's their job to give way," I instructed Bill, who was on the wheel. A very big cargo boat of unusual design was bearing down on us. The day was bright and clear, a 20-knot wind from port astern was piling up white caps and the *Whai* was rolling and surging a little with its peculiar "stiff" motion.

"Hell, it's getting very close! I don't think it's going to alter course!" Bill got decidedly nervous and I did, too, as the ship drew nearer, its great white bow tearing the waves apart. High up on the bridge we could see some characters sauntering about, not deigning to look our way. Why should they? This was the nuclear-powered *Savannah* rushing along at 20 knots.

"Hard aport! Idle the motors!" and the enormous bulk slid past. The bow wave arrowing away took us head on and the *Whai* dug in as if hitting a cliff.

I learnt another lesson from this—if you're bigger, you're boss. For the rest of our voyage I played chicken and watched the chances taken and the bluffing of heavy traffic near big ports and, in particular, in the Japanese Inland Sea. It would have shaken my instructors at the Marine Department course to see what went on.

Taiwan was dead ahead—Cape Garan lighthouse shining white against the green mountains and grey cliff-faces. Away out to starboard, faint and hazy on the horizon, was Koto Island. The chart had warned of what we could now see ahead, but even so I wasn't prepared for the short and steep 20-foot walls of water. One minute we were cruising quietly and the next were rearing and rolling in an extraordinary sea. I was on the cabin roof and just had time to grab Robbie. Together we clung to anything handy: rails, the engine ventilator, each other. The rolling was so violent the two side ports overbalanced to crash down with frightful bangs. Luckily Bill had both hands gripping the wheel —he'd have lost fingers if his hand had been hooked around the porthole's rim. Converging currents struggled together at this spot in an endless combat of blue-green ridges, and the wind added to the turmoil. It lasted for 20 frightening minutes and

the boat was a shambles when we came out the other side of the
heaving area. Books and clothes, dishes, spearguns and cameras
were scattered everywhere. The dinghy had worked free of its
lashings and was wracking back and forth. Thank goodness, it
was so very light and strong—a heavier craft would have been
tossed overboard. Thoughtfully I helped clean up the mess.

"Well, after that I've complete confidence in the *Whai!* There
wasn't a creak out of her and we've not shipped a drop of
water!"

"Man, she'll do me," said Bill. "I could feel the currents heaving at the rudders but the motors could steer her on their own!"
We found that in emergencies the two propellors, 13 feet apart,
gave us extraordinary control and manoeuvrability.

Taiwan, dark and mysterious, slowly drifted past, mile after
mile. The occasional lighthouse led us up the coast and lights
gleamed in golden beads and clusters. Way up on the mountain-
sides bright lights shone in meaningless flashes as if we were
being handed on from one secret watcher to another.

Dawn came—beautiful and serene; blue-grey cloud lay in long
thin layers softening the rocky coast. Mists climbed the valley
slopes and the sun, huge and red, slid above the sea to tip the
mountain peaks with splendid colour. There was a nip in the
air. The sun rose higher, driving the shadows down the mountain sides in silent retreat. Now the glassy sea became alive.
Cormorants and gulls passed overhead and far off a faint white
"tadpole" crawled across the china blue above. And another and
another, heading our way. Then we heard the muted thunder of
powerful engines a long way up. The murmur rolled and muttered, trailing the pencilled lines now lengthening into fluffy
con-trails pointing to the west. In front of each—a tiny black
dot on its way to Vietnam and each tiny black dot carried 30
tons of violent death. The drifting cloud veils ashore turned to
smog and factory smoke, and suddenly the day lost its sparkling
freshness and the joy of dawn was gone. It was not Nature's
clouds that stained the earth and sky. Silently we went about our
petty chores.

"We'll put in at Hualien—I can't see anything else marked on
the chart. I don't want to go any further north than I can help
'cos we're short on fuel. Lord only knows what we'll find there
—I haven't the faintest clue!"

This was quite true of most of the places we'd visited. If you
are going to explore why read all about it in advance? Cook
didn't, couldn't. I'm no Captain Cook—just a bumbling be-

ginner, but at least I was truly exploring. Charts for safety, yes; a Baedeker, no.

A procession of fishing boats streamed out from the harbour moles of Hualien. They were in pairs, each pair tied together by thick rope hawsers and a big net looped across their sterns. They looked for all the world like catamarans and their cheery crews waved as we slid by.

Hualien is entered through a narrow channel. The mountains had receded from the shore line where their cliffs and shale slides dropped steeply into the sea and a plain spread out in front of us. We slowly cruised between the shoreside rocks and outer sea wall, into the big concrete trough which paralleled the coast, and then turned sharply to port into a harbour basin. After circling the basin I took a chance and tied our cat behind the battered stern of a gunboat. No. 111 bristled with guns; she was gay with washing strung across the fantail. A cloud of filthy diesel smoke poured from an exhaust, to the heavy knocking of an ancient engine.

A figure in immaculate khaki drill and peaked naval cap strode along the wharf towards us. Here it comes, I thought. What now?

"Hulloa—do you speak English?" The standard opener.

"A little—please to speak slow. I duty officer on warship."

And so we met the Chinese Navy. They were good to us, but in the end we disgraced them dreadfully.

Arrangements were made to contact Customs and Immigration—the wharf police were just over the dockside. A bland policeman arrived, complete with folding chair and umbrella. He took up a position with his back to some crates and sat watching us. He adjusted his plastic helmet and pulled a large holstered automatic pistol into full view. Day and night one or another sat guard. On us? For us? And little us right next to one of their warships.

"Ten copies?" I was dumbfounded.

"You will fill in ten copies of each form. It is the regulation," said Immigration. Two Customs men and a policeman dressed in neat boiler suits and wielding torches presented me with a form. It read, in effect, "Assist these examining officers voluntarily or we'll force the issue."

I grabbed Mike, big and obviously awe-inspiring to these slight Orientals. "Quick, hop down and try and block off the gun cubby-hole. If you run into trouble, don't worry—just play dumb!"

We'd put clothes over the rifles and the automatics were hidden in the enginerooms. Apart from the French in Noumea, no one ever asked if we carried arms and so I said nowt.

"Come down this side first," I suggested to the officials and down we crowded port side. I showed them the grog and our medical kit. The Chinese flashed their torches very briefly—it was soon obvious it wasn't contraband they were looking for but spies, illegal immigrants, stowaways: who knows? They didn't bother about our grog and they completely missed the guns.

I sat down to fill in 40 forms. How I prayed for some carbon paper. Four different forms, ten copies of each. The morning wore on.

"Say! Look at this!" Rafe came in with nine curious dead-white shiny spheres. "The Navy sent it along—Chinese bread!"

The heat was stifling. I got Cobber to go to the warship to ask for water—the novel experience would do him good, and muttering with hopeless doubts Cobber disappeared, only to return triumphant with a huge hose. The crew sloshed water all over the *Whai* to get rid of the sticky salt, filled our tanks, and everyone had a shower much to the huge entertainment of the Chinese, civilian and Navy, crowding the wharf. When the two girls, golden brown, appeared in bikinis to rinse off, there was a terrific chirping and clicking. Light-coloured skins are considered beautiful by Chinese and for a woman to expose herself deliberately to the sun was beyond the pale. The American girls must have seemed shameless hussies of very low class.

The duty officer came aboard again.

"Our captain sends compliments. Would your crew have dinner aboard our ship?"

"Yes! Thank you very much. Please give your captain a little gift from the *Whai*," and I hauled out a bottle of vodka.

"Please not to be late. We eat at 12.30. The naval commander for district guest too."

I got out a bottle of gin and we climbed the high-sided wharf by clambering on the rubber buffers and heaving the leggy girls up ahead, to the huge delight of the crowd. I gave our guard a cake of chocolate to ensure his goodwill and we strolled down to the 111. Self-conscious in shorts and open-necked shirts we trooped up the gangplank, ducked under wire cables and so into the officers' mess. We were introduced by the captain, a tough-looking Chinese of about 40, to the Hualien naval commander, then to the 111's first lieutenant and executive officer, and so on to the political officer (this *was* a sur-

prise—we were in Nationalist China). This officer sat withdrawn and said little. Later when things got warmed up he un-
bent and gave out some little screw-in lapel-badges: portraits of
Generalissimo Chiang Kai-Chek. I didn't hesitate to puncture my
best shirt and fasten this natty gilt souvenir in place.

"Thank you for the New Zealand wine," said the captain,
pouring himself a glass of vodka. "A happy voyage to us all."
And we were off on another king-sized party. Mike nudged me.
"Do you see what they're doing to the gin!" It was awesome—
our two bottles of spirits only made one round. There were 14
of us crowded in the tiny mess. A large table filled the centre
and the *Whai's* crew lined one bulkhead and the Chinese officers
the opposite. Two big fans droned and tried to push the hot air
into motion.

Smiling crewmen with tureens of pork and soup, rice and
noodles, cabbage and bean sprouts, kept loading the table. Exotic
sauces and pickles and hot rice wine were offered for approval.
The Lazy Susan turntable kept going round and round dispen-
sing seaweed, salted melon, sunflower seeds and lychee nuts. The
girls, round-eyed and thrilled to bits, sipped their wine and
covered their shudders nobly. We rugged Kiwis struggled with
the neat vodka and gin but had to cry quits and ask for lemonade
to break it down.

The commander slapped me on the back, laughing. "Your
wine is good—but try some of ours. It is made with reindeer
blood!"

We eyed the mystery bottle with misgiving—the liquor was
dark red and smelled like a corpse in an oil well.

"Whew! My God! Watch it!" But it was too late and Bill
and Rafe were spluttering and coughing. I grabbed the nearest
glass and drank deep to quench the liquid fire. It was the duty
officer's gin, neat and pungent. Involuntarily I gagged and
coughed in distress. The Chinese roared with laughter. These
people are supposed to be impassive but that's nonsense. Their
cheeks flushed red and tears ran, and helpless with delight at
having surprised their guests, the officers' day was made.

We found out too late that the first course was but a beginning. "Their wine makes neat gin taste pleasant," said Mike, as
with numbed lips and trembling hands we waded through one
dish after another. Course followed course; raw fish (not new
to me—I'll often eat a speared leatherjacket on a long lonely
swim in New Zealand); octopus, squid and, horror of horrors,
hundred-year egg, black, slimy and completely beyond our
tastes. There was bean curd, too, like an evil-looking junket.

Different wines for us to try and Chinese beer, insipid and warm. "Get some more grog, boss!" whispered Bill, "I can't take this Chinese stuff."

But it was over—we'd spent two wonderful hours and the commander wanted us to join him at golf. In 95° of humid heat? We had a quick conference. Robbie, Bill and Cobber decided to return to the *Whai* to sleep it off and the rest of us, martyrs in the cause of politeness, staggered into the sunshine, heaving and swallowing in the last stages of food narcosis, and so into a blue Navy minibus.

The commander addressed his ball shining white on its little red tee. Small women in coolie hats pottered around the greens armed with rake and hoe and completely swathed against the sun. Anti-aircraft guns pointed their ugly snouts to the sky from grassy revetments set in the rough.

The commander swung with gusto and followed the soaring flight of a 300-yard drive. He started up the fairway with a bemused smile of satisfaction but the captain of the 111 tapped him on the shoulder and pointed to the ball still perched on its tee. The commander blinked and gazed in disbelief. He again smote a mighty drive, again was referred to the ball inexplicably unmoved. Five times he followed in his imagination the flight of glorious drives and five times the captain diffidently drew him back to reality.

We dared not laugh—one doesn't laugh at Chinese and certainly not at one's host, the Naval Commander of Hualien. The vodka and gin, the Chinese wine were fuming in our heads. The sun beat down in shimmering waves—we were all very drunk and I just had to laugh or burst.

Suddenly the unreality of the situation hit me—what the hell was I doing here, 5,000 miles from home, playing golf with the Chinese Navy? And I didn't even like golf.

It was obvious we couldn't keep on. The commander had fallen down once or twice. The captain, however, was of sterner stuff and the duty officer, too. We called it a day after four and a half holes because we ran out of balls. Some Mike and I had deliberately driven into fields of cabbage lining the course. Some had fallen into water traps and some the captain had pocketed. At least it looked that way.

We poured the commander out at his home and gathered up the others. The captain was pleased to escort us around town which, of course, meant the night clubs. We ended up with a bout of singing, loud and coarse, unintelligible, thank goodness,

to the polite Chinese—anything and everything we knew and
eventually when we ran down in fits and starts like clockwork
toys a monumental bill was presented. Of course we had to be
short. The club manager insisted on coming back to the *Whai*
to collect and our captain of the 111, mortally mortified at this
loss of face, left us in a huff, taking with him the bus. As we
bedded down for the night we could hear the unfortunate club
manager snivelling at lack of transport and the three-mile walk
back to his clip-joint club.

Our policeman on the wharf cheerily waved good morning.
"Velly happy las' night! You no smile now?" All right for
him; all he had done was sit under his umbrella and watch the
T.V. set taken on to the dockside by the sailors off the 111. We
milled about, moaning and trying concoctions of Alka Seltzer,
aspirin and pep-up pills. Apart from our guard we seemed to
be in Coventry—the Navy kept strictly to themselves. I went to
see the port captain or harbour master.
"You must have agent!" the little man said.
"I don't want one! Why should I? We can get our own vegetables and diesel. We aren't an ocean-going liner! Hell, we only
need about 200 gallons of fuel and a few dollars' worth of
groceries!"
"It is the law. You must have agent. I fix for you." And that
was that. The retired naval captain, now Hualien's harbour
master, introduced me to a fat-faced, bespectacled Chinese, oily
and placid.
"Now—what you want?" continued the harbour master.
"Well, here we go, but you'll see it's stupid. We need 200
gallons, Imperial gallons, of first-quality diesel, 2 tinned chickens,
2 cabbages of about 2 kilograms each, 1 kilogram of rice, long
grain if possible, and about 5 kilograms of potatoes."
"Is that all?"
"Yes. I told you we don't need much; we're just a little boat
and I want to get most of our stuff from Americans in Okinawa."
The captain conferred with the fat merchant.
"Can do." It was arranged to refuel first thing in the morning.
We decided to hire a taxi to see the countryside. The roads
weren't good away from the docks and the main highway north
out of town became a narrow tarsealed road with pot-holed
verges. Gangs of men and women with simple hand tools were
resealing a strip. Women, swathed in rags, shovelled and pumped
as hard as the men. How they stood the heat, working energetic-
ally and wrapped up like mummies I'll never understand.

We passed several shrines all red, blue and gold and guarded by stone lions and gilded dragons. Paddy fields and market gardens lined the road and peasants topped by large conical sun hats stooped among the lush crops. Little cane and brush shelters were tucked among the fields.

There were betel-nut vendors and baskets of strange fruit. Curious sweetmeats and unhealthy looking sticky confections alongside huge cabbages. Girls and women selling postcards pestered us at every halt. It was obvious that tourists were no novelty and a taxi meant people with money to spend.

We were off to the Marble Gorge—everyone in Hualien had said we mustn't miss this, the seventh wonder in Asia, and they were right. We crossed a concrete bridge over a small milky-blue river and entered a big canyon. The gorge walls closed in, huge and rugged. Great outcrops of rock, some weathered smooth as sculpture, others cracked and jagged, forced the roadway to wind and twist. The road bored into dark tunnels cut through bluffs to emerge into brilliant sunshine and again and again to hide itself underground. The driver stopped at an underground lay-by and we climbed out into cool darkness. Swallows flickered in the shadows and a steady draught of cold air swirled and tugged at our light clothes. Balconies and balustrades had been cut from the living rock and out from the cliff face we could look down into the ravine. Most of the smooth faces of rock were solid marble, dove-grey or icing-sugar white. One of the drivers threw a piece of paper over the edge and it fell in fluttering swoops a hundred feet before being snatched and hurled aloft in the rising draughts high above our heads. Again and again we tried the trick and each scrap of paper fell, only to be rounded up and blown skyward out of sight.

The highway weaved in and out of the rock wall and below a big curve the river tumbled over the rocks and idled over white sand shoals. I was hot and sticky, my head throbbed and I wanted a drink of water. We were miles from anywhere and the descent to the river looked fairly easy. I left the others and clambered down the boulder and earthen slope. There was a huge pure white marble basin full of milky-blue water, cool and gently flowing. Our party was a hundred feet away and above so I slipped out of my clothes and into the water. Cool at last and plenty of bath-water to drink.

"What's it like, Peter?" Mike scrambled down to the water's edge.

"Mother's milk, fountain of youth—you name it! Don't just stand there, hop in—it's bloody marvellous!"

"You must see Ami peoples," advised the driver. "Pretty girls dancing. Much pleasure."

We came to a complex of small booths with a central theatrette built in the form of a big "U" around a gardened courtyard. This was the "Cultural Centre" of the Ami village—actually a tourist trap with a difference. The booths were simply little shops each selling various handicrafts of the Ami, a mountain people. These Ami were indigenous Formosans and had built the cooperative; they catered for the tourist trade and picked out talented and pretty girls as entertainment. A single male dancer completed their troupe.

The evening performance was about to start—a gong sounded, sweet and mellow. Coloured lanterns were lit as we filed into the little theatre with its tiers of cane armchairs surrounding a circular wooden stage. About 20 girls poured out from the wings, laughing and giggling, eyes sparkling; short, robust girls with ruddy cheeks, and black hair. Linking arms they gathered into a circle facing outwards and slowly danced around so that we, as it were, met each one. Their leader stepped forward to make a little speech of welcome, first in Japanese (or was it Chinese?) and then in quaint English.

The Japanese tourists smiled and sucked in their breath politely. We were so very close to the entertainers we were almost part of the show. The girls were so near and so vivid in mime and costume that it wasn't long before we were entirely caught up in the spirited tempo of their dances. We felt the communal joy of a good rice harvest, knew the thrill and satisfaction of a great day's hunting.

The dances enacted a dozen vignettes of village life. The girls whirled and stamped their bare feet, barbaric in costume and energy. A man, much taller than the little dancers, leapt into the circle and shouted encouragement. He, too, was dressed in Ami splendour. Coloured cloth leggings were bound with curious bandage-like strips below a kilt of tassels; strings of coloured beads clashed and jangled on his bare chest and a magnificent cap of dark cloth sported small pointed horns flanked by splendid pheasant plumes.

The last spectacular was us: we were singled out for the unique finale. One by one our crew were led on to the stage by giggling girls and dressed in embroidered smocks and fancy hats. Strings of beads were hung around our necks and curious palanquins brought in.

"They can't do it! For Pete's sake, they'll strain themselves!" But do it they did. Four small girl-women heaved Mike up and staggered around the stage in a sort of dancing shuffle; then Bill, even heavier, was collected by four more, who proceeded to grunt their way along. Soon we were all bobbing and wobbling around the ring, hilarious and petrified at the same time, our little steeds sweating with their exertions. The Japanese and Chinese audience were rolling in their seats, tears streaming down their cheeks.

For a horrid moment I thought we were being made fools of— stupid foreign devils being taken for a ride—then dismissed the unworthy idea. Everyone was having fun, even our little horses.

The show ended; we stood hot and happy on the stage. The troupe leader came to me.

"You English peoples?"

"No; we're from New Zealand."

A blank stare then a flashing smile. "Australian?"

"Not quite—from near there."

"Ah so—you stay—we dance—have joy?"

"Thanks—that would be fun."

But our style and theirs were a world apart. Music in half and quarter tones were beyond us and, an untalented lot, we couldn't even do a haka for them. Monique borrowed a mandolin and put on a surprising performance—quickly she had the friendly Amis gathered round and taught them a simple song.

Next day, and a bright hot sun. A crisp wind raised little dust devils which blew along the wharf. Our guard announced the arrival of the agent with the fuel. I gazed open-mouthed at the ancient three-wheeler truck and battered rusty drums. I had expected a tanker-wagon, but this outfit was ridiculous.

"How do I get the fuel into the tanks? There are two tanks on each side! Have we got to syphon the bloody stuff?"

I was furious—it meant mouthfuls of diesel, spillage and consequent waste. And hours of swabbing the cork-covered decking with detergents to clean up.

The bland agent presented an account which rocked me—he wanted over 90 U.S. dollars for 200 gallons of fuel! I was sure it was a come-on but who could I turn to? I decided to fuel now, argue later.

"Put in 150—that'll get us to Okinawa."

I got about five thicknesses of fine cloth and we filtered the fuel. It looked all right for colour but flakes of rust and beads of moisture clogged the top layer of cloth. At last it was over and I made the unfortunate truck driver drain each of his horrible containers into a bucket and from this into the ship's tanks.

I wrote a note to the harbour master about the overcharge and sent it off by a small boy who was hanging around.

An answer came some time later: "Please see me. I think I can save you 50 dollars—Harbour Master."

That fetched me out in a rush—it was 4.30—would he still be there? I took a bicycle leaning against a shed and was on my way.

The harbour master had the agent in his office. Not the impassive man of the day before but a pale, sweating fellow with fluttering hands.

The small official presented some papers for my signature—heaven only knows what—handed me a roll of Chinese dollars and told me where to pick up my clearance papers for Okinawa. Thankfully I shook his hand and left a bottle of gin on his desk. The agent stood silent, looking at the floor.

I collected the clearance from the harbour police, leaving the bicycle where it would easily be found and in the meanwhile be safe, and walked to the *Whai*.

"We must be out before 12 tonight as the harbour is sealed then," I told Bill. "Make sure all the others are on board—we have to go! I intend to sail at 11.45 definitely, ready or not!" And with that I tottered back to bed. Our diesel had cost us less than 18 dollars and I wasn't going to hang around while on top, not after nearly being gypped. At about nine I was woken up again, this time by Mike.

"Jesus, Mike—what's up? I'm on the wheel at 11.30 and I'm flakers!"

"The cops want a sample of the fuel!"

"What for?" Oh gawd! What had the fat bastard sold me! We tried sucking fuel from the tanks but they were too deep down from the fillers on deck, so we had to lift floorboards, remove a tank inspection plate, lower a coke bottle tied on a string and then replace everything. The police took the bottle away and half an hour later came back to search the boat. I was scared stiff the guns would be found but again it was stowaways they were after. At 11.45 I started the donkeys.

The night was pitch black. I shouted cheerio to our guard, threw him a bag of Minties and he cast us off. Behind the *Whai* the 111 lay dark and silent. In tribute to the friendly sailors I pressed the horn button but the twin trumpets only made a rude noise which sorrowed me. They were full of salt water again.

I steered around in a slow half-circle and headed down the channel at three knots. It was impossible to see the shore line and

I had to judge the centre of the channel by the lengths of golden light from street and dock lamps lining the route. The *Whai* lifted and rolled a little to the uneasy swell on the bar and I turned her north-east towards the Ryukyu Islands and Okinawa. The next stop would be in Japanese territory.

CHAPTER SEVEN

Okinawa: Americans and Others

WITH ABOUT 300 miles to go before reaching Okinawa, I had time for introspection and to face up to personal problems and those which were becoming critical in the *Whai's* machinery, equipment and crew.

I have always tended to bottle up reaction to petty annoyances, but eventually the sum total of little stupidities, laziness or selfishness of crew life reached a point where one last infraction caused me to blow my stack. It must have been a shock to the current Count to have me burst into a towering rage over a trifle. I was sick of things left lying around, tins of butter or meats being freshly opened when one or two were already in use; toilet rolls finished and not replaced, lashings undone, tools not put away—a host of things, piddling in themselves but indicative of general laziness of mind and body. The heat, I think, got us all down, resulting in "scratchiness" and selfishness, and an effort was needed to pull us together again. The motors needed an oil change and thorough check-over—the injectors were due for service, and all the fuel and oil filters needed renewing. The radio transmitter was blowing fuses for some obscure reason and the echo-sounder tracings were becoming vague and indistinct.

I reasoned that the Americans at Okinawa would have the facilities and technical know-how to help me get the cat in good shape. My method of deciding where to go for refuelling was simple: I'd look at the small map of the Pacific and, if a place was big enough to be mentioned and was within 1,000 miles of our last refuelling point, that was it. Naha, in Okinawa, looked the most likely, and the *Japan Pilot* confirmed it as the chief Ryukyu port of entry.

So that was all set—lean on the good old U.S. military for facilities to get the *Whai* into shape, let the crew refresh themselves ashore for a few days, and then I'd read the Riot Act. Having two new members on board, Monique and Robbie, provided a first-class excuse to re-brief the entire gang on how the cruise was to be run in future, and I set about writing a list of do's and don'ts.

Morning dawned with a burnished sun almost dead ahead and a choppy sea of white horses flecked with gold. In the main cabin Robbie was cooking eggs and bacon, coffee and toast. The aroma drew us out of our bunks to yawn and stretch, blinking at the bright new day, as we skirted the East China Sea.

Iromote Island, green and steeply cliffed, was about an hour away and beyond it, low on the horizon, others of the Sakishima Group and Ishigaki, the largest. Two big junks were seesawing back and forth in perfect unison over to port.

"Let's see what they're up to. Head over behind them." The *Whai* eased around and as we drew closer all the crew came up on top of the cabin to watch the curious manoeuvres. First one junk motored forward with puffs of smoke from its high exhaust. It would cover perhaps 100 yards, pause, and then reverse to its original position. The other boat did the same, each alternating back and forth as if in a strange nautical dance. The junks were about 150 yards apart and almost at right angles to each other. They appeared to carry very large crews, some of whom wore diving masks. About ten men in the bows of each boat hauled in a heavy rope when their craft moved forward. As soon as it finished its run and paused, the crew belayed the rope around a big bollard for the pull backward.

"Good grief! They haven't got winches and they're hauling in a net!" cried Bill.

Not quite. The thick rope had what appeared to be bunches of raffia or flax tied every six to ten feet or so. This was no net but a version of a trick I'd seen in the Tongan Islands. The Tongans (and other South Sea islanders) tie bundles of greenery to a long rope and then draw it across a lagoon, driving the frightened fish ahead to be speared and netted in the shallows. The fish go crazy and come out of their coral caves instead of staying put.

We drew closer, taking care to idle along well clear and to the rear of the junks. Suddenly a man jumped into the sea from the high outstretched pulpit of the forward boat, then another and another. Soon some 20 young men were splashing and shouting in the water. They swam to form a half-circle lining the outer edge of the rope. A little praam-like dinghy was lowered from a junk and more divers leapt into action. The dinghy towed a net, with floats and leaden weights, across and between the sterns of the two junks and the trap was complete. Heaving and straining, the deck crews slowly hauled in the balance of heavy rope while the swimmers redoubled their commotion. The fine-meshed net was drawn together and hauled aboard. We eased in close now that the fishing cycle was over and counted the catch. Three largish flying fish. The fishing party did not look pleased and started eyeing us with disfavour, as if we could have been responsible for the pitiful results.

"Open her up! Let's get out of here!"

Cobber looked at me: "Cripes, there must have been at least 50 men there! No wonder they're coming out to New Zealand to fish!"

We passed Miyako Island in the night—just a dark mass speckled with a hundred winking lights. I had calculated on reaching the Islands of Karama, just south of Okinawa, at daybreak but something went wrong. There are strong currents up here amongst the Ryukyus and then the Count woke me with "Peter! Peter! There's an aircraft-carrier dead ahead!"

I heaved myself up, groaning and cursing. I wasn't due on watch for another three hours and had slept badly. Expecting to see an aircraft-carrier, sure enough I saw one. Big, black, with a string of porthole lights down its flank and a cluster of lights where the bridge-island reared darkly. If it were landing or launching aircraft it would be heading into the wind and we were up wind and right in its path.

"Go 90 degrees to port—we'll have to pass behind it." I looked for its green starboard light but could see only a flashing white light which blinked three or four times and went out.

"I think it's stationary. Damned if I can see any steaming lights, and there aren't any aircraft operating that I can see either. Switch off for a minute and we'll listen." The motors coughed and rumbled to a stop and the *Whai* ghosted along. Not another sound.

Mike came up and gawped around, blinking and yawning: "I can't sleep. What's up? What island is that?"

"It's an aircraft-carrier."

Mike looked long and hard: "I can't see it. Where abouts?"

"Right in front of you! What the hell do you think it is?"

"An island. You need your eyes tested!" And with that Mike went to rattle around in the galley.

We two Counts peered, and slowly the carrier faded in our imagination. A string of street lamps replaced the portholes and the bridge island with its glittering sparks of light became a hillside village.

I learned something from this—never to take anything for granted, to come fresh to an emergency, mind clear and eyes open. The power of suggestion can play strangely vivid tricks. A sort of *folie à deux* is created.

We'd made very good time. A current of at least 2 knots had brought us right along with it and we were amongst the group of islands south and west of Okinawa, about two hours before scheduled.

I had quite a job trying to establish our position, for the whole area was a mass of pinnacles, reefs and islets. Several aircraft droned above heading nor'east, and as we crawled across our blue carpet I calculated our approximate position. By the grace of Lady Luck we'd got through a very hairy situation.

Naha ahead—the *Pilot* was almost incomprehensible and years out of date. Several huge smoke stacks on Okinawa were adding to the sea haze but I could just make out some small craft in front. The echo-sounder was picking up the depths and with everyone sunning themselves and keeping a look-out I felt confident of a safe entry. More and more jets screamed overhead— this was a thrill for us—we were seeing stuff we had read about but which were strangers to New Zealand skies.

Naha, Okinawa's main city, is entered past a concrete break-water and up a channel lined with docks. It was our first Japanese port, and, not knowing the drill, I did my usual stunt of cruising around and around the wharves displaying our disreputable yellow flag, trying to draw some reaction. The left side of the harbour was untidy and obviously commercial, but on our starboard the metal-faced wharves were more ordered. Long low buildings and piles of huge crates, tier upon tier, formed a backdrop for rows of badly-battered army trucks.

Jutting out into the final reaches of the harbour basin, dividing it in two, was a clay promontory topped by a flag mast. Old Glory hung limp from the yardarm of a signal tower and a

large sign read "U.S. Army Port Authority". This must be it.
There were landing-barges tied to a jetty and I pulled alongside.
"Try and get the boat hosed down and the water tanks filled,
Mike, if you can." Some indolent sailors, hardly more than boys,
were hosing decks and skylarking around. We could have been
a boat from the other side of the harbour for all the interest
they took.

"How can I see the harbour master?" I asked. "We have to
check in with Immigration and Health, too."

"Yeah." Gum being chewed around and pushed to one side.
"Over there on the hill."

"May I cross your boat?"

"Sure, why not? Who cares? Say, guy, where's you from?
Britishers?"

"No, we're from New Zealand."

I clambered over the barges' hot decks to hear my young
sailor answer his friends:

"Yeah, Australians."

I marched across the hot bitumen, past machine shops redolent
with the smell of engine oil and up the slope to the signal station.
Then up two flights of stairs and into an office. An ice-water
dispenser couldn't be resisted and I helped myself. Telex machines chattered away and a big top-sergeant in summer drill
strolled over to the counter.

"Can I help you, sir?"

"Yes, please. We've just arrived here from Taiwan in my
yacht (even a power boat, or any small craft privately operated
is a yacht. Sounds grand, doesn't it?), the black catamaran down
there alongside the landing craft. I want the Immigration and
Health authorities. Here's my clearance from Hualien in Taiwan."

The sergeant studied it, stalked over to look down at the
Whai and then excused himself to confer with his major, the
Port Captain. As I slurped away at the water fountain I could
hear the rumble of voices in the major's office. He came out,
covered with enough ribbons to make even Monty envious.

"O.K., Skipper. You return to your boat and I'll get the
medics. I can handle the immigration part as long as you're here
for only a few days, and all your passports are in order. Forget
Customs. This is an Army port."

I was tickled pink. No stupid forms to fill in, no prying and
poking about. Whistling, I went back to find the crew soaping
and hosing each other off on the dockside with a huge crystal

jet of fresh water. Two Army medical orderlies came down and
presented us with small forms to fill in and that was that.

"You can't keep your ship here; we're moving in 20 minutes."
Oh hell! Just when I thought we were set. It was Friday and I
had assumed the barges were tied up for the weekend.

Eventually we crossed to a broken-down wharf alongside a
creaky old crane used for loading sacks of silica sand, coral and
chunks of stone. The dust was awful, blowing into eyes, hair
and mouths. But it was better than the place the Army had first
put us in, next to a sandblaster cleaning down a rusty tug. About
a hundred yards away a huge pontoon was moored—a U.S.
Army floating power station which billowed clouds of carbon
cinders from its twin stacks each night.

The day was nearly over and the crew had gone exploring. I
had a few chores. I wanted to arrange for the fuel injectors to
be serviced before the Army base across the harbour closed for
the weekend. Taking my passport I wandered off the dock,
skirting the harbour towards the huge complex. There was a
bridge crossing a river that smelt to high heaven—its nickname
was "Sweetwater" I found out later.

There was about half a mile of high wire-mesh fence around
the base. Outside the gates I asked a G.I. in civvies how I could
get inside. He pointed to a small vine-covered shed and told me
to ask there.

The guard on the gate barred my way. I showed him my
passport.

"You have to get a pass! You can't come in here!"

"How do I get a pass then?"

"You get it in that office over there." He pointed to the shed.

"Thank you," I said, wandered over to the shed, went behind
it and kept on walking towards the air-conditioned two-storeyed
block beyond. So far so good; Spurdle the secret agent was in.

The good old U.S. Army hadn't changed a bit. There must
have been well over 1,000 male civilians as well as uniformed
G.I.'s wandering about. I might have been denied a pass, so why
worry about one? I wouldn't get shot if challenged.

The hallway was long and cool; offices led off on either side.
The usual old nonsense of meaningless abbreviations—letters
which had been contrived to make up childish words. DOLL,
Director of Loading Logistics; and MADS, Marine and Dock
Services. They must spend hours at it. What I wanted was some-
thing that could read ARSE for all I knew. Like Army Repair
Service Experts. But this was a bit much to hope for. So I

knocked on the first door. It read ABLNS and turned out to be toilets. That figured.

The next room was occupied by a large civilian, olive skinned, with big brown mournful eyes. He listened politely to my request for assistance over the fuel injectors.

"Listen, Limey, it's too late now. Everything is shutting shop. How's about coming and visiting with me on Monday? My name's Sam Spencer—here's my card."

Crestfallen I took the card; it meant going through the same performance at the gate and on a Monday they might be more alert.

"Where's your boat? I'm going into town and I can drop you off. I've finished here now and I'm going to lock up." He carefully emptied his ash tray into a trash can. Then his waste-paper basket contents, and the can was pulled into the middle of the floor for collection. Every paper and article was removed from his desk and everything locked up. Even the empty top sheet of his desk pad was torn off and put into the safe. Either he was most security conscious or he was a very tidy man.

I was introduced to his car, two blocks long and with enough chrome to decorate a dozen English models. At the wharf I invited him on board for a drink. We knocked back some Scotches just as Cobber arrived, hot and brassed off with the dust and confusion that is Naha. He joined in; we demolished a bottle.

"Cobber, you should see Sam's bloody car—it's terrific!"

"Is that yours? Man, it's mighty!" enthused Cobber. We went on to the docks to admire the monster. Immensely pleased, Sam asked us to go to the Skyview, a servicemen's club started at the end of the war in a Quonset hut. Now it was four storeys high with several dance floors and restaurants, a dozen bars, sauna baths and so on.

Would we ever. We slid into the car, fiddled with the electric windows and air conditioner and were off in a cloud of chips and dust.

Sam was a Hawaiian-American and very proud of his Polynesian blood. We found a lot to conjecture over such as the ancient migrations of the Maoris from Hawaiki. Sam was conversant with the writings of Sir Peter Buck, the famous anthropologist, and the evening progressed pleasantly from Japanese Kirin beer to rye whisky and experiments with bourbon. The little Okinawan waitresses captivated us—smiling, always attentive, and trying so hard to please.

"How about your wife, Sam? Shouldn't you ring her?" But

Sam had reached the brave stage and was confident all would be well.

"No, it's all right. I'm in pretty solid at home! Drink up—have another!" And so we carried on until the club shut and we were assisted into the humid night air. Sam surprised by ordering two cabs—one for himself.

"Aren't you driving home?"

"Can't," was all Sam could get out, so we helped him lock up his monster in the car park.

Next morning, shortly after breakfast, a runabout came charging across the harbour straight for us, a bearded figure at the wheel. I stared at the familiar face. The beard was new but those bold blue eyes and roué moustache could only belong to

"Ted Scott! You bastard! What are you doing here?" The greeting was quite in order, Ted being an Australian. The last time I'd seen him was in Port Vila in '65. We'd been out with Cooki, a little Chinese who ran a bar daytime and went out after turtles at night.

The night I met Ted we had motored over to a lonely bay enclosed by a shallow coral reef. The procedure was simple, but it was my first night dive in coral waters and I felt uneasy.

"You no worry—shark eyes show red. Turtle lie with head under rock. You knock on shell, bang-bang, and when he come out put hook in neck."

Cooki handed me a sort of huge barbed baling hook with an eye welded to the handle. Through the eye a nylon rope led to the dinghy which was manned by a Melanesian.

Ted said, "It's a piece of cake! If it's a big one I'll shoot it."

"Bugger you, Ted!" shouted Cooki. "You spoil shell, no bloody good! You use hook, too!"

"Oh, balls! I'll get them in the head!" and Ted waved his spear, tipped with a wicked 12-gauge power-head.

We slipped into the tepid water, eased our bare skins so carefully over the spiney rough corals and floated into the guts and channels. It was pitch dark and the torch beams wavered and probed in sweeping arcs. Tiny organisms, excited by the light, flared into brilliant flashing stars to hang in the water, glow briefly, then fade into darkness. Our very arms glowed and created a living fire which swirled and eddied around us.

I found a small turtle fast asleep, with its flippers drawn in under its horny shell and its head stretched out. I called Ted, who promptly grabbed it, called for the dinghy and flung it in. I felt a bit stupid but "know-how" is everything and now I was all set for another. Except that the next one was about five feet long and must have weighed 300 pounds or more. I saw Ted dive and bang his speargun on what I thought was a barnacle-covered rock. The rock heaved and moved backwards. It started to turn and there it was, ponderous and as irresistible as a tank. I could hear Cooki shouting instructions and saw Ted put the power-head to the beast's huge scaly head. There was a thump and the spear bounced off—a misfire.

"The hook! The hook!" Cooki shouted. "Give me the bloody hook!" There wasn't enough free rope, so Cooki heaved. The dinghy turned over and the dreaming Melanesian was flung screaming into the water. The monster turtle just barged ahead uprooting and pushing coral lumps aside as if they were rotten logs of wood and, getting up speed, flippered away in a cloud of whirling sparks.

"That shell worth £30! You no-bloody-good Australian bastard!" Cooki was beside himself. "I no take you again with that bloody power-head!" Then he lapsed into Chinese. But we could understand every word.

Ted looked at me.

"Well, I'll be buggered! Peter! What the hell are you doing here?" And so we met again—two of a kind.

"Yeah, the Yanks were knocking themselves off with scuba and I got in touch with the Special Service crowd and talked them into letting me set up a school to teach skin-diving," Ted explained. "They lost quite a few guys and now I run classes and look after the marina at Fitzwoody Beach. I've got four or five runabouts and take out diving parties in a 40-footer. How about you doing some charter work while you're here? You'll make a bomb!"

I was sorely tempted but we just had to keep moving. Ted was a great help. He organised my two sets of injectors to be serviced and bought us dozens of cans of fruit and groceries through the military P.X. stores. The crew were enjoying themselves, making friends and seeing the town.

Naha is a mess—reconstruction since the war seems to be to no overall plan. The city is poorly paved, dusty and dirty. Army trucks rumble about with small Japanese taxis and jeeps scuttling in and out in reckless sorties. The whole place seems geared for the easy American dollar, honky-tonks, bars, souvenir shops and clip-joints. The Americans have been there since the war, over 25 years, but I could see no sign of cooperation between the Okinawan authorities, the U.S. civil administration and the mili-

tary. Either the Okinawans are a peasant people, crude and un-
cultured, or the domination by indifferent Americans has choked
civic pride and planning.

Here, as in Palau, the United States had a wonderful chance to
create a living memorial to their occupation—something given
that would endure for generations so that they would be remembered not as conquerors, crude and careless, but as rebuilders
from chaos.

Rafe returned to the *Whai* with a bluff Army sergeant-major
he'd met working on his yacht. Pat Pettingill had offered him
some carpentry and painting jobs on his boat, which suited Rafe
fine as extra cash was always welcome.

"How's about you boys coming up to my place for a barbecue
and a few drinks? I'd like some friends of mine to meet you all.
My wife's one hell of a fine cook—she'll make up some Japanese chow."

We met Pat's wife Yoko. She was tall for a Japanese woman,
about 5ft. 5in. and very lovely. Perhaps she had had plastic sur-
gery to change the shape of her eyes—a lot of Asiatics do,
although I don't understand why. Perhaps it is a practice similar
to Negros trying to unkink their woolly hair or the white man
disliking his pallid skin.

It was strange to see this talented and cultured woman taking
such a subservient role in her own home—sitting in the back-
ground or quietly serving her husband's guests. A Western
woman would be right in the thick of the conversation and quite
likely to tell her hubby to belt up if she so decided. We were
all rather envious of Pat.

One of Pat's guests was an Army captain who promised to
take us to Kadeena Air Base. "If you're lucky you'll see B52's
taking off for Vietnam! The tankers usually take off half an
hour before and the bombers refuel down towards Taiwan. The
bombers can't get off the ground with a full bomb load as well
as full fuel tanks."

This we had to see. Next day we took plenty of film and
drove to the base. We watched a tanker take off, huge and
shining silver in the sun. The B52's, a dozen or more, lined the
far perimeter. They had enormous pointed tails and great drooping wings.

"We'll go down the highway near the end of the runway—
they'll pass right overhead." We found a hillock topped by the
remains of an old rock-crusher on which we perched like birds
on a roof. We could hear the rumble and whine of jets and see
the big brown bombers taxiing before take-off.

"Here it comes! Just look at the wings lifting!" One of the monsters rolled forward faster and faster. Each of its wing tips was supported by crazy little oleo struts and wheels and as the machine gathered speed you could actually see the anhedral of the wings alter as they started to lift the enormous load. It seemed to roll for 1,000 yards before it heaved itself into the air on eight thick clouds of fuel smoke.

Three of the planes roared off to climb and disappear on their way to targets 1,200 miles away. For a long time the sky seemed to throb and re-echo as, in my mind's eye, I followed the bombers. The sky was a different sky, the men and machines of a different generation, but still the sight of warplanes setting out on a raid excited me. It was for me a deep and disturbing experience. How many many times I had flown fighter escort for bombers—and here we are, still at it. The wicked waste and futility of it all!

Some friends of Ted's had lent him their flat while on furlough in the States. The crew went along for a farewell party and stayed the night. I spent the evening replacing the starboard fuel injectors and preparing for departure. The Japanese harbour authorities charged me 30 cents port dues and 50 cents for one ton of water. We carried about 100 gallons of water only, so used the balance to wash off the dust and soot of Naha just before sailing at 9.30 a.m. The crew weren't much good for anything, moaning and groaning with hangovers.

"It's turning into a giant pub crawl—we don't seem to be able to get away from the filthy stuff," said Mike, flopping on the aft seat where there was a little breeze.

"Well, you must admit that there's nothing else to do at night. After all, you've seen all the museums and art galleries during the daytime. Haven't you?" I demanded.

"You go to a museum! And get stuffed!" was the rude rejoinder.

It was time we had our little lecture on shipboard routine and discipline and as we left the harbour moles I gathered up the sorry-looking gang and held forth. But they were tired and grumpy and my sage advice went in one side of their fuming heads and out the other to blow away in our wake. I knew the lecture would have to be repeated, some time later.

Darkness caught us skirting the Amami Islands on their western side. The weather stayed fine and the following night we were off the Tokara Group. I had been looking up the various islands in the *Japan Pilot* and noted that Suwanose is an active volcano.

We saw the glow from its crater and showers of red-hot boulders flung high into the air to crash bouncing down the mountain sides. The *Pilot* said that that was quite normal.

Next day great dark clouds came down from the north-east and in the distance Yaku Island was blotted out. Lightning stabbed the horizon. The wind became a gale, moaning past the radio aerial, and our wind-indicator, a length of bandage tied to the mast, snapped and flickered in panic. I got in a bit of a panic, too—this was typhoon alley and the Army meteorological section in Naha had advised that a typhoon was developing north of the Marianas.

I had hoped to be in sight of Yaku all day and night but now it meant approaching the large group of islands, their reefs and shoals in darkness, heavy rain and wind. I didn't like it at all. The currents up in the Ryukyus were variable and strange. I was certain that the steering was getting sloppy because landfalls had been as much as 25 miles out in less than 50 miles travelled. Although it took us some seven hours to cover 50 miles I wasn't ready to agree that our drift could be as much as three and a half knots. Two, yes, perhaps even two and a half. I suspected the Count was back on the job so watched the telltale compass set near my bunk, and shouted rudely at the slightest wandering off course. It was going to be a bad night so I caught up on a little sleep, knowing we were safe from landfall for at least four hours.

Lightning stabbed again and again in searing mauve and silver. Rain drummed on the cabin roof and streamed off the canopy over the rear deck. Everything was damp and howling gusts of wind, white with spray, swirled around the rear platform to soak the two outside beds and vegetable locker. It was impossible to see 20 feet except in the momentary glare of lightning, when an eerie circle of waves was exposed, wildly heaving under a dome of crystal raindrops. Frightening crashes of thunder, only a second after the flash, actually shook the boat more than once and I disconnected the aerial lead to the radio.

Twice passing vessels were seen, their steaming lights misty and vague when the rain lifted momentarily. I was keen to reach Kagoshima, our port of entry, next day so pressed on, taking a chance that my dead reckoning was accurate. I wasn't at ease because of the tiderips and currents marked on the charts for this area. I doubled as lookout and stayed up all night making endless cups of cocoa and peering into the desolation outside. At midnight we had to reduce speed in the face of mountainous seas.

Morning was grey and cool with clouds lifting and no wind. The seas flattened and we cracked on full revs to head for a nearby island which I confirmed as Ioshima. The precautions of slowing down and easing away had paid off, even if it had delayed our arrival by half a day. More and more shipping came into view, and a few airliners passed high overhead, pointing to our destination with long white contrails. I estimated we'd arrive at Kagoshima just on dusk; we cleaned up the *Whai* and had the first decent meal in 24 hours.

1 July: Passing around the lower end of Io we cruised between it and neighbouring Takeshima. Low fog covered the sea and beaded the *Whai* with glistening droplets. We were isolated in a white world of our own but, knowing exactly our true position, it was a simple matter to set course directly toward the entrance to Kagoshima Bay.

The fog wilted and in the distance the perfect cone of a hazy volcano lay dead ahead on Kyushu, third largest of the Japanese islands. Again the crew got channel-fever at the proximity of land and the thought of getting ashore in a strange country. As usual I started to worry about our time of arrival—would it be in daylight? Where would the Harbour and Customs office be and where would the Japanese have us moor?

A brisk breeze pushed at us and wavelets rose, forward into ranks to jostle and heave us forward with little surges of power. The *Whai* pitched up and down and spray flew, not to wet us but to blow ahead and fall on either side as our cat purred along. It was a long moment of intense satisfaction for me, both with the ship and crew. We'd come over 6000 miles and were in great shape. Here all around us was Japanese land—we'd made it! And the doubters, so many, could now dry up and blow away.

Of course, to really confirm my faith in the *Whai* and its novel design, we had to get back safe and sound to New Zealand, but of this I was quite confident. I had managed this far, by taking all my problems in navigation and the whole complexity of supplies, refuelling and anchorages, one day at a time. This is the crux of a long journey, the crux, in fact, of living itself. Plan what you want and need to do, anticipate and prepare if you can for pitfalls, and tackle problems one day at a time.

More and more ships of all sizes, as if in convoy, ahead, abeam and astern. As the bay narrowed we could see industrial complexes lining the flats along the shoreline below high green hills. It was mountainous land—already we had passed the

high cones of two old volcanoes and ahead to starboard was the
towering bulk of an active cone with a thin plume of vapour
streaming from its crater. The lights of Kagoshima started to
wink and spark in the dusk.

Again the *Pilot* was incomprehensible—to the navigation officer of a large ship, standing 30 feet above the sea's surface and
with radar and large-scale charts, it would be simple to identify
the port facilities. But with our limited horizon and with charts
that were definitely not up to date it was wellnigh impossible.
Later we were to find that whole islands had been connected
with causeways, small bays reclaimed and built on. In one place
in the Inland Sea I was hopelessly confused for an hour or so
as we motored past an oil refinery covering hundreds of acres,
with a new deep-water harbour and super tankers, which was
indicated on my chart as two little islets and a reef. Japanese
industrial growth is so rapid that our Admiralty charts are way
behind. We found whole shallows charted as dangerous, even
for small craft like the *Whai* to have been dredged completely
out of existence.

At last we got amongst the concrete protection walls and
docks of the city. Harbour beacons flashed in red, green and
white from towers and buoys that followed no pattern that I
could identify. And so we motored slowly past liners, ferries
and junks, past dockside cranes and terminal buildings. It was
getting dark and our yellow flag became a lazily flapping grey
blur. In desperation, I drew alongside a small tug tied to a jetty
off what appeared to be a scrapmetal yard. The sole crewman
on the tug couldn't speak a word of English, but he was friendly
and didn't object when we tied up. I gave him some chocolate,
indicated on our tattered Pacific chart where we were from,
and we were O.K. for the night. I had been warned by other
yachties about Japanese officialdom and their insistence on formality, so was most uneasy at this unconventional arrival.

"Clean up the boat, make sure everything is O.K. for inspection. I'll go ashore and see if I can find out what's what. For
God's sake don't go ashore until I tell you!" Off I went, passport
and ship's papers wrapped in a plastic bag, to stumble around in
masses of scrap metal, old trucks and derelict machinery, and
over the cobblestone of poorly-lit dockside streets.

At last small shops and curious little stalls replaced the warehouses and factories. I entered a maze of dark alleys and in
pools of light from open doorways, small groups of Japanese
sat or leaned. Several times women called "How much? How

much?" as I passed. I wanted bright lights and some form of authority; even a policeman.

A man started to follow me, keeping about 50 feet behind, in the shadows on the other side of the street, but after many false turns I reached a main thoroughfare with bright lights and hustling traffic. My unwanted companion disappeared—perhaps he just happened to be going my tortuous way. All shops were shut, except for a small bar/eating place. I tried to make contact but no one spoke English, so I made an exit with an embarrassed "sayonara" which brought howls of laughter. Outside I managed to flag down a taxi but had to let him go as again my enquiries for the police, Customs and harbour master were incomprehensible. Tired, disgusted, I made my way back in the general direction of the *Whai*. I saw a bar ahead—a plastic sign for Ankor beer lit the pavement and thankfully I entered. Two girls behind the bar stepped forward and when I asked if they spoke English both had a smattering. It turned out that this was a red light district, so having finished a bottle of beer I plucked up courage and ventured into the night again.

"We'll just stay here and take a chance. In the morning we'll drift around and locate the Customs. Better have an early night 'cos I want to get cracking at first light."

We cast off in the morning and found what turned out to be the main Customs office. They were good to us in some ways, letting us use their ablution facilities, complete with a curious little square bath, automatic washing machine and toilets. The bath was too small for either Bill or Mike, who had to fold up to get down into it. The toilets were an earthenware trough in the floor, flanked by two ribbed tiles as foot rests. Squatting like this was hard for us and somehow demeaning. There were, however, some European-type toilets complete with instructions for their use, in the form of "stick-man" cartoons, for both sitting and standing. They were hilarious!

We had a bit of a tussle with the Japanese Customs, Immigration and Health. The police were brought in, too. Luckily they didn't bother about looking too hard and the guns weren't noticed. It was my introduction to the Japs' fetish of officious paper work. Form after form and endless questions. It seemed hard for them to understand we were tourists—merely private citizens on holiday.

Except for Mike, the gang went exploring and the two of us stayed behind for a breather after the morning's form-filling and tension. A coaster came in and I was requested to shift the *Whai* as the wharf space was needed. We motored a couple of hundred yards in front of the harbour office buildings where there was plenty of space, and where a Navy patrol boat was moored. Immediately a car dashed up and Customs officers jumped out, suspicious and demanding to know if we had permission to move.

"We were asked to make room for that cargo ship," I explained.

"You have permission to move?"

"I don't know—someone just told us to get out."

"You must not move without permission!"

"Well, I'll get permission," I countered.

"You not allowed to leave boat!"

"Well, if I can't leave boat how do I get permission to move?" I asked.

There was a long silence as the officials appraised the impossible situation. There was much chatter and then the leader said:

"Ah so—we not say anything if you move—you no say anything, we no see anything!" And with that problem out of the way they departed.

Mike and I looked at each other.

"You know, the only things we've in common with the Japs seem to be officials and Coke bottles. They're the same all over the world!"

Back at the Customs we squeezed up against the wharf and were left alone except for the sightseers who came at all hours of the day and night to look at the cat and its curious crew. The interest must have been generated by a newspaper article which I had encouraged, as I wanted pictorial proof of our arrival to send home.

That first afternoon Mike, Rafe and I walked into the city centre to look at the shops. Bill and Cobber had gone off shopping. The thought of those two Kiwi farmers out buying a wife a wig was too funny for words. How they'd get on I couldn't imagine. We'd learnt two new Japanese words from the Customs men: Arrigato ("thank you") and Konnich-iwa ("good-day").

The girls had gone off to a travel bureau to arrange a conducted tour of the city, so the three of us were free to wander. It was fascinating to browse in the huge department stores—in so many ways like ours, but yet so very different. At the doors and at the foot of each stairway and escalator, pretty girls bowed sedately to each passing customer. We understood they took it in turn to greet a hundred each before being relieved. The people were neatly dressed; they seemed well-ordered and disciplined.

During the whole of our stay the only police we saw were those activated by our presence.

The toy departments were fantastic—a child's dream world come to life, with every kind of mechanical toy imaginable walking, crawling, swimming, wetting its pants or sucking at miniature milk bottles. Or barking, wagging their heads, shooting out sparks or zooming. The whole huge floor clicked, buzzed, hummed, while a thousand small batteries expended themselves demonstrating the marvels to wide-eyed kids.

Yet in all the stores we visited the simple little compressed flowers of my childhood were absent. Remember how you could put tiny, pithy grains into a glass of water to watch them swell and expand into full-sized blooms? The shopgirls tried their best to help but the nearest we could get were plastic flowers and plants to put in aquariums.

In a back street we came on a curious, carved stone arch. At the back of it, framed as it were, was the bust of Francis Xavier, the first Christian missionary to Japan. This arch was all that re-mained of his old church, destroyed by bombing in World War II.

While we were taking photos, a Japanese priest in black soutane came over and introduced himself as "John". He in-vited us to go for a sightseeing drive around the city.

"This hotel is our best. Come look at the view."

We passed through the foyer and out on to a lawn to stand behind a barrier fence at the top of a high cliff.

Kagoshima was spread before us, and across the harbour the volcano steamed and puffed away to itself. Gay rice paper lan-terns hung in strings from tree to tree and an artificial waterfall splashed in glassy sheets from rock to mossy rock. There were dozens of small metal-clad tables scattered across the lawn, all connected by a plastic hose which fed propane gas to burners set in their tops.

"Yes, Japanese peoples like to cook own food family-style. Tonight I take you to special restaurant. You like." Father John was beaming. We provided him with a heaven-sent opportunity to practise his English.

In the hotel dining room was a pool or fish tank. It was all of 30 feet long by 12 feet wide and probably 4 feet deep. A cat-walk ran along its centre and we watched a dexterous waiter scoop up a salmon-like fish in a long-handled net. He trans-ferred it to the chef's work table by wrapping a wet cloth around its head so it couldn't slip. The chef filleted the unfortunate creature, taking care not to injure its spine or stomach and entrails. While another cook skinned and sliced the fillets, the chef impaled the gasping and heaving fish on to a board with wooden spikes at head and tail. He then garnished the whole thing with little radishes, grated carrot and lettuce. Several times the fish had to be forced back on to its spikes as it struggled in agony. The thinly sliced flesh was put back more or less in its original position and the completed dish taken out to be served quivering and twitching to the waiting gourmets.

We are ardent skindivers and knock off lots of fish. I admit that often we leave a fish alive in a damp sack so that it stays fresh a little longer. These fish die by asphyxiation which is relatively painless. No doubt spearfishing, like all blood sports, is cruel, but this was something else and revolted us. John laughed and said, "I never see that before—it very good—very fresh." Mike and I took movies of another horrible performance and went off with very mixed feelings.

"I pick you up about eight. We need taxi for the others."

"O.K. John, thanks. Now how about the girls—we won't want to leave them behind."

"Well, women cannot go to this restaurant. I bring down some of my students to entertain them."

"Sorry, ladies, that's the way it is," I told them.

John arrived with three charming lasses who wanted to try out their schoolgirl English. Before we left the boat they had transformed it for a magic moment into a little theatre; with two singing, the third girl danced an ancient classic, in kimono, greasepaint and lacquered wig.

We drew up outside a small single-storey old-style building of wood with curious eaves and projections from gabled windows. It was starting to drizzle and Father John was concerned about parking his small car. There was space, but little enough room for even a good driver to manoeuvre, let alone our friend John.

"Let's pick the bloody thing up," demanded Bill, and in a trice the little Datsun was in the air and bodily carried into a vacant spot—to our friend's amazement.

"These are my New Zealand friends. They are on their way to Expo. I want them to have real Japanese style meal." John introduced us to the proprietor, a smooth, well-groomed man. We felt privileged. Not many tourists would have it quite so authentic. This place catered for local businessmen and not the carriage or tourist trade.

"We'll have sukiyaki. You like," decided John.

"What is it?" Bill and Cobber were suspicious of strange foods and much preferred steak and eggs.

"It is kind of soup and we cook it here on gas flame. We cook meats in it—very good!"

A tiny woman bowed deeply and removed our shoes. She slid open the partition leading to a little room, and we stepped inside and squatted around the low table. In the centre was a gas burner. A girl brought in a large heavy metal bowl of spiced brown soup. Then plates of raw meat and fresh vegetables were placed on the table and we were all busy cooking wafer-thin slices of beef and greens in the bubbling pot. It took only a few seconds for the meat to turn white, ready to eat.

As usual I fumbled with the chopsticks and longed for a fork and spoon to stop all the messing around. Others, more dexterous than I, were recovering my pieces of meat and having a feast. There were several condiments, some based on seaweed. We tried raw squid as an extra, but I could see most of us would have preferred to get on the outside of more solid food. In the next room a group of young men were laughing and laughing. I thought I could hear sobbing, too, and it intrigued me. I slid the partition aside a little and there they were, eating away enjoying themselves, all but one youth who sat bolt upright, tears streaming down his crimson cheeks. He was being "picked on" by the others, who thought it a huge lark. It was a mystery to us—a Kiwi would have gone berserk or gone out.

Back on the boat, Monique and Robbie were delighted with their little guests. They'd cooked Western-style food for them, taught and been taught simple songs.

There was a note for me from the Navy. It read:

"Tomorrow morning at 0800, Japanese patrol boat *Amatsukaze* will guide you to the bay Shindai for sheltering typhoon. Follow her. If necessary she will tug you."

Typhoon? What typhoon! It was too late to check now. The morning would come quickly enough, and luckily no mechanical work was necessary.

"I think I'll stay ashore tomorrow. I want to try this Japanese massage and baths they talk about! You don't mind do you?"

Bill was dead keen to have a little Japanese woman run barefoot up and down his back. For a barefoot massage on Bill, a Sumo wrestler might have been more satisfactory.

"No, we'll be O.K. Does anyone else want to stay ashore? Personally I think this typhoon experience might be fun."

And so it was settled. At eight o'clock a large launch arrived spic and span and flying the Rising-Sun flag.

"Are you ready? Follow us!" and we were off across the harbour and into the shelter of the volcano's north-eastern slopes. Shindai Bay was a tiny inlet formed by two arms of broken lava and rock shale. It was baking hot and the sun beat directly down into this natural ovenpit. Dozens of boats, barges, floating cranes and fishing vessels filed through the narrow entrance and took up positions according to size and construction. To my horror I found we were to be lashed between a Navy tug and a work-barge. Because we were all-steel, the *Whai* was put in the front rank. Behind us wooden fishing junks and light craft were tied in rows.

The whole organisation was probably centuries old—the skippers new exactly what to do. There was no fuss, no messing about. All the boats (except the steel front rank) were laced in such a way that they were separated by three or four feet and could work a little without knocking each other about should the waters become rough. We steel hulls had big tyres for fenders and I could just see us grinding and gnawing away at each other in torment while the lucky second and third groups lay in calm water.

Every four or five hours the *Amatsukaze* came around and gave the latest reports, first in Japanese and then, for our benefit, in English. Their loud-hailer boomed out across the harbour to echo back from the crags and rock walls. That night we slept on deck, some under a big canvas stretched across the foredeck.

Next day, and no sign of the typhoon. At about 11 a.m. the patrol boat came back and said it was O.K.—the storm had passed far to the south, we were free to go. In a remarkably short time all the craft dispersed. As we cruised back we passed huge floating frames of wood. These were the cultured pearl-oyster beds being towed back to their normal positions. They had been dragged mile by painful mile from across the bay and anchored outside our refuge.

"Well, how did it go, Bill? Were they very good? What did it cost? What do the girls wear?" But Bill shut up and just grinned. My guess was that it cost a lot of money and was perfectly respectable.

In our first experience of a Japanese city (we don't count Naha) many little things struck us as unique and strange. To our surprise the Japanese drive on the left side of the road as we do. Sure enough, as in films and in books, the Japs do say "Ah so"— the first time Mike and I heard it we both burst into laughter.

It is true, too, that a large proportion of men wear horn-rimmed spectacles and all suck in their breath politely on occasion. They, along with most Asiatics and the Filipinos, love capping their teeth with gold, whether for beauty or as a sign of affluence I don't know. We were surprised at the number of tiny elderly women bent almost double—the crippling legacy of malnutrition as children and backbreaking work in paddy fields. The school children in natty uniforms, all carrying knapsack bags on their backs, were delightful. We were upset at the sight of women in rags working with shovels and concrete mixers on building sites: it was so much in contrast with the dainty kimonos and wooden clogs of others more fortunate.

5 July: We pulled out at 5.30 a.m., dodging the little illuminated floats of the rod fishermen at the end of the jetty. The weather was blustery and vast mats of brownish-white pumice scraped and scratched past our waterline. They made me think of a craft I'd heard of in the New Hebrides which had had its steel sides polished by passing through acres and acres of the floating abrasive rock, and I began to worry about the *Whai's* expensive paintwork. Signs of the typhoon were visible once we left the bay and headed down the coast towards Cape Satano— great bunches of brown seaweed torn from the rocks and shallow-water bays. More and more debris appeared, this time man's handiwork: plastic and glass bottles, jandals, children's toys, plastic wrappers and bags, dunnage, empty boxes, old mats—if it could float you'd find it in Japanese waters. The mess was indescribable. Later we were to find in the beautiful Inland Sea, bands of rubbish drifting like long thin sea-serpents, rotting, filthy and obscene. The Japanese, so clean and neat ashore, seem to dump anything and everything into the sea; this is strange because the sea and its delicate ecology is so very very important, indeed vital, to them.

We entered the narrows between the island of Awaji and the mainland of Honshu. A couple of Japanese Army planes droned by. Lots of shipping; once again we were being surrounded by giants who pushed us aside like a piece of driftwood. It was a foretaste of the fantastic pressure of shipping we would meet in the Inland Sea proper.

Afternoon, and we were well into the Osaka bay. Now thick brown haze hung over the waters and ferries materialized to rush past with creaming bow waves. Small freighters and curious-looking workboats with strange superstructures came through the haze from all directions. I tried to pick up landmarks, but the smog was too thick and only vague distant hilltops appeared. Evening, and the sun set behind Awaji, blue-grey behind us.

Osaka with its teeming millions and its docks and wharves lay somewhere very close. The *Pilot* gave the port light system and, as we motored past a supertanker at anchor in the roadstead, I thought that I could identify the harbour entrance. On my chart it looked simple but, as with most ports, the blasted red and yellow neon signs, the flashing greens and blues and whites of hamburger bars, clubs, insurance offices and whisky advertisements and so on ad nauseam, made it a nightmare.

Mike and I struggled with the chart, the *Pilot* and the maze of lights. We were more or less sure that the channel ahead, lined with two rows of buoys, was the correct one. About a mile up the channel, however, the wharves came to an end and a bridge barred further progress. For two hours we cruised up and down gloomy reaches, past docks and piles and warehouses outlined black against the glow of the city. Then, thoroughly brassed off, I called it a day. We had come on a little harbour with a few small fishing junks, a tug or two and some tiny yachts at anchor. This was good enough for me and we dropped the pick in a heavy ooze bottom. Tomorrow we'd find our way in daylight.

CHAPTER EIGHT

Japan in July

7/7/70. With a date like this we just had to be in luck. The sun struggled with the smog and climbed above it, crimson from holding its breath. We on the *Whai* had to breathe and the stench from the filthy waters was appalling. I got Big and Little Stinky going and we glided out of the small harbour into the major port that sprawled all around. I conned the *Whai* past cargo boats, looking for one with a red ensign so we could ask our position.

I found a Filipino ship discharging logs. A grubby looking sailor pointed to the north and held up four fingers: "Osaka—four mile" and disappeared below. A white-coated steward looked down on us from the top deck as we drifted alongside the rusty steel cliff. He, too, disappeared and next instant a pail of slops and rubbish cascaded over us from above. It may have been accidental but the howling curses from our crew weren't.

Ahead a stream of small cargo ships, fishing sampans, even a little tanker were queuing up to enter the moles leading into harbour. It was Osaka all right: a large sign over a concrete building indicated the Customs and another the harbour police offices.

I tucked the *Whai* in close behind the extraordinarily small tanker—it couldn't have been more than 100 feet long. We were really close, not 50 feet from its stern, and our cat hunted from side to side in its bubbling wake. A Jap came aft, looked hard at us, dropped his pants and sat himself over the stern.

"Well! said Robbie, "I didn't know they ate so much!" We burst into laughter. Our blasé friend heard our hoots and, looking over his shoulder, spotted the girls laughing at him. He retreated in frantic confusion with much loss of faeces. And thus we arrived in Osaka, the end of our outward journey.

Once more I cruised slowly until I decided to enter the harbour police area and then tied up alongside a floating jetty. I climbed the dockside stairs and crossed to the Customs offices. About 20 neatly-uniformed Customs men were lined up in a hallway, being addressed by a senior officer. At a word of command they saluted, then broke ranks; the parade was over. I found an English-speaking officer who organised the Medical and Immigration people. We trooped on board the *Whai* and the fun began. Another forest of forms, little rubber stamps and ink pads. Our passports, the *Whai's* papers and, for the second time, a list of articles to be declared.

It mentioned firearms. I decided to declare them and straight-away the fat was in the fire. The harbour police were called. I explained that the guns were for hunting food on some of the lonely islands of the New Hebrides and Solomons. It was as good a yarn as any. I explained they were sporting rifles—not military—not for armed insurrection. The Japs were in an up-roar and more forms were sent for and wire clip-on seals and more rubber stamps. By a lucky chance the English-speaking Customs man had travelled to Australia and understood our free and easy way with weapons. In the end all three rifles and the shotgun were wired together and sealed into a cubbyhole.

"Yacht Club? You want Yacht Club? Not here. You must go Nishinamiya—about five miles around bay. To north more." We were off again. The officials stood in a dishevelled group on shore. I shut all hatches so the cabins would be hot and un-comfortable and any unwanted visitors would complete their business promptly. It always worked well. At least until we reached Japan, where the Customs and Immigration are true-blue dyed-in-the-wool officious pests, poking and prying, sus-picious and downright disbelieving. I like Japan—it is truly fascinating—but I'll never go by private craft again—it's just not worth the effort. It took two hours to complete the formalities.

We found Nishinamiya—my Customs lieutenant had taken me to the harbour offices in Osaka and had secured a chart of the little port. The yacht basin water was filthy, black and smelly. But the Kansai Yacht Club buildings were excellent. We were shown where to anchor and we rigged an endless-rope arrange-ment so we could pull the dinghy back and forth between cat and jetty.

Some blue uniforms on the jetty.

"Customs here," one figure called out.

"What for? We've been through Customs in Osaka!"

"You in Kobe now! We come on board!" There was a police-man too so, grumbling, Mike pulled the dinghy to the wharf and four grinning Japanese got in.

"Papers please; all documents and passports."

"But we've just been through Customs! Look, here are our receipts. Jesus, we just spent two hours with your people!"

"Jesus? Explain please!"

I looked at the now serious Jap. I looked at Mike, at the instrument panel. I looked out at the distant clubhouse where there were cool showers and a bar waiting. I got pretty shirty.

"We've been through Customs in Osaka! What do you want?"

"You now in Kobe prefecture. Have you clearance from Osaka for Nishinamiya? What you say Jesus mean?"

"No; I haven't any clearance from Osaka. This lieutenant here (pointing to his signature) told us to come to this yacht club to moor. We're here for Expo 70."

"Ah so. Jesus word?"

"A prayer word." (Now I know what they mean by taking the name of the Lord in vain!) "Doesn't mean anything at all—forget it!"

The little monster gazed at me with flat stone eyes. "Ah so. No clearance. Let me see guns."

Now I knew they must have been informed of our arrival at and departure from Osaka. The officious cretin was putting on an act.

We all climbed below and inspected the guns. And the wire and seals. And the registration papers. And argued over no papers for the shotgun. I unlocked and broke the seals on the drug and ammunition cupboards. We re-counted the ammunition, re-listed it and re-locked it away and re-sealed it. We presented our passports and they were re-stamped. Twice on the same day, on the same island of the same country! The grog was unsealed, re-inspected and re-sealed. Six more forms in quadruplicate. The *Whai's* registration papers were demanded. I refused pointblank to hand them over.

"This is a British ship! You don't have to take the papers and they stay on board! I'm sick of this—get off my back!"

"Get off back? Explain please!"

Oh Lord! I'd done it again! I realized that idioms must be avoided at all cost! How could I explain this? I took a chance.

"Get off back? You mean get off boat! We want to get off boat for a shower and a drink. Go see Expo."

"Ah so!" With that they were gone, along with 3000-odd yen carelessly left lying on Mike's bunk.

"Are you sure?" I asked.

"Yes! I left it on my bunk like a fool. I was getting ready to go ashore when they asked for the passports. What can we do?"

"Nothing. It's gone; forget it. What a bastard!"

Poor Mike—so flush with cash—buying cameras and lens in Kagoshima, plastic models of the sunken Jap planes of Nila and other goodies. And now almost broke until his traveller's cheques, lost in Kagoshima, turned up.

In the yacht club was a sunken tub of blue-white tile. It must have been all of six feet square and three feet deep. It was enormously refreshing to have a long cold shower and then hop into deep sudsy hot water. There was an electric washing machine and huge cartons of soap powder. I confess that the *Whai's* depleted stock of soap powder recovered completely during the ten days we stayed here. Also the toilet paper, but this Japanese stuff was terrible, being made of something unserviceable that just went into holes.

There were squads of young men living in temporary-looking dormitories or barracks lining the yacht basin. They launched their sailboats to shouted instructions and chanted Jap heave-ho's in unison. They jogged along the sea wall in close-knit phalanxes, calling cadence with martial yells. It reminded me of the German shadow air force, drilled and trained in secret before Hitler declared his hand. If these weren't naval cadets, I'm a Japanese Customs officer!

8 July: A new day! No more formalities! No more sea travel for a week or more and all of Expo to see and enjoy! We piled into the dinghy fairly festooned with cameras. As we clambered on to the jetty, a group of our young sailors surged along the top of the sea wall. They chanted and ran in step, hardly deigning to look at our unusual party.

"They're Navy all right," grunted Bill.

"Must be," said Cobber. "They're all the same age and their boats are all identical."

"Could be a sailing school," remarked Rafe. "There are quite a few in England."

"No fear! Too much ordering about and doing by numbers! They'll be down our way again some day!"

We straggled along looking for the railway station. I ruminated how there is nothing much more helpless than a sailor separated from his yacht and dinghy. I loathe walking. Legs are made to straddle a horse, a motorcycle—they're made for working a car's pedals or to balance on a rolling deck. Walking is strictly for unfortunates without taxi-fare or wheels of their own.

The factories and warehouses gave way to a shopping centre and at last we found the miniature station. Where to? Being the oldest and theoretically the leader, I approached the ticket office. A pretty girl eyed me and said:

"Good morning! Where you go?"

"Hi Joe!" the children chanted

The Chinese "green-girl" on the golf course at Taiwan

Fish-holding baskets line Shindai Bay

Sheltering from a typhoon in Shindai Bay, Japan

"Good morning!! Expo 70 please!"

"You go Osakashima. Catch another train there. You ask please!" And it was all settled. I can't imagine how a Japanese would fare in New Zealand if he had little or no English. We must be the most insular yokels in the Western world.

We entrained with a rush and a whistle, swaying and jiggling, clutching the plastic hand grips of the crowded train. Once before, when surrounded in the crush of Filipinos in Rizal Square, Manila, I had experienced this feeling of unreality and here again, in the jam-packed train I felt cut off, almost trapped. These were yesterday's enemies, now our valued customers. There was plenty of time to study them in repose, eyes shut or attention fixed on the roof tops and factories zipping past.

Here, clutching a briefcase, an elderly man, face sallow and drawn. He looked tired out and yet just off to his office. A young mother was next to him, her doll-child gazing fixedly at Mike. He must have been a storybook giant come true as he towered over the others. A man of my own generation looked at me with a cold glare that 26 years had failed to dim. We stared, eyes locked and memories in mesh. To hell with you, I thought, you started it but we finished it.

But had he? His generation, perhaps, but look what the survivors and their children had wrought. This was the world's third industrial giant. Soon it would be second only to America. The teenagers of his day were exposed to the full power and thrill of national pride in its military heyday, and then to the burning humiliation of defeat and thwarted ambition. These youths, now men, were beginning to take over the reins of industry and commerce on a scale far greater than their elder brothers had dreamed of. What path would they follow—these men who were forged in yesterday's furnace?

The glare was hooded and the moment passed. He was just another stocky Japanese with a hard brown face, and I a camera-clutching tourist.

"What was that all about?" asked Mike. "Did you know him?"

"Yes, I knew him—long ago. Forget it!" And with that we rocketed into the underground station of Osakashima.

Our unwieldy group filtered and barged along from one concourse to another, passed from one white-gloved guard to another until we were pushed into the right train. With a sighing of released air brakes and a whining surge the train took off. Again we were standing—Robbie and Monique clutching at the straps along with the men. I noticed no man gave up a hard-won seat for a woman.

We drew into the special main station for Expo and climbed the stairs along with thousands of cheerful jostling visitors. More and more Westerners were seen converging on the ticket booths and turnstiles.

"Six hundred yen! Let's see; that's about $1.50! Hope we don't have to pay for each pavilion!" Mike muttered. Rafe rejoined us once past the barriers.

"Only cost me 400! Said I was a student!"

Robbie and Monique set off for the U.S. pavilion and the rest of us for the N.Z. site. The building complex was unique and the Geyser restaurant was absolutely first-class, a tremendous credit to the designers, architectural and engineering. There was nothing to touch it for polished sophistication in the whole exhibition. Nothing that is, except for our film "This is New Zealand". I confess to a few involuntary tears, not of homesickness, but of sheer delight and pride in seeing our lovely land so dramatically brought to the screen. The excited whisperings of the Japanese told of its impact.

We spent six days exploring Expo and didn't see it all. We didn't get to the amusement section. Each day we paid over our 600 yen and trudged on miles of tar-seal roading and endured one queue after another. The U.S. exhibition's queue was the longest and often it meant a four and a-half hour wait. I never did get to see it—the human snake twisting around the site four coils wide was too much! I did get into the Russian pavilion, however, and was disappointed to find the main floor devoted to glass cases displaying early Bolshevist books and memorabilia completely incomprehensible to every non-Russian, which meant 99.9 percent of all present.

There was too much to see and do and too little time. Cobber and Bill had to return to New Zealand: stock and crops can't look after themselves and we had already spent some four and a-half months—the time planned for the entire trip. I was sorry to see them go; both solid sorts—dependable Kiwis. Bill flew home via Hong Kong but Cobber had some problems. His beloved guns were to be got home and he'd a shortage of dollars for air fare. I had decided to try to ship the *Whai* back, if it was not too expensive. My idea was that it could be put on a timber (log) ship as deck cargo, but after days of enquiries and negotiations the charges arrived. It was out of the question—$5,000. This was madness, so I secured a berth for Cobber on the *Port Albert*, a cargo ship with limited passenger accommodation and the fare only £153 sterling.

Cobber went to the Customs to see about transferring his weapons. And ran into trouble. He came back furious.

"I spent four and a-half hours filling in forms! Sixteen of them! Then the bastards brought in two more, so I gathered the lot up (waving his muscular arms in vivid pantomime) crunched them up and threw them on the floor! I shouted at them 'That's enough! I've bloody well had it! The guns can stay where they are! You're nothing but a pack of officious pricks!' The Japs just gaped at me—never said a word!"

Every third day while we were anchored in Nishinamiya a Japanese patrol boat came alongside to enquire when we were leaving, to inspect the weapons and generally check us over. After Cobber's experience I got fed up and when the rumble of the launch announced yet another visit, I erupted.

"We'll go when we're ready! We're visitors, not criminals! We'll go when the weather suits us!"

The Japanese official said, "You can go now—rainy season finished on the 13th!"

He was serious—it was the Japanese official end of the season, regardless of the actual state of the elements.

"Well it looks like bad weather to me! I'm going to shift to Kobe harbour to transfer the guns to Mr Hurley's ship."

"You must not leave here without permission."

"Bugger permission! I'll leave when I like!"

And with that we parted, the Japanese stiff and bristling and myself hopping mad.

One evening I found a message pasted to the cabin door: an invitation to dinner from a young man curious about New Zealand and Western life. Through him we were able to visit the colossal Kawasaki shipbuilding yards where a 100,000-tonner is completed in three months—only part of the production of some 18,000 workers. It was an awesome sight—a tanker being readied for launching while in the next building-berth another grew while we watched.

Mighty cranes working from either side swung prefabricated sections into place, and welders like helmeted ants tacked the numbered pieces to the giant carcase with flashes of man-made lightning. On the cutting-out floors thousands of men with gas torches and electric arc, with rollers and grinders, with rivetting guns and shears, shaped and fashioned steel plate to the master plan.

Completed sections were numbered and whisked up and away in great swoops by the never-resting cranes. These rumbled up to reach out over the laying-out floor and then attach themselves to the still hot steelwork with slings and hooks that looked too spidery to carry the great weights.

I had been a Yamaha motorcycle dealer (along with car franchise) back in Wanganui and was keen to look over the works. These were at Hamamatsu some 200 miles distant, over halfway to Tokyo. We travelled on the Kodama limited express—the "bullet" train, at speeds of over 130 miles an hour. After New Zealand's slow, narrow-gauge trains this was a fantastic experience. We rocketed along the built-up permanent way; Osaka's suburbs dwindled and paddyfields and quaint villages swept into view, to fade as the train ate up the miles. It was a two-line system shared between the Kodama and Hikari super-expresses. The whole complex was elevated—no level crossings and controlled by computers. We were nervous and ill at ease especially when passing a unit coming from the opposite direction. At some 260 miles an hour almost 3000 people passed by in less than five seconds with a thump and a roar as the compressed air waves collided.

At Hamamatsu—2500 motorcycles were being churned out each week, plus outboard motors and snowmobiles. For Mike's benefit the famous V-four Yamaha road-racing bike was wheeled out. We were not allowed to photograph this from certain angles, as secret development work was being experimented with, and actually we were enjoying a special privilege in just seeing it.

I began re-provisioning the cat for the voyage home. I intended to travel the Inland Sea down to Shimonoseki at the western entrance. En route we would call at Hiroshima and in particular the sacred island of Itsuku with its famous Tori standing in the water. Through this gateway, in ancient days, all visiting vessels were obliged to pass to show their friendly intentions. It was a clever device to channel strangers to a definite locality and to limit the size of vessels. I wanted to take the *Whai* through, just for the hell of it.

The morning of departure was bright and a brisk wind blew towards us from Kobe, a few miles across the bay. As we headed out Cobber undid the seals and wires from his guns, arranged them on the cabin table and we prepared for the coming wordy battle. I cruised slowly past the wharves and cranes, past a visiting Royal Navy cruiser and moored just in front of Cobber's ship, the *Port Albert*.

"Hop ashore and see your pals in Customs! They'll probably

do their blocks but I don't care! Do you want me to come with you?"

"No, she'll be right." And Cobber was off, to return half an hour later with a policeman and the chief Customs officer—the one who'd been witness to Cobber's outburst. He was friendly as could be—the guns and baggage were taken off the *Whai* and put on the ship without fuss. From this episode I learnt to stand up to officials from the word go—not to budge an inch if convinced I was right.

We slowly coasted beside the white walls of Cobber's new home. He looked down from the promenade deck and waved farewell. "Wish I were finishing the trip with you!" he shouted. "I think you'll have the best part to come."

We sailed on. Out into the narrow channel between Awaji Island and the mainland. The sun was reddening in the thick haze. We anchored behind a Japanese frigate off a village on Awaji. Without Bill and Cobber we rattled about the boat. There seemed so much more room and so much less cooking and fewer dishes to do. It meant, however, longer spells on the wheel and I warned Robbie and Monique that from now on they'd be expected to do their share during daylight hours.

The *Whai* yawed and the hiss and slap of a fast tiderip kept me awake. The anchor warp creaked and strained uneasily. Eventually I dropped off. My sixth sense awoke me. There was an uncanny silence and a curious bobbing motion. I peered at the landmark I'd picked out before going to bed. The lights were different and far away. Of course! The tide had changed and the cat had turned in the current. But the anchor couldn't be holding—there wasn't a creak. I climbed up top to find the *Whai* gently drifting right into the shipping lane. The anchor warp hung straight down and a quick check with the echo-sounder indicated well over a hundred feet beneath the keels.

"Quick Rafe! Call Mike—we're drifting. Get him to help you pull the anchor up."

It was about one a.m. and a huge moon silvered the waters. The anchor was pulled into its locked position and for a while Mike and Rafe stayed up to watch the lights on Awaji slide past. More and more ships were seen. There were literally dozens coming and going. I found myself threading across, in front and behind, edging away and sometimes towards the black shapes of the sea traffic. As we had to round the north-eastern tip of Awaji, we were obliged to cross the main shipping route to take the right-hand "lane".

As far as the eye could see there were the steaming lights of vessels. It was as if there was a highway on the sea. In fact it *was* a highway. Each time we put to sea it was an exciting challenge—our seven knots made it dicey crossing a lane, but took the necessity for decisions away once we were motoring along it. Overtaking ships have the right to pass on whichever side they choose, so we just ploughed along while all types of traffic forged past, sometimes coming very close to inspect the stranger from New Zealand.

Large chunks of dunnage thumped against us, run down in the darkness, and fiery phosphorescence rippled and splashed in sparks from our bows. I have never seen it so brilliant as in these waters. The moon set and for an hour we cruised a world of black velvet inset with green and red stars. They appeared as sparks, faint and far away, to grow into the steaming lights of ships with bow waves of luminous green.

For the next week or so, we would be in sheltered waters. Islands were all around, all connected by sea traffic. After days and weeks at sea, south of the Equator, with nothing but an occasional native canoe paddling close to jungle fringes, the shipping generated a feeling of camaraderie and we cruised along, our minute Japanese flag at the masthead flapping bravely. The smog and stifling heat of Osaka Bay had cleared and we lazed on the cabin roof or on the day-beds enjoying the lovely seascape.

Water-pump trouble again. The spares which were cabled for from Manila had not arrived from New Zealand. I decided to put into a sheltered harbour, a tiny out-of-the-way spot where there would be no pestilential officials. There we could strip the wornout pump seals, renew the bearings and patch up from bits and pieces. I found a little bay, shallow, with a good holding bottom of heavy mud, and a little jetty of fitted stonework on Hiroshima Island (not of atom bomb fame). I had seen a ferry pull in and hordes of children disembark. It meant transport to a city on Shikoku Island, where parts could be bought. There we found a different Japan, unhurried and quaint. A village with a small fishing fleet, a small guest house and two pavilions built out over the beach for day-trippers seeking a change.

There was nothing to attract Western tourists or businessmen and we aroused tremendous interest. I was the first Occidental to use their tiny post office, the first in the barber shop to loll back in luxury while a diminutive woman shaved me with tremulous hands. She was very nervous and soon I was, too—I've never liked cut-throat razors—and here I was stretched out under the shining blade of a visibly upset Japanese of my own vintage. Had

she lost a lover? A brother? Had she been waiting for this day?
Time for payment and I held out a handful of small change.
It was the only way, as counting in Japanese was beyond us.
She selected some 50 yen (about 12 cents) and motioned me back
into the chair. What now? Holding one hand above the other
for weight and strength, she proceeded to strike my shoulders
and to pummel at me in a form of rough massage. Then a tiny
cup of pale tea was brought and to much smiling and sucking-in
of breath and tea the episode was over.

"Mike, take the ferry to wherever it goes and try to get four
bearings to match the pumps, plus some seals. Better take a
pump with you. The bearings are inch sizes and if the Nips have
only metric then the housing will have to be re-machined. You
know what we need."

Mike gathered his cameras and was off. The rest of us explored the village—it was a little gem and quite unspoilt. Old
men, gnarled and bowed from years in the paddyfields sat in
the sun yarning the days away. Bright green frogs croaked and
splashed among the reeds bordering the flooded fields of rice.
Butterflies, splendid and gay in the sunshine, floated over wild
flowers growing on the grassy verges of the dusty roads winding
around the bay.

Every few hundred yards curious stone figurines, obviously
very old, stood or sat in silent communion with their surroundings, religious relics of earlier times powdering to dust, forgotten
yet unforgotten. We came on a little cemetery where stone
plinths had fallen at crazy angles. Some graves were recent, and
tiny bamboo shelters with paper streamers were erected over
them, protecting the mouldering offerings of rice and sweetmeats.

It was night when Mike came back, footsore and worn out—
he'd left the pump with an engineering shop in Marugame. He'd
return next day to pick it up. In the meantime we could carry
on exploring, and went ashore to a little eating-house we'd discovered. The village may have been the permanent home of a
couple of hundred people—the entertainment was nil until we
arrived, but as we ordered rice and raw fish, neighbours dropped
in to talk with our hostess and watch the strangers eat.

Again I ran into a veteran, aloof and angry, who glared at us
and spat on the footpath whenever we passed. Full of Japanese
beer, I was prepared to have him on, but without communication
we just eyed each other. He spat on the ground in front of me,
so I spat too. I was better lubricated than he and in the end,
fairly dried out, he slouched off into the darkness. The girls
were in hysterics. It must have been very funny to watch but we

were deadly serious. Lord knows the punishment for assault in Japan, but whatever it is, the risk of it kept our hands in our pockets.

Next evening the pump was refitted and, two hours later removed again. The Japanese engineer had done a poor job and water poured past the seals. We rebuilt it and at first light moved off.

The Japanese islands and landscape are exactly as painted—blue and grey mists shade the hills and mountains into beautiful perspective. Ridge by ridge, the high ground fades into obscurity. I loved Japan—the teeming cities, modern and dramatic; the villages peaceful and rustic; the vitality of the people, the variety of insect and bird life. There is something dynamic and yet enchanting about Japan that is hard to put into words. Even the butterflies are different. Ours flit about, aimless and erratic. In Japan they are bigger, more colourful and fly purposefully from one place to another more like birds. The heron standing on its rock, the rice, green and rustling, a cargo ship with diesels pounding—all belong, all in counterpoint, one to another.

Apart from the officials, the occasional truculent veteran or arrogant youth, I liked the Japanese people. Quick, intelligent and industrious, they were also friendly and helpful. I think they sincerely believe themselves to be superior to all other races. I also think and sincerely believe that in looking to the future, so entwined with ours, we should remember the past. There are dragon's teeth planted in so many fields.

More and more shipping—hydrofoils like huge water-spiders skimmed across our path. Catamarans, ferries, 200 feet long and transporting cars and buses, joined the parade. Sometimes we managed to overtake a tug with barges or a floating crane. It was now our turn to sidle alongside and eye the stranger. Ashore, along the coastlines, arterial roads wound and traintracks, too. We could see streams of cars, trucks, buses and motorcycles in an unending flood.

It was grand to be skipper on my own at night—the challenge of the shipping lanes, the analysis of ships' intended movements and the decisions on courses to steer were enthralling. I even thought with gratitude of my unfortunate instructor at the Marine Department's navigation school. The hours of fiddling with little wooden models of shipping lights, of buoys and other navigational aids were paying off. In all the Inland Sea not once did we see a yacht or so small a craft as our own when out in the sea lanes.

Kurushima Kaikyo was ahead—a narrow channel between islands of stone and scrubby trees. Lighthouses and beacons were on every headland and fierce currents sucked or pressed at the shores. Mist hung over this dangerous place and ships' horns echoed from crag to crag. At some places the *Whai* could scarcely motor forward against the current and we edged slowly past the rocks of hidden shorelines, keeping well to the right side. We could hear ships passing each other, like huge bellowing dinosaurs. The echo-sounder clicked and hummed away to itself, rolling out feet of jagged lines as the bottom rose and fell in underwater canyons. We arrived during the tide-set against us and it was slowly, slowly that we edged through the narrows where a million tons of water flows back and forth each day.

We cleared the complex island group and entered the Aki-Nada (open waters) at evening. It was plain sailing until dawn when Ka Shima was reached.

We headed towards Hiroshima. Oyster "mats" became more numerous, anchored a few hundred yards off the coast. I couldn't find a port entrance and eventually edged into what looked like a creek outlet lined with concrete walls. A small ship was discharging gravel and a most smelly "tanker" was moored just ahead. The channel between the walls was narrow, perhaps 30 feet wide, and the echo-sounder showed some 6 feet depth. I hoped to moor alongside the tanker but the smell was appalling—she was the marine equivalent of a "honey-pot", the carts that shift nightsoil in backward areas! What they did with the stuff I didn't wait to find out. We cast off and drifted, motors idling, up the channel to a small turning basin. A white-shirted man paused to watch our approach and hastened forward.

"New Zealand? New Zealand! I George Sakai—J Force batman. Welcome to Japan! How long you stay?"

And so we met a man who, as a youth, had been "adopted" by some New Zealand unit. Our thanks to those unknown soldiers who so impressed and influenced him that he was genuinely pleased to offer hospitality to strangers. To comply with maritime regulations I had had our two lifebuoys marked with our port of registry, but on the obverse side the words "New Zealand" were painted. This was the side we always displayed and how it had worked in our favour! George was manager of a tourist hotel at Ono and laid on free rooms, meals, beer and a car.

We wanted to see Hiroshima, to spend a few days in the area. It was obvious that this little harbour was unsuitable—dirty, dusty, and the small wharfage space fully utilised by local shipping. George Sakai suggested we cruise up the coast and moor alongside his company's ferry wharves where there were nightwatchmen, water supplies and, of course, the hotel.

"Leave your car! Come with us—we'll pay for a taxi back to collect it!" So George climbed on board, we opened a bottle of Scotch and enjoyed a hilarious hour weaving in and out of the oyster farms until we arrived in Ono.

"It's like Blackpool!" muttered Rafe. "Look at the revolving restaurant and the ruddy piers!" There were fountains too, and clipped formal gardens. It was a mighty tourist trap.

"That Itsuku Island—a sacred place. No one is allowed to die or be born there. It is most beautiful and you must go see. You take ferry—I get tickets." We chose a dragon boat—fat and ungainly but resplendent in blue, gold, red and green. It had a great carved head on its long scaly neck and at its stern, the tail. As we chuffed over the channel separating Itsuku from the mainland I spotted the huge red Tori of Miyajima.

"Look at that!" I said to Mike. "Reckon we could get the *Whai* through it?"

The great gateway stood in the sea a few hundred feet from the shore. Behind it an ancient temple rested in a fold of the hills, grey and weathered. Itsuku was mountainous, but beeches and pines, oak and larches clad the slopes. A cableway hung like a spiderweb in enormous loops up the hillside and disappeared over the top ridge.

"Let's go on that!" We hadn't climbed anything steeper than the ladders on the *Whai* or the stairways at Expo for months, and the walk through the woods up to the cableway station was rough. Butterflies danced in the glades and green dragonflies hovered and darted across pools trapped by tree roots and boulders. Leaves, red and gold, carpeted the floor of the woodland. Were the trees planted for effect? Was the stream contrived to fall in shining sheets from rock to rock and gravelly shallows? The whole parkland was beautiful.

With many a rest we arrived at the first cableway station: only a couple of hundred feet up, but it underlined our weakness.

"I reckon meat's the trouble! We need good solid Kiwi tucker. I'd give anything for a fat juicy steak!" said Mike.

We climbed into one of the gondolas and with a clank and lunge were off. Off over the tops of the firs and beeches, past gondolas descending towards us. At the top of the first ridge was a station and another set of cars. This time two pretty

Japanese girls, attendants, got in with us. The cameras clicked and whirred.

"Plenty monkeys and deer up summit," one girl offered. "Many photos—you save film." But the monkeys had got weary and gone to tree and the little spotted deer were pretty blasé with the end of the day's tidbits.

"You come Hiroshima tonight—see bomb damage. I take you after ten. I work until ten tonight—then go."

Ten o'clock and George arrived with a limousine. We were miles from Hiroshima and on the way bare patches were pointed out where the paper and wood shanty-town suburbs had burnt and not been rebuilt. Nearer the centre of the city, large areas of open waste ground marked the sites of what had been shopping arcades. We stopped on a river bank.

"Here many peoples stood in water from fires," said George. The buildings had disappeared and only the stark wreckage of the town hall stood—illuminated by floodlights and preserved as a monument to the tens of thousands who died in the atomic blast. It was in silence we looked and in silence we walked to another memorial shining in the glow of concealed lights. It was a curious cone supported on legs of concrete. Hanging from its apex, like the tongue of a bell, was a mass of tiny white folded paper birds. Thousands and thousands strung on nylon threads.

"Little offerings to the dead—little peace offerings."

"It's all wrong!" said Monique. "They never should have done it! They had no moral right to do such a beastly thing. I'm ashamed of my people."

"Nonsense," said I. "They killed thousands to save millions. If the Nips hadn't seen the writing on the wall with the atomic bomb, they'd have gone on fighting island by island. Germany fought right until the end and Japan would have, too. Only the Japs wouldn't surrender in the face of conventional weapons— they gave in to fight another day. These people don't love us— they'll make use of us until it suits them."

I don't know what George thought about it. He kept very quiet. He did, however, tell us a strange thing: every day for half an hour a survivor of the blast talks on the local radio of his or her experience. Every day since 1946.

CHAPTER NINE

A Cruise on the Coast

BEFORE leaving Ono I intended to take the *Whai* through the big sacred Tori. High tide was about 11 a.m. As far as the eye could see were the frames of oyster "mats" anchored in parallel rows. I could see I was in for some problems taking the cat through them and into the channel between the Sacred Island and the mainland of Honshu.

The Tori was dead ahead—there were no boats nearby.

"Rafe, how about you taking your Nikonos and getting a shot of us coming through the arch? We can drop you off, circle behind the Tori and pick you up as we come through. It should make a great photo." So Rafe loaded his waterproof camera, pulled on his wetsuit jacket, fins and mask, and jumped over the side.

We cruised very slowly behind the red arch, lined up and edged forward between its six legs. Above us the huge wooden beams and curved "roof" seemed to press down and scrape our tripod mast. But there was plenty of room and the *Whai* had about four feet clearance on either side.

"I don't think the Japs are very impressed with this stunt," remarked Monique. "Some of them are waving at us and shouting."

We moved out from under the Tori's shadow and Rafe climbed on board.

"Should be a super picture—I got the temple framed between the hulls!"

Should have been, but all Rafe got was a balled-up roll of film, somehow misloaded in his camera. It was too late to turn back—the tide was down and we were miles away when the failure was discovered.

The evenings in the Inland Sea were cool and delightful, but the days muggy and hot. We were disappointed in the sea's discoloration—we could do no diving as underwater visibility was limited to six feet, if that. The cat was getting sluggish with weed and barnacles; the stay in the Nishinamiya yacht basin had allowed a slimy growth to develop. I decided to hole up for a few hours in a sheltered bay while we cleaned her. It was good to get in the cool water with a scrubbing brush and work on the hulls.

We arrived before dusk at the narrows where the islands of Honshu and Kyushu are joined by a great bridge. The Inland Sea ends here and the tide flow is very strong. As this was a focal point for shipping and a very interesting coast, I decided to anchor for the night and go through in daylight. There was a little shallow bay on the Honshu side with a fishing village built against the hills. A concrete seawall separated the beach and roadway. The anchor splashed down and I reversed the *Whai* towards the beach so that the Danforth was well embedded. We dropped a stern anchor and were set for the night. A hundred feet or so away a small cargo boat lay at anchor; the place should be safe. There was a very small village, primitive and of no account, but in less than half an hour we were eating steiki and drinking pilfered U.S. Navy whisky.

Rafe again had struck up a casual friendship—the Japanese are fascinated by fair hair and delight to try out any English they know. He had wandered from the little store, where I had been bargaining for eggs, and had been invited into a fisherman's cottage. As soon as the Japanese realized he had companions, we were rounded up and a party began. It was a small, poorly constructed house, built into the hillside.

The woman of the house was a cheerful laughing sort, stocky and robust, pretty in a way. We couldn't fathom the set-up—there were three men, two with gnarled hands and knotted muscles, the other a quite different type, slight and with a clever mobile face.

An old woman, bent and shaky, hobbled to meet us—she bowed deeply and Mike helped her straighten up to the merriment of the men. A huge bottle of whisky was produced and when Monique pointed to the blue U.S. Navy seal, the two hard cases laughed and slapped each other on the back.

"Plenty! Plenty!" one cried, tears of laughter running down his cheeks. A pan of grilled steak appeared: this was either a wealthy household or a den of racketeers. But it was the first decent meal of solid meat we'd enjoyed for a long while. Its origin didn't worry us.

I have always admired the Samurai swords of Japan. I don't remember how the subject came up—my Japanese was limited to "arrigato" (thank you) "konnishi wa" (good day) "sayonara" (goodbye) and for good measure, "mushi mushi"—the equivalent of our "hulloa?" when calling on the telephone. But anyhow the young man stood up and excused himself. He returned dressed now in a loose kimono type of robe. In his arms he cradled a long shape swathed in old threadbare brocade. The other Japanese fell silent and the food and drink were cleared away. The women withdrew and Robbie and Monique fidgeted in case they, too, were expected to leave. For this was a ritual.

The young man knelt on the central mat and placed a lacquered box to one side. Gently and slowly, he unwrapped a beautiful sword in a shining black scabbard. Then he stripped the sword by removing the peg which locks the blade into the hilt. Next he slid the hilt, washers, guard and habake (socket) from the sword's tang. These were carefully laid out on a folded cloth and, taking a little bag of white powder from his "tool box," he proceeded to polish the blade by dusting the shining metal and rubbing it with tissue. No oil was used and we were allowed to examine the blade only by holding it carefully with the tissue paper. The cutting edge of tempered steel showed the mokume (or pattern) forged into the metal by hammering. This sword was old, an heirloom, and with pride the owner showed us its registration document. It could not be sold or exported from Japan.

The Samurai of ancient Japan looked on his sword almost as a living thing. It was created by a master smith living an almost religious and abstemious life. No sex, no animal food or intoxicating drink could be taken and all food was cooked over a sacred fire. Not even members of his own family were permitted to enter the smithy while the forging of the blades went on. For the final, critical stages of creating a Samurai's sword, the smith put on the ceremonial costume of a court nobleman. At this time, his workshop became a sanctuary and over the gateway was hung Shinto straw-rope (shime-nawa) to ward off evil influences.

The ancient weapon was re-assembled; he re-wrapped the lacquered scabbard with its pearl-shell butterflies and beetles. The gold and silver inlay was covered. He bowed over the sword for a few minutes, stood up, stared at us each in turn and left. We did not see him again.

Who was he, and how had he come by this weapon? Just a little mystery in a little village of no account.

With arm-waving and weird signs we indicated that we wanted our hosts to come out to our boat for a party—for a drink. In the morning we'd be leaving early and there would be no time for farewells. So we piled into the dinghy, all nine of us, and paddled a wobbling course across to the *Whai*. It was impossible to pick her out until we were within about 30 feet.

Climbing out of the dinghy one of the Japanese fell into the water. Within a minute he'd stripped off his clothes and was swimming around, laughing and calling to his friends. Then we were all in; it was pitch dark and the bay re-echoed to shouts and laughter.

Dressed and dry again, we broached our liquor stock. It's a curious fact that women seem to be attracted by novel homes—caravans or boats arouse their nest-making instincts. Our living quarters fascinated the Japanese woman.

"Where you sleep?" asked our former hostess in the best English we'd heard all night. So I showed her, everyone crowding down to the port hull. Immediately she climbed on to my bunk and, lying on her back, almost helpless with laughter, shouted "Captain's woman! Captain's woman!"

The menfolk seemed to get restive and, however interesting the prospects might have been, it was time to say goodbye. We bundled them over the side and paddled them ashore.

A beautiful morning as we left the little bay, the big bridge spanning the narrows towering over us. Hydrofoils skimmed past, crowded with commuters, and the coastline came to life with the new day. Streams of cars and trucks on the highways on either side of the channel flowed along, tooting and jostling. We climbed on the cabin roof to take in the spectacle as we passed through the Shimonoseki Straits. We were out of the Inland Sea.

Winds were light and variable down the coast of Kyushu. It took a full day and night's cruising to reach and pass through the Iki Straits between Iki Island and Kyushu. We were nearly entangled in nets strung between fishing vessels at night—the lights shown must have followed a local system, not the international pattern at all. Once we actually rode right over a line of floats and by sheer luck missed picking the net up around our propellers.

On 26 July, as we cruised along the coast the glitter of a spire caught my eye. It was a great gilded pagoda, built on a promontory; it didn't look Japanese somehow. Further around the coast, a concrete building in the stylised shape of a junk stood among trees near the water's edge.

And so we came to Hinura. It was a little harbour and being only 7 a.m. no officials noticed our arrival.

"Be back at the boat by two o'clock at the latest—don't let me down. I want to get clear of the islands down the coast before dark."

Mike wanted some film and he and Rafe went off with the

girls while I gathered up a shopping bag and some dollars. I was out of yen, and it meant finding a bank or business that could change them—small shopkeepers always seemed confused and chary about handling U.S. dollars or travellers' cheques.

I took a taxi, saying "ginko" (bank). It needed time and a pantomime of waving dollar bills in front of him before he cottoned on. The bank was shut. As was another and another. It was Sunday—I'd forgotten the days and the only thing to do was find a business house open so I gave the driver a dollar and got rid of him—he well knew my quest was hopeless and had, indeed, taken me for a ride.

What appeared to be a shipping office was open, and five or six pleasant-looking giggling girls crowded around. One went to a lot of trouble telephoning around and in the end took a chance and called her boss, who was upstairs. As soon as I saw him I knew there would be trouble. He was short and stocky and about my age. We eyed each other and I explained I was from New Zealand, in the harbour with my boat and wanted yen for buying fuel and groceries. He grunted, turned towards the girls, barked out an order at which they all moved back to their desks. Then he must have berated my little helper severely, for she suddenly flushed and hung her head. Her eyes watered and she stared at her typewriter.

The manager, or whatever, turned on his heel and stalked out of the building. As he did so, he shouted at one of the girls, who said to me in a frightened voice that I was to remain.

Five long silent minutes dragged by. Then the outer doors flew open and a policeman rushed in, glaring around until he saw me sitting quietly in the corner.

"You trying change dollars! Come with me!"

I rose, put my wrists together in mock submission, which brought a little giggle from the girls. The police station was just over the road and as we crossed we passed my betrayer, who got my No. 1 look of scorn.

Now began a performance which ended only when the police admitted defeat and were forced to ring a professor of English at some nearby university. I had decided not to understand the police—I was sick of Japanese officialdom. Let them stew around and upset themselves. If I pretended to misunderstand their enquiries it would shake their belief in their command of English. Civil servants had made things difficult for us and I now enjoyed a new outlook—one of passive awkwardness. I let the perspiring, shouting characters jump up and down.

"This very serious! You defy law!"

The huge Tori of Miyajima

One of the many
churches at Uvea,
in the Loyalties

Melanesians at Rabaul with their palm umbrellas

It seemed that U.S. dollars could be changed only through a bank—that it was a serious offence to traffic in them and that I'd have to go to Sasebo, an American Naval base 100 miles down the coast, to change them.

"Well, how do I get there if I need food and fuel! I want to go tonight—not stay here after two o'clock because of navigational hazards to clear before dark. Sasebo's miles out of our way!"

The last thing I wanted was to stay overnight and have Customs, etc., to contend with.

But they were adamant and so the old rigmarole of forms started up and I filled in dozens—I'd have to go to Sasebo now or there'd be trouble. Anyhow I could get my clearance for Okinawa from this port. After a lot of discussion, one of the police changed a 20-dollar bill and I was solvent again.

Two o'clock came and no Robbie or Monique. Restively I studied the charts again, trying to decide on a port for the night further down the coast. I wanted a quiet little place with no Customs.

"Welcome to Hinura!" a voice called from the dockside. "We would like to converse."

On the dock were a group of smiling Japanese. One had a carton of beer.

"Welcome! We teachers and students from university. We do not often meet English peoples."

We had them aboard and toasted one another in warm beer. It turned out that after the police station affair my English-speaking professor passed the word on and these visitors wanted to practise their English.

Monique and Robbie arrived, hot and flustered—they'd taken a wrong bus and got lost and were worried in case I took off.

We waved goodbye to our students. "That was nice of them," said Mike, polishing off a bottle. "I like the civilians, but you can keep the officials!"

Darkness caught us in the midst of a milling fleet of fishing craft. In the end I had to shut down the motors and drift the night away, the Japanese cruising all around us, no doubt wondering what and who we were. At dawn we started up again on a sea almost clear of shipping. It was 27 July. A most pleasant day with little dancing wavelets capped with white. The wind, about 10 knots on our starboard stern, helped us along. We passed island after island, green but treeless with grey rocky foreshores. I studied the charts and, deciding we'd put in somewhere for the night, chose a bay which looked sheltered from any direction. A tiny village was marked and we would not be bothered by officialdom.

Mike, at the wheel, was having an animated discussion with Robbie, who was preparing the evening meal. I was due "on" at the end of Mike's spell so that I could take the *Whai* into harbour.

"How are we doing?"

"About five minutes to go," answered Mike, who had unknowingly joined the aristocracy.

I had a rule that the relieving helmsman made a quick inspection around the decks immediately before taking the wheel. After all, the helmsman was in full charge during his watch and was responsible for loose lashings, opened ports or hatches.

I strolled around the cat, checked everything likely to shift or cause trouble, and relieved Mike. On checking the island ahead it didn't seem to match the chart, but I didn't worry—the harbour I had decided on opened out in front and I conned the *Whai* in through the big buoys marking the channel.

It was a curious inlet—the buoys were rust-streaked, uncared for, with bent and broken light standards. A few small junks, off for the night's fishing, headed towards us with diesel smoke puffing from their exhausts. Cliffs and hills hemmed in the bay and on the shore several brick buildings stood, roofs fallen in and grass growing through the broken roadings around them. Twisted iron work lay half in and out of the sea where loading cranes had fallen across the wreck of a wharf. There were the remains of a power substation reduced to twisted ironwork and broken insulators. Pylons leaned at crazy angles or lay in the debris.

"That's bomb damage! I wonder what it was? It's been a very big complex—look at the wrecked trucks under that rubble!"

"Hell's bells! Look at the size of that anchor!" said Mike. On the edge of the bay a giant anchor lay, encrusted with rust and dirt.

"They must have had very big ships in here—those are moorings, not marker buoys. See the workers' flats on the skyline!"

On the hilltop surrounding the bay, stood a line of three-storey concrete buildings. Rows of them. No washing hung from the balconies, there were no window curtains, just barrack-like empty apartments.

We cruised past the remains of the factory, past more derelict wharves, and crept around the last buoy to turn into the calm waters of a tiny port. A fleet of small junks lay at the rickety wharves and tough-looking, silent men watched us manoeuvre and draw up alongside a decrepit floating crane.

"This should do us. It'll be safer than alongside the wharf and no tide movement to worry about. Rafe, hop over and see if anyone's on the barge and ask if we can stay here for the night."

There was no crew. We made fast and sat down to tea.

"I don't like the feel of this place. Something's wrong. I feel we're more than unwelcome," said Robbie.

"Yes. It's a queer place. Those apartment houses and the warehouses. Did you notice the hovels on the other side of the harbour—I'll be pleased to leave. We'll go at first light," I replied.

Rafe decided to go walkabout. He clambered over the barge and wandered along the wharf, a group of ragged urchins trailing him, but not too close.

"I hope he doesn't try chasing women here. I hope he doesn't get into trouble!" I was worried.

"He's a big boy—not to worry!" said Mike.

But he did get into trouble: within ten minutes he was back, escorted by an armed policeman.

"This man say crewman. Who you? Where from?"

"We are tourists. We are going to Sasebo. Here are our papers."

Out came a notebook and our particulars were carefully written down.

"I take these," stated the policeman, a pleasant looking chap, reaching for the *Whai's* registration papers.

"No you don't! They stay on the ship."

For a moment I thought we'd be in real strife; then he pocketed his notebook and stood up.

"You stay here. I call superiors."

Here we go again, I thought. More ruddy nonsense.

"We leave at first light for Sasebo—tomorrow morning early! We sleep here tonight," I told him as he clambered over the rail.

"I send friend. Speak good English." And he was gone.

"He caught me asking for a beer—I could find only one scruffy little shop. The people were damned unfriendly. I was pleased to see him!" explained Rafe.

The evening shadows crept down the hills, covered and hid the wreckage and crumbling buildings. A sea mist rose from the black harbour and a few lights flickered among the shanties. Something solid splashed into the water nearby—something thrown from shore.

"I'll break your bloody arms!" shouted Mike with a bellow, and little feet scampered off into the darkness.

Mosquitoes, big and thirsty, found us. It looked as if it would be an unpleasant night—dark, no moon and a brooding stillness. Sitting in the dark on the foredeck we heard someone clicking along the wharf.

"Good evening! I am (unpronounceable). Can I come to see you?" A disembodied voice from the shadows.

"Yes, welcome! Be careful of obstructions," I replied.

The Japanese was dressed in a simple kimono and wooden clogs.

"I am schoolteacher—teach English in college. My friend the police officer tell me you here."

We offered him whisky and we sat drinking, giving the mosquitoes infusions of a rare treat.

"This was city of 30,000 peoples six years ago. Big coal field and mines now finished. Only 6000 peoples live here now."

The girls were happy enough with the yarn but I'd seen enough bomb damage to recognize it—even after 25 years. No wonder the locals had been unfriendly. They were off the beaten track and had to live with the wreckage of what had been the main source of local wealth and security.

I don't know why the teacher didn't tell the truth—it wasn't the first time, nor the last, that Japanese dismissed or covered up for the war's defects.

Back came the police—this time two of them and I was carefully questioned as to our previous movements. A full report was required by the chief of police for the Saga Prefecture.

"We come back in morning. We see you eight hours."

"O.K. Goodnight." And we were off to our bunks, leaving the disgruntled "mossies" to their usual diet ashore.

At six a.m. the sun's rays struck the hills with gold. Dozens of junks puttered back to harbour and in the confusion of movement we left. Out past the fragment-scarred walls, past the derelict dolphins and jetties and into the open sea, with the *Whai* bobbing and bowing politely to the incoming grubby junks.

Once outside I searched for landmarks to establish our position—according to the chart the next island, Sakito, our turning-point east for Sasebo, should be an hour's steam ahead—but nothing was in sight. I backtracked in my mind and through the log book.

"Mike, you Count! You were so busy talking to Robbie you steered for an extra hour! We stayed the night in the wrong place!"

"Well, we had some fun and we're an hour further on our way," replied Mike. But that wasn't the point. I was upset, as it had meant a clash with the law and maybe repercussions yet to come.

No more chattering or reading at the wheel was the edict, and long faces became the order of the day.

There was a stiff current against us going into Sasebo harbour. Long trails of brown foam flowed past, dotted with dunnage and rubbish. I got in behind a tanker and in its wake we edged forward. A Japanese cruiser appeared from around a headland to port, then another and another. All told, nine grey warships cruised past and from their bridges and superstructures crewmen and officers looked at us with much interest. As each drew abreast and our "New Zealand" came into sight, the officers studying us through glasses became very excited and waved and drew each other's attention to us.

"Those must be some of their 'home defence' vessels. They look pretty modern and efficient," I said. Rising-Sun flags fluttered from their jackstaffs and we gazed after them with mixed feelings.

Sasebo is a large bay. I had no intention of running into more officials if it could be avoided. If I could find a U.S. Navy pier it would do me.

A large Stars and Stripes hung limply in front of a group of buildings. Grey Quonset huts, whitewashed picket fences and American uniforms indicated a U.S. base, and at the water's edge was a marina with naval pinnaces.

We went alongside and Rafe and Mike made fast. We had made it O.K.; now all I needed was fuel and food for the trip to Okinawa and a clearance for the *Whai*.

A pleasant Yank breezed up: "Say, guys, this is the Admiral's jetty. How long are you staying?"

"About 24 hours, I hope. Can we stay here for the night?"

"Waal, I don't know about that. I'm dockmaster. This is a naval base—no civilians."

"Could I see your boss? We need fuel and provisions and a clearance."

And so I was led ashore and met a commander who "visited with us" and helped polish off a bottle of vodka. He organized our short stay. He made us welcome.

"The port authorities are after you, Captain," he said. "They say you disregarded their signals at the harbour entrance!"

"Didn't see 'em—was too busy keeping behind a tanker and bucking the current."

"Oh, well—get your papers and we'll fix it up."

No fuss, no bother, and what a marvellous change. Would it

have been as easy if our cat was called "Katinka" and registered in Vladivostok?

Fuel was a problem and I don't know who actually got the dollars paid out for some 200 (U.S.) gallons. But at last we were set, clearance signed, and ready to leave. I checked my watch for correct G.M.T. and got the latest weather bulletins—a typhoon was forming up in the Marianas and it was time to go.

We sailed before the new day could bring problems—out into the open sea into a head wind of some 10 to 15 knots and short, breaking seas. In clear weather, day and night, we passed the Koshiki Group, the Uji and Kusayaki Islands and on to the Tokaras. I decided to go down the eastern coast of the Ryukyus this time, but the wind changed to the east and so we crept along under western high bluffs and crags in sheltered waters. On the 29th we had our first spearfishing swim for a month— off Amami Ō Shima—off a rocky point with kelp and stunted corals and few fish.

We'd been in the sea less than a quarter of an hour when the high wailing of a siren blared across the water. I looked up to see a grey patrol boat edging towards us, a crowd of Japanese in the bows. She crept forward and the siren moaned to a stop. To the mutter of its diesels I muttered too. If words could sink ships, the Japs would now be breaking out their lifejackets.

"We're on our way to Naha! We're catching our dinner! Food! Food!!" and I waved my speargun, turned my back on them and dived below. I stayed down as long as I could. If I'd had a lung, I'd have stayed down half an hour, but after half a minute I came up, redfaced and angry. Again. The Japs looked us over—the girls sunning themselves on the deck and the three men swimming in the water.

"Naha! Naha!" I shouted and from then on ignored them. Presently they reversed and made off. They had gone, but the day had been spoilt—the fish were tiny and scary, there were many stinging jellyfish, and the coral was stunted by cool waters. Rafe got four crayfish and a small coral trout and I shot three fish. Fresh fish for tea. We had a scrumptious meal and left. Tomorrow we'd make Buckner Bay and the Okinawa Yacht Club. Here we could refit for the next long hop. Here we could eat huge steaks and drink Bacardi cokes and meet friends again. And no more Japanese officials.

CHAPTER TEN

Encounter with a Typhoon

Buckner Bay is entered past low-lying coral and sand islands with reefs breaking the sea in long creaming swirls. Troop transporters, the odd tanker and supply ships of the U.S. Navy were anchored off White Sands beach. Jets screamed and tore the sky to shreds.

One of the Naha port pilots had given me a chart of the bay, as getting to the Okinawa Yacht Club's marina was a bit dicey with sand bars and coral reefs spread out like an obstacle course. When I went to find the chart it had disappeared, but I did find Mike's book of travellers' cheques, mislaid among the charts, pencils and navigating gear.

Mike was very relieved—he'd been scratching for dollars and now his troubles were over. Some of mine, too, as I needed to put the nips in and borrow some money. We were solvent again.

I conned the *Whai* slowly around the bay; past hills of kunai grass, past fields of sugarcane. Curious stone and concrete structures dotted the hillsides—almost stylized portals or gateways. We studied them intently through binoculars but couldn't make out their purpose. Later we were to find out that they were tombs. Once a year, on a religious holiday, the Okinawans take a picnic meal to their families' resting place. They dust and clean the bones of their forebears and generally tidy things a bit.

The breeze grew cool and shadows lengthened. It was unnerving with the echo-sounder on the blink and not to be trusted. Reefs were getting more difficult to see and the odd buoy meaningless without a chart. I drew alongside a rusty workboat and an Okinawan crewman indicated with a crude sketch where we were to go—half an hour yet and the sun already red and sombre.

A crowd of hilarious Japanese youths roared past in their outboard, but shout and gesticulate as we might, we couldn't get them to come over and guide us.

"Just have to take a chance and follow them—I'll keep on the outside of those buoys though." And so we arrived at two small moles jutting out into the dull waters. A flagpole and burgee marked the club and a row of yachts and power cruisers lined

the basin. Thankfully I manoeuvred the cat around a vacant
floating dock. In five minutes we were secure and descending in
a cheerful gaggle on the clubhouse. This was something like!
Air conditioning, a lounge of easy chairs, soft lights and a semi-
circular altar to Bacchus with worshipful attendants. The *Whai's*
crew advanced on the bar.

"I'm Lois Lyons. Mark, my husband, is club mooring captain.
He's at a committee meeting and I'm to look after you. Welcome
to the yacht club! You are invited to a complimentary meal.
Would you care to have dinner here tonight?"

Lois was a most attractive hostess. She laughed when we
settled for the jumbo-sized steaks—we had the choice of 8oz or
16oz T-bones—the first really solid meat meal in months.

Little Okinawan waitresses served us—short, stocky women
with black, black hair. I think they are prettier than the mainland
Japanese, or perhaps these had been carefully selected.

"Now, no interfering with the help, you guys," said a new
friend, an American civilian called Floyd. "They're hard to train
and we don't want to lose any of them having Kiwi kids."

It had been all of a week since the crew had had a thrash and
we were dehydrated after conserving water on the way down
from Japan. Someone rang a bell, which was mounted on a
pillar, and immediately a loud cheer went up from all present.
The club members had a novel method of celebrating a triumph
or good fortune (or too much to drink) by "ringing the bell."
This meant a round for all present, and this night the bell clanged
again and again as we were introduced to late arrivals and the
party gained momentum.

The first night we were a novelty. The next night we established closer contact through Rafe getting a black eye.

"How did it happen? What the hell did you do?"

"I didn't do anything! I just mentioned 'Ugly American.' And
Joe said, 'I don't like that expression.' I said, 'Oh, I don't mean
you—I mean Army types.' Joe said, 'I *am* Army, and proud of
it! Don't use it again or I'll fill you in.'"

Well, anyhow Rafe said it again, a slip of the tongue no doubt,
and whop! a shiner of many colours worn for a week.

On the third night we were fully confirmed as true members
by joining the inner circle of club life on this steamy island.

It was sweltering hot outside and heat lightning flickered
across the hills separating Buckner Bay from Naha. Mike and I
were irrigating our parched carcases (we had been working in
the *Whai's* engine rooms all day in over 98°F.) with Floyd and
the secretary. Outside the dust swirled, but inside the air condi-

tioners whirred while we played darts. Tried to play darts in between Bacardi cokes, rum Collins and Bloody Marys. It was pleasant; we were relaxed and happy. That evening the girls had gone into Naha with friends and Rafe into hiding with his eye. There had been a marvellous thrash at the bar and all had left but we four.

Suddenly, with a crash, the swing doors were flung wide and in rushed Joe's tearful and panting wife.

"Help me! He's going to kill me! Help me! He's gone mad!"

She ran stumbling past chairs and tables, headed for the back rooms.

Again the doors were thrown open and in he came—big, glaring and full of fight. Joe was Floyd's friend and normally an easy-natured, kindly man. A little touchy over anti-American expressions, perhaps, but all-in-all an average joe. But not now.

"What's wrong? Come over and have a drink," called out Floyd. It is common practice, well tried and true, to offer enraged persons more of the medicine which enraged them in the first place. This has two virtues. It can divert them by making them forget the object of their rancour or it can put them out of their trauma if administered in quantity. Anyhow, it's an excuse for carrying on the party. Who wants a party pooper?

We got him outside. We got her outside and into Floyd's car in which she promptly locked herself, wound up the windows and cowered, crying.

"Come out or I'll come in!" raved Joe and with that he punched his fist clean through the side window, showering his spouse with glass and cutting himself badly.

"Hey! That's my car," shouted Floyd and was promptly flattened with a roundhouse swing. He slowly folded over his car's bonnet, backwards, to lie there blinking at the stars.

I saw the diminutive Okinawan gate-guard duck out of sight below the windowledge of his hut. This wasn't his night—or his problem.

"Hell, we'll have to do something!" I yelled to Mike—but what!

Mike, 6ft 2in and all muscle, grabbed Joe and next minute they were rolling in the dust. I jumped across the flailing legs and, finding an uncovered area, thumped it hard three times. Anything to incapacitate the raving figure below.

"That's three times you've done that, Peter! Don't you do that again!" he roared. And then,

"You'd better get off this island tomorrow, Mike, 'cos I'm gonna get a gun an' shoot you!"

But the wind was out of him and when he promised to "be good" we let him up, to stand swaying and dripping blood.

Floyd was got going again and we breathed a sigh of relief as all three drove off to hospital, crying, groaning or cursing.

"Well," said the secretary, who materialised from the shadows. "I must apologise for that. It's most unlike him. Come on and we'll have some drinks on the club."

We relaxed again, but darts seemed tame after the excitement and we decided to pack it in.

With a crash, the swing doors were flung wide and in rushed another tearful and terrified woman. When we'd seen her last she had been dancing seductively—the attractive centre of attention. Before she'd got married (to an ugly-tempered drunk) she had been a model and a dancer. Now she was tear-streaked, with widly disordered blonde hair and torn stockings.

"Help me! My husband's gone mad! He's trying to kill me!" And she, too, raced for the haven out the back.

Again the doors were thrown open and in he came: big, but not as big as the other, drunk, but ugly drunk, glaring and full of fight.

We got him outside, lured with a drink. It was getting monotonous.

"I know you've got a bottle behind your back!" he shouted.

"Yes, and I'm going to use it!" I promised. But Mike's size must have unnerved him, for he gave up and drove off in a cloud of dust, vowing to "finish her off when she gets home."

"I'll divorce him! Tomorrow I'll fly back Stateside! I've had enough!"

"I don't believe it!" Monique and Robbie were excited and furious at having missed the entertainment. "You're having us on!"

"True! Straight up! You should have stayed behind. Look at my pants—they'll have to be dry-cleaned to get the blood out. And sewn up!"

One of the club's boatmen drove up. "Captain! Telephone for you! I give ride."

I hopped into the utility and we went to the clubhouse.

"I want to apologise, in the name of the club, for what happened last night! It was inexcusable. Sorry you had to witness it!" The president was very upset.

"Think nothing of it—it was amusing while it lasted. These things happen."

"Yes, sure—but not twice in the one night! I'll get the members concerned to apologise in person."

"No! For heaven's sake not that! We'd be terribly embarrassed. Forget it—we have."

"Well, thank you for taking that line. Oh, by the way, better contact Mark Lyons—there's a typhoon on its way and expected to hit here in a couple of days." And with that cheerful news he hung up.

Mark warned it was going to be a big blow—a typhoon designated "Wilda" was coming up from north of the Philippines and curving around towards the South China Sea. It was expected within 24 hours and now was the time to prepare for it. Mark had four men bury anchors in the compacted coral of the dockside. The club marina was closed after Mark's two charterboats were brought in. A web of nylon ropes leashed each craft clear of its dock so that the buffetting winds could not bash them to pieces. Ropes crisscrossed the water, tied to the buried anchors, tied to piles, tied to heavy machinery. A fitful, uneasy, gusty wind tugged at the tethered craft, making them bob and pitch. Big jellyfish, brown and obscene, with slimy fronds and a wicked sting, heaved and pulsed their blind way among the boats.

Mike and I had to swim across the little harbour several times, towing light nylon ropes. With these we heaved across heavier, stronger moorings until the *Whai* was secured, three feet off the wharf and riding free.

"Looks bad. Better stick around until this blows over—the typhoon should hit us tonight," advised Mark. "We can expect winds up to 90 knots and gusts up to 120! I've seen seas break right over this mole, so don't wander around in the dark." And with this cheering prospect we settled on board instead of in the bar. I couldn't start up the *Whai's* motors, as we'd removed the injectors for servicing. And one of the water pumps was in pieces for new seals and bearings.

We sat in the gloomy and moaning dusk while the waters rose higher, pressed into the harbour by the gale, now whistling across the entrance. Waves started to break into white clouds and be carried across the mole. We could hear some unfortunate craft being ground and smashed against its dock. And the shouts of the yard men trying to secure it.

"I can't stand this! Let's go up to the club. We can watch from there. We've done all we can and if 16 tons get free, I can't see there's much we can do. Everything is battened down and the ropes can't chafe." With that we forced our way against the wind to shelter in the lee of the boatsheds which huddled back towards the blasting gale.

The spume was so thick that a solid wall of white completely screened the harbour. Sixty feet away the boats on the other side were invisible. It was as if giant hands clutched and pummelled us as we were bowled along in a half run to the comfort of the clubhouse.

I took my mind off the nightmare outside by ringing around friends made during our stay in Naha. There was great satisfaction in being able to invite them to the club as our guests, and so repay in small measure the hospitality given us.

"Come over next Wednesday night. We'll have a Typhoon Party if we're still afloat." And so it was arranged.

It was a long, uneasy night, the *Whai* heaving and straining at its bonds. At about three in the morning, calls from the other side of the basin dragged us on deck, bleary and redeyed. The wind had veered and the Durr's trimaran had screwed around so that its mooring lines were being chafed through against a float's sharp stem.

Mike and I were the only ones on board—the girls were staying in Naha, and Rafe with Yoko and Pat. It was easier to swim the 50 feet separating the craft rather than struggle with the wind and long walk around the perimeter to the other side.

We dived into the soapy water. It was pitch dark and spray flew in stinging sheets as we splashed across, climbing or ducking under the straining mooring ropes that crisscrossed the harbour.

"Just as dry this way! If we'd walked we'd have been soaked," mumbled Mike, fending off a hawser. We quickly had the tri repositioned and were safe aboard, drinking coffee and rum.

"How about taking a job with my firm," suggested Mike Durr. "We're short staffed and you could earn a few bucks."

"Go on, Mike. I'll be a few days more now that the weather has loused up. You could rely on a week," I suggested.

This was a good opportunity, and so every morning the two Mikes set off to a machine shop to swelter over their lathes. I was busy checking gear and reinstalling the overhauled pumps and injectors, changing oil and filters—the thousand and one things to do on boats. The typhoon had faded away, missing Buckner Bay by about 30 miles; a few Ryukyu islands further north had copped it with some deaths and damage. We'd been very lucky.

One morning I found Rafe talking to two huge men in the main cabin. I'd met them before, in Naha; they had come to see me when they heard we'd come through the New Hebrides. It turned out they were salesmen for some real estate at Hog Harbour in Espiritu Santo Island. Some local Americans had asked me about Hog Harbour, and one at least had changed his mind after yarning to us and lost interest in the project. And now these two had come along to see the man who'd scotched their sale.

I didn't feel like marching in—one was reputed to be 6ft 9in tall and a very, very rugged individual. The other, the baby of the duo, was at least 6ft 2in and built like his friend. They were sitting, heads forced down by the low ceiling, overflowing the space normally sufficient for four or five ordinary folk. I called Rafe out.

"Do you know who they are? They're salesmen for that Hog Harbour deal; For heaven's sake don't annoy them! I'll come back when you've got rid of them!"

I made my way to the clubhouse, ordered a huge root beer and awaited their departure. But it grew boring, so I started off for Naha on foot. A jeep pulled up and the driver, short and brown as a berry, leaned out.

"Care for a lift? How far are you going?"

"Into Naha—if I can. It's too hot to walk, that's for sure."

And so I met Ray Rapoza, born in Hawaii of Portuguese parents. He became a fast friend and helped with all manner of problems. I needed the echo-sounder repaired and a serviceman was found. I needed tinned foods and liquor and he helped me secure them from a commissariat. Well-known and well-liked, Ray drove me around for miles; I bought two 12-volt car fans to cool the cabin and a small electric refrigerator; a water pump and fittings, a host of items bargained for and reduced in cost. I'm no good at bargaining; I get angry at the demeaning performance. But Ray took a delight in matching wits with the shopkeepers and saved me many a dollar.

He was concerned at my electrical problems and secured a surplus 12-volt generator which hammered away on the dockside keeping our batteries charged. Another friend was also concerned about our electrical shortage and, working independently, surprised me with a beautiful little 110/230-volt unit which he'd "found."

"I can't buy that! I just haven't got that sort of money," I protested.

"Buy? Who said anything about buying? It's yours—take it!"

"Hell! I can't take it! It must be worth a fortune!"

"Well, I can't take it back, that's for sure!"

A moral impasse perhaps, but if it couldn't be returned it might as well disappear over the horizon with me. It was surely welcome.

I was toiling on the boat, Mike at a lathe, and Rafe doing carpentry for Pat and Yoko. Robbie and Monique decided to earn some money too, becoming very secretive and excited.

"Go on! You can tell me. What's up?"

At last it came out. I was horrified.

"You're both mad! You can't do it! You'll get into all sorts of trouble!"

"No we won't! Mrs. —— is a pet and she's going to chaperone us! All we need are some long frocks!"

They were to be "hostesses" in some Naha night club. They were going to make money being friendly to servicemen and Japanese civilians. The "wages" were to be paid in the form of commissions on drinks bought for them.

I was upset. I'd grown to like them and this seemed a chancy way to earn money, ever if it was mostly for the hell of it and as a daring adventure. I was right. The night—the one and only night they experienced—was hot and still. The girls were keyed up and insisted that Mike and Rafe were not to know, and certainly none of the club members was to be told.

But I was really concerned and checked with Lois as to their safety. She too, was horrified: Monique was furious.

"You promised not to tell!"

"Well, I don't care! You're young enough to be my daughters and this is just about the last thing! I can't stop you, but you tell me where you'll be and we can keep an eye on you."

But it was no use—the two clammed up and we didn't see them again until about 2 a.m. when they arrived back, almost hysterical. It seemed that Mrs. —— was a madam and had put the word out among her Asiatic customers. They weren't nice "clean-cut American boys" but leering, toothy Orientals, who pawed and tried to get them drunk.

To get away, the girls had encouraged the two best-looking and persuaded them to come out to the boat "for a party." They were the two most disappointed lechers when they gazed in awe at Mike as he came up grumbling and rumbling to order them off.

A couple of days later I found Pat and Yoko sitting in their car parked near the *Whai*.

"Hulloa! Come on board and have a cup of tea."

Pat looked uncomfortable and Yoko, too.

"Peter, you shouldn't have those people on board—they'll cause trouble."

"Who? Have we visitors? I've been down at the clubhouse. What's up?"

"They live near us—they're pot-peddlers," said Pat. "I think the girls are talking to them."

I marched on board ready to order them off, but they were already on their way, and I was introduced briefly as they left. I decided to tackle the girls later and not cause an uproar in public. Much as I liked the hospitality of Okinawa, things were getting out of hand. It was time to go. Tonight was Typhoon Party and next afternoon we'd leave.

"Did you hear Pat's broadcast?" asked Yoko.

"No. What about?"

"Pat got into touch with the local service radio people and said you were looking for crew members to go to New Zealand."

"Yes; hope you don't mind. There are plenty of G.I.'s signing off and one or two could be a big help. I had a ball—gave you and the *Whai* a big build-up," Pat laughed.

That evening, before the party, I had a visit from a decent young chap who'd heard the broadcast and had come along to see what we were like and what it would cost. Mark stammered slightly because his thoughts out-raced his tongue. He was terribly unsure of himself—he read too much that was controversial and had developed a real complex about his country. He had just signed out of the Air Force, was mixed up with an Okinawan girl and was confused over the reports of unrest and violence back Stateside. He thought a long sea trip might bring back perspective and I agreed. I would have agreed with anybody! It would bring me another pair of hands at the wheel and a few welcome dollars, too. Declining to come to the Typhoon Party but promising to move aboard next day, Mark took off to farewell his girl friend, pack his gear and sell his rattling old bomb.

Sam Baron lowered himself ponderously to sit on the little fridge. I wanted to shout in protest—he must have weighed 200lbs. But he and his wife had been good to us—had brought a big carton of foodstuffs and given us the use of their dockside shed. I could straighten out any bent steelwork later. The cat was crowded, both hulls and the top cabin. The wind was gusty and unpleasant, the rear platforms unusable. It was stifling, and eventually we retreated to the clubhouse and its air-conditioning.

We took our own grog and the club turned a blind eye. The bell started clanging and our party was on the way.

The following morning Ray called with roast chickens and ice cream, so we would not have to stop our last-minute clean-up and reprovisioning, to cook. It was a kindly thought. The Americans had been very decent to us. We were strangers and not of any account, but we'd been welcomed in a way which far outstripped anything we could have provided back home.

So we finally climbed on board the *Whai*, fired up Big and Little Stinky and cast off. There was quite a crowd on the dock —all our old friends from Naha and the Yacht Club members waving and calling good luck. There were loud pops as projectors sent showers of gay streamers curling over our boat. On shore Bill and Judy Baxter waved goodbye, Floyd, Laverne and Mike Durr, Pat and Yoko. Mina was having a little cry and Mark's girl, too. Ray Rapoza was there, a sturdy figure waving hard, and as we headed out to sea, the streamers stretched, parted and fell into the water.

Mark Lyons sounded the horn on one of his boats and Lois waved farewell. I was both glad and sorry all at once. We had some 350 miles to go, the cat was in great shape, we had a good crew and plenty of supplies. We cleared the last reef off Okinawa and headed sou'-west to Hualien.

CHAPTER ELEVEN

In the Wrong Bay

WE HADN'T bothered with visas for Taiwan this time—we were stopping only for fresh water and the latest typhoon forecast. I saw my friend, the harbour master, and gave him another bottle of spirits. The 111 had gone and the little port was deserted apart from two small freighters. The heat was stifling and along the hot concrete dock the little dust devils still whirled and scurried between bundles of bamboo and aromatic timber.

It was a little depressing after our hilarious previous visit. I had given the girls 20,000 Chinese dollars (the 50 U.S. dollars' worth of Chinese currency that was refunded by the dishonest agent) and they had a shopping spree. The change was spent on tinned fruit. There was a typhoon reported developing 900 miles to the north-east, so when the girls returned we cast off. It was noon on the 18th of August and we had over 700 miles to go to Manila.

Once again, high on the mountain sides, the mysterious lights seemed to signal something as we cruised down the rocky coast. This time I kept closer to the shore line and missed the turbulent waters off the southern tip, and by morning we were well out into the Bashi Channel. Ahead was a freighter of curious construction, preceded by a smaller craft. Something flashed intermittently between them.

As we drew closer, on a converging course, the strange duo became an armed Chinese tug heaving away at a *Seatrain* line cargo boat. The hawser lifted out of the sea to flash in the sun. The *Whai* had about two knots advantage and we angled in under the overhanging stern, narrowly missing the log and a couple of trolling lines towed behind.

"What's up? Are you under arrest?" I shouted to a bearded sailor who stared down at us from the railings high above.

"Broken tail shaft—going into Taiwan for repairs. Where are you off to?"

"Manila."

"What! In that?" was the rude rejoinder. Perhaps not intended to be rude—probably the very insignificance of our pygmy alongside the lumbering giant made our journey seem incongruous.

"Don't s'pose he'd believe us if he knew we'd come from home to Japan and back here again," Mike murmured.

"Have you any typhoon warnings?" I shouted.

"Hold it!" Our friend disappeared topside, to return with another bearded character who stared hard at us, waved and turned into a doorway.

A few minutes later he reappeared, holding a sheaf of papers. From them he recited enough wind velocities, barometric pressures and directions to confuse a meteorologist.

"Thanks! Thanks!" I yelled. "How long before it reaches the Philippines, or will it miss there?"

"You should be O.K. for three or four days."

"Can you sell us any fresh bread?" I begged as we motored alongside. We had a dozen frozen loaves flung down as gifts and, waving cheerily, we turned away.

I tried to raise someone on the radio to get weather forecasts but the fuses kept blowing and it looked as if some feedback or electrical surge was causing it. Or a short in the extension speaker. Mike disconnected it and taped up the plug so it couldn't be plugged in by accident. I got an extra battery, given me in Okinawa, and wired it directly to the set, also the windscreen wiper which was the only piece of equipment earthed through the hull.

A wind started to rise and the seas ruffled with catspaws streaking from many directions. We were on a compass course of 187 degrees and tracking down the 121 degree meridian towards Luzon. According to calculations based on the freighter's figures, the typhoon was some 960 miles to the east-nor'-east and moving south-west at some 15 to 20 knots. We had about 400 miles to reach the shelter of Fuga Island. The typhoon should be near enough to affect us within 40 to 50 hours and Fuga about 53 hours away. It was going to be close if the typhoon continued its present course and speed. I studied the charts and the *Pilot* for suitable shelter in the nearer Babuyan Islands. Nothing! To hell with it! The *Whai* was sound, a grand bad-weather craft, so we headed for Calayan Island.

All night in rising winds and driving rain we pressed on. The wind was behind us and we made good time. It was evening on the 20th and because sun shots had been impossible, I altered course slightly to starboard to aim between Calayan and Dalupiri Islands, which would give plenty of sea room should our time be better than estimated.

It was early dusk the following evening before we saw Dalupiri on our port. The driving gale had swung around in the night and a tide set had carried us 15 miles to the right of our course. The wind veered again, and just as violently started to tear and buffet at us from ahead and to starboard. The rain poured down and the air was thick and sticky with incredible humidity.

Sixth-sense premonition was nagging at the edge of conscious thought, filling me with unease. I went on deck to search the limited circle of sea for danger. There was no sound, no warning—just a huge dark shape rushing out of the downpour. A supertanker, coming up astern was pushing a great wall of water from its bow.

"Hard to port quickly!" I fairly jumped to the throttles to ram them fully open. And to help wrench the wheel over.

The *Whai* churned slowly around, heaving in the cross sea, then the bow-wave hit our sterns, lifting us effortlessly. We were picked up a dozen feet to glissade downwards as if surfing. We could hear the beat and thump of the tanker's propeller as we were pushed aside like a piece of driftwood. The bulk of thousands of tons of steel slid by and left us rocking in its wildly boiling wake.

"God! That was close! They must have seen us on radar!" But conjecture was useless and, much disturbed, we scanned the circle of wild waves shining dully in the afterglow of the sun now setting behind the clouds.

Then again, but this time on the fringe of our vision, another great tanker slid by, huge and irresistibly forging ahead. We must have been in a shipping lane and it was with great relief I took the cat in close to Dalupiri and the shelter of its cliffs. This was a curious island, no trees, just acres of rolling grassy hillsides. Lenny had told us it was famous for racehorse breeding. We dropped a grapnel, to catch in coral. The wind was blowing in great swoops and gusts with a swirling motion that worried me. I felt something was dreadfully wrong and when the meal was over I had the pick pulled up and Mike took the cat down the western coast towards Fuga while I calculated our course.

I estimated that it should take us an hour and 40 minutes to reach the safety of Fuga, once we rounded the rocky southern tip of Dalupiri. Here there was no shelter—just gravel and rock shores and bleak wind-swept hills. At Fuga, if we could enter the channel, we would be safe, with a good anchorage and friends ashore.

At the southern tip of the island it grew dark, and an unbroken carpet of whitecaps reared and fell to rear again in wild rushes against us. I shut off Little Stinky and, with only 1500 revs on, proceeded to bash away into the head sea. We were making about three knots and it looked like a three and a-half hour slog. Even then I was doubtful if we could enter the narrows with the reefs, niggerheads and shallow sand bars in the darkness. There was no moon, only scudding clouds, and sudden downpours of rain, which vied with the spray to make visibility minimal. It was a lousy night; uncomfortable. Everyone went to their bunks to sleep, leaving me to the wheel and the monotonous hours ahead.

The wind increased and the spume and heavier spray from breaking seas continually burst over us. It was a nightmare, with the *Whai* pitching like crazy. I tried to angle off to port but for some reason the wave pattern and our speed caused the odd crest to bash up at the decking between the hulls, and while safe, the bangs were unnerving. It was just a question of enduring. At least it was warm and dry inside.

A bright glow on the horizon appeared to be on the mainland of Luzon, which could be seen occasionally as a black line. I estimated we were now clear of Fuga, west of it, and started to angle across to Mairaira Point where we just might gain shelter in Claveria Bay before dawn. Stars came out to glitter coldly and the clouds were all gone. But the wind still tore at us. The glow on the mainland must be the town of Claveria, I thought, and kept edging over towards it.

It was suddenly still. The *Whai* was cruising steady as a rock, in flat black water. For a moment I gaped at the glow which had been drawing me like a magnet. It was near—very near, and the horizon pitch black and strangely rugged. A fear came over me and I pulled the throttle lever shut and rushed on deck. A low black mass of land slid past just to port and tiny fish skittered out of our way across the glassy surface. We were heading for rocks in shallow water—but it was impossible! I rushed to the wheel, pulled Little Stinky into reverse and frantically started up the other motor. As it rumbled into life Mike came up blinking and yawning.

"What's up?" The stock expression.

"Quick! Hop outside with the spotlight! We're bloody near ashore!"

The *Whai* came to a stop, started to ease back, and I put it out of gear and switched on the echo-sounder.

"Hell! We're right in a little bay! There's a sort of low cliff ahead and all along the port side!" shouted Mike.

"Hang on—I'll have the depth in a minute." And with that the first faint tracings started to appear on the creeping recording paper.

"Thirty-five feet! Thank goodness. I'm coming out."

The beam of the spotlight swept around. To port, astern, the low coral wall faded into darkness but ahead it curved around, an unbroken barrier, until it ended abruptly a few degrees off our starboard bow.

"That was close. I don't know where we are. We'll put the grapnel down—there's bound to be a coral bottom. Then I can work out where this is."

Mark and Rafe came on deck. Then the girls.

"Where are we?" I had to admit I hadn't a clue. Just over the coral cliff, the glow of lights were seen. It was impossible that it was the mainland. I checked my watch. Only an hour and a-half since Dalupiri. It must be Fuga, but how?

Time and again we tried to get a grip on the coral bottom, but the three-pronged grapnel wouldn't take. It seemed flat and smooth. Sometimes it would catch for a minute, only to slip, and we could feel it scratching across the bottom. We could hear, too, the wind soughing across the land and the crash of rollers breaking against the other side of our sheltering barrier.

"We can't stay here. If the wind veers we'll be in trouble. I'm going to re-assess the position. Mark, you and Rafe stay up top with the light and let me know if we tend to drift in close. Put down the Danforth—the weight of the chain will help hold us till we're ready to move."

Mike and I studied the chart.

"I reckon we're here. The wind and waves are from this direction and we must be jammed in this little bay. It's the only possible spot."

We were at Mabag (Driftwood) Island, just off the north-west end of Fuga. Just a tiny place and so nearly the end of our voyage. There must have been a terrific set with us and against the wind to have carried the *Whai* so far and so fast.

I gathered the whole crew together. I wanted every mind on the job, with a clear picture of our position.

"Look at this. Here is where we are. We'll cruise out and back along this coast for about a mile. The spotlight should pick out those rocks at the entrance. With a bit of luck the light in Miguel's house will be on (it was about ten o'clock) and we can feel our way up the channel and anchor in the old spot off the shed.

"Now—when the chap with with the light says 'On'—everyone else shuts their eyes till they hear 'Off'. I want everybody to have full night vision, so be careful."

We took off with both motors idling and the echo-sounder clicking out its vital measurements. We crept along the 20-foot coral wall, with shoals of small fry leaping and splashing at our approach.

"On—off" the light switched, with the crew blinking in unison. The sea mist was dense and the light could penetrate only 80 yards or so. Slowly we drew nearer the channel until at last we picked it out by the two big rocks off Mabag's eastern tip.

We motored up the channel to safety. A tremendous feeling of accomplishment and cheerfulness seized us all and we laughed and shouted, and swung our beam on to Miguel's house. So we came to rest again at Fuga, which also means escape. Haven or escape—we were safe.

Just as the sun rose a chuntering sound woke us. It was the *Nely Dante*, with a smiling Lenny on board. The *Nely Dante* was an incredible creation with a permanent list to starboard. Puffing and wheezing it drew alongside and Lenny leapt on board as it slid past. It was good to see him again, although his Salvador Dali moustache had gone and he didn't look half as dashing as on our previous visit.

"Hulloa, Miguel! We're back for that dive on the old wreck!"

Miguel was quite effusive; he actually smiled. He could see the bottle of Black Label cradled lovingly in my arms. We got down to business. We were to be allowed to visit the Jap caves, dive the wreck and visit the ancient Spanish monastery around the coast.

"The caves were part of the Japanese defence system. Fuga was just a staging post," said Miguel.

"Miguel was a regular in the Filipino Army," remarked Lenny. "He was captured by the Japs at Bataan."

"Yes; I escaped, or I probably would have been killed."

"How did you get away?"

"Oh, the Japs have very bad eyesight," said Miguel. "Three of us just walked out during the siesta."

"But didn't the guards see you?"

"No" was his extraordinary reply. "We stood still when they looked towards us and walked when they looked away."

I lunched with Lenny and his wife, with the lieutenant at the head of the table. Two Filipino girls stood behind us waving large whisks to shoo the flies. It was a strange meal of tinned fish (why tinned?), the inevitable rice, tiny shrimps and peppers, sliced and floating in oil. Washed down with whisky. Miguel was a taciturn company man—the factotum of this cattle station. Only there were no cattle. But there was the strange house on Barit Island which was surrounded by big brilliant lights, turning the cleared area into a floodlit exposed place all night. The lights which had nearly caused our destruction.

And the mysterious light aircraft which came and went, but no one saw the crew or cargo. And why did we have an armed guard with us whenever ashore? It could be dangerous to ask. Dangerous for Lenny at the very least, and he wasn't talking. Not at all.

We trudged to the caves. Guava bushes scratched our legs and dragonflies zoomed across the grassy patches. In the stillness and shadows of the trees, against a gentle slope, were three cave entrances. They were dank and cool. Manmade, with shallow drainage channels on either side of rotting duckboards, they penetrated 100 feet and more, to twist and turn, providing shelter against bomb blast. Nothing of value was left—the local villagers had stripped out anything of use long ago.

We up-anchored and coasted the half-mile or so to the end of the channel, to anchor over the ancient wreck.

"It was a tax-gathering steamer sunk in 1894," said Lenny. "You'll find it just near here. There's a cannon there somewhere, too."

In a trice we were over the side. The wind had died to a gentle breeze and the disturbed coral powder and sand had drifted away or settled.

"Here it is!" someone shouted, and for the next hour we dived, examining and searching.

The *Gravina* had been caught in a typhoon while running for shelter. She just missed and had sunk at the very entrance to safety. An iron ship, not steel, she had withstood the sea's corrosion remarkably well. Though smashed and rent apart, one could still trace the general shape as she lay in the sand. Coral growths in pink and cream, gay crinoids and sea tulips covered much of the wreckage. The propeller shaft lay along the bottom, pointing to the primitive cylinders of the engines.

A myriad little fish flashed in the dappled light as we hung 20ft above the hull. Brown speckled coral trout emerged from nooks and crannies to watch us. The water was too warm to be refreshing, but it was so clear that we hung as if suspended from the ceiling of an underwater room.

Mark was enchanted. Beginners to skindiving, he and the girls splashed noisily and missed a lot of the more unusual and timid creatures. The squirrel fish with their large black eyes and iridescent scales darted to cover, and plumed lion fish backed slowly into coral caves and out of sight.

"Here's the propeller. I think we could salvage it!" But on examination, the screw was too eroded and too far buried to be worth the effort. Besides, we couldn't lift it or stow it on our boat. A bronze porthole complete with glass and, wonder of wonders, working hinges, kept me struggling until, completely exhausted, I had to give up trying to wrench it free.

It was time to leave for our next attraction. "The best place to land is in the next bay. You can get in close enough to see the rocks and you can anchor on clean sand. The monastery is over the cliff top," advised Lenny.

We left the *Whai* at rest like a tethered horse. It was hot and sticky climbing the earth and rock slides, grabbing at gnarled and twisted roots and scrabbling up the wet clay slopes. At the top we came out on to a large flat covered in guava bushes. Their fruit was woody and poorly developed. In the foreground stood the ruins of what had been a 16th century monastery. Great brick and stone pillars supported the arches which had, in turn, held up the roof now so long fallen and rotted away.

Villagers had re-roofed a little chapel and on a makeshift altar two painted effigies stood. These were no better than crudely-made, jointed dolls of wood and very old. I had seen the same things on sale in Manila's art and curio shops. Here they were in their authentic surroundings. On one, the rotted robes which had given it personality and meaning, hung in tatters. It was a gloomy and depressing place. No air movement, just dust motes twirling slowly in a solitary thin beam of light which fell to die in a corner of nameless rubbish.

Subdued, we crept out. From a low doorway a stream of tiny black swallows darted to twist and turn at frantic speed and fly off among the bushes and eroded pillars of a courtyard.

We picked our way through the guavas to the "citio" or village. It sprawled haphazardly among bushes on the flat ground above the cliffs. Red-brown earth tracks meandered from hut to hut and dragonflies pounced on blowflies attracted to the stench of ordure under the rickety hovels. In the one house we entered, the sight of a hole cut in the floor and the pile of human excrement below sickened us. This was a poor place with demoralized people. The few dogs, scratching and limping, were emaciated, sickly things and the children huge-eyed and with distended bellies. Lenny muttered something about no work or money—that they were squatters and could be evicted from the island.

But the clean waters of the sea were just below the village and the earth was rich enough for food crops. All these people needed was a good headman to lift them out of their hopeless sloth.

Great banks of cumulus cut off the sun's last rays and a gusting wind began to moan past the aerial. The sea became ruffled, dark and unfriendly. We got the anchor up in double-quick time. Monique and Robbie started to prepare a meal, but had to give up as the *Whai* heaved and tossed leaving the bay. Lenny's wife turned green and cried with mortification and distress as she was forced to use the "laughing" bucket. Johnny lay on the deck and groaned, oblivious of the stinging spray which whirled out of the darkness.

"I don't like this, Peter! We might lose sight of the shoreline and there are a million reefs around here!" Lenny was concerned.

"I'll put Mike on the wheel and Rafe can relay steering instructions from us. We'll get on deck and con the boat along the coast."

We were wet through and cold. A flood of warm salt water, spume and spray would cascade over us, but the wind quickly chilled us again. It was dicey and miserable for Lenny and me and I had to stir the others, safe and warm in the cabin, into taking it seriously. We were in trouble, as only the breaking seas indicated reefs and shoreline in the darkness.

The wind was howling now, driving the stinging rain and spray against Lenny and me like bullets. "Give her 2000 revs," I shouted, and the exhaust stacks poured out smoke as the diesels started to really work. But we had to slow down and creep along, feeling an uncertain way past beaches and coral niggerheads only half-seen.

Lenny's wife was very sick, but I needed his help more than she did. We stood, shivering and wet, peering and peering into the gloom. The seas rose and broke against us, but we had to stay there searching for the channel entrance, the lights of Miguel's house, anything to fix our position.

For over an hour we struggled along and it was sheer good luck that a momentary break in the rain gave us a glimpse of the light near Miguel's hacienda. It was a very relieved group that paddled ashore and a very worried skipper who was warned by Miguel that the typhoon, after several delays and turnings, was now definitely headed our way.

"There's a big storm developing—you'd better decide whether

you'll stay or leave now," advised Miguel. "I've just got reports in from the shipping company network and it looks bad."

"Okay, we'll leave at dawn if the weather is clear. And get some sleep because we may need it! Once we get around Negre Point we should be O.K."

We swapped books and magazines and paddled back towards the *Whai* in the dark. A tantalizing smell greeted us 100 feet away—Monique, who had stayed aboard alone had prepared a full-size dinner—two roast chickens (collected on the previous day's expedition), yams, baked bananas—the works. We cracked a bottle of gin and sat down for the first really solid meal in days.

"Monique, this is marvellous!" (It was: Monique tended to be a little lazy.)

"Monique, you're a champ!"

"Monique, I could kiss you!"

"Oh, well, there was nothing else to do, and you all can do the dishes."

But there was a catch in it (there always is) and Monique, furious with us and more so with herself, retired in a paddy to puff away, chain-smoking in the darkness of the after-deck.

She'd assumed the chickens had been cleaned out, and had cooked them, entrails and all.

Next day the sun shone once more. It was hard to recall last night's fears and discomfort. It was harder to imagine the dangerous giant away to the north and east gathering strength and veering across the sea towards this tranquil place.

We said goodbye to Miguel and Fuga Island. Goodbye to Lenny's child-wife and, last of all, Lenny. He gave me a Bolo—"the .44 of the Philippines"—a beautiful little weapon, or tool, whichever you needed. Razorsharp and sheathed in wooden scabbards they have to be withdrawn with the left hand holding the scabbard between fingers and thumb. To wrap one's hand around the sheath is to risk a nasty slice, owing to the peculiar shape of the cutting edge.

"Goodbye, Lenny—look after yourself. Cheerio, Miguel. I'll write to you!" I shouted across the water. "Keep in touch!" and we were off to Manila—300 miles to go. Lenny looked a little forlorn. He hadn't much to talk about to his girl-wife and Miguel could be heavy going. And someone had eaten his dog, which had been devoted to him.

At the channel between Mabag and Barit we dropped the mud anchor and stern ladders. As we swam over the coral sand 30 feet below us, little piper and garfish streamed ahead of our path. All manner of fish browsed the coral growths and the thunk of discharged spearguns promised fish for tea.

25 August: Corregidor ahead in the early dawn. Curtains of rain fell silently and over Manila lightning flashed in mauve bursts of energy. The music of the clouds hissed and crackled on the radio. There was a humid tension in the air, an uneasiness and feeling of depression. We were looking forward to Manila, to the comforts of the yacht club, the hot showers, the iced drinks. We pulled into the club marina flying our decrepit yellow quarantine flag.

"We thought you'd sunk!" shouted Ernesto. "We thought you must have gone down in a typhoon! You're just here in time—there's a big one coming. Typhoon Pitang—already there's been a lot of damage!"

We moored securely near the sea wall and sat and sweltered in fantastic humidity while my friends the Customs, Immigration and port medico regaled themselves in the clubhouse at my expense. In the end I could stand it no longer. We were sticky, hot and short of water. The thought of cold drinks, green salads and refreshing showers, combined with the bitter knowledge of three or four fat bastards eating and drinking their heads off, forced me into action.

"Close all the ports and hatches and open the engineroom doors. Make it really uncomfortable!"

I whistled up a boatman and entered the club.

"You shouldn't have left your boat, Captain," murmered Immigration.

"Come out to the boat and have a drink or two," I countered.

Wiping their faces and belching, the trio downed their drinks. There was a fine fug in the main cabin and the heat from the engineroom welled out in oily waves.

"A cup of coffee for our friends," I suggested and Monique, almost melting, put on the kettle. The formalities were over in double-quick time and our unwelcome guests departed to the clubhouse to recover. We cleaned up and, clasping toilet bags and fresh clothes, were taken ashore.

Sure enough they were drinking away merrily and I caught Ramon's attention.

"Take these blokes three large glasses of iced water with my compliments. I'm not paying for one drink more, or any food. They've had enough—and so have I."

There was a moment of suspense as the smiling officials raised their glasses in silent toast. I watched for a few seconds to savour their disappointment before retiring to the showers. They were gone when I returned. Ramon presented me with the bill.

"Fifty-eight pesos! The bastards! They won't catch me again!" I resolved to sneak out from Manila without worrying about a clearance. It was a decision which was to cost me some anxious moments later.

For two weeks we sat in safety at the yacht club while the great Typhoon Pitang howled and screamed around the Philippines. More than 150 people missing in small craft, believed lost, and 42 more dead. For days it poured with rain and Manila was awash. Public transport broke down and the unfortunate Caingñin huddled in their miserable shacks. Roads were impassable and workers were stranded where they happened to be. People slept in picture theatres and children swam in flooded subways. On the *Whai* our clothes mildewed, and the window glass dripped condensed water. Mould grew on woodwork and food fermented.

"How can you criticize—how can you air any opinion if you've never tried it? You drink alcohol and it's far, far worse than pot!"

"I don't care; there's no need to add another vice. If it was legalized you'd have guys turned on at their lathes and getting caught up in them. You'd have drivers getting high and pranging all over the place. You could smoke at the wheel and no one would realize what was going on. If someone waves a bottle around in a car or factory it's soon noticed and stopped."

"You don't know what you're talking about. You're like the rest of the squares. You'll see! It'll be legalized within five years."

"Well, if it's harmless, what's the fuss about? Don't you get happy on it? Don't you get exhilarated and, to use your own language, 'stoned out of your mind'? I've seen you two with your eyes rolling round like roulette wheels!"

"Listen, Peter, we'll get some and then you can see for yourself!"

"I don't smoke—how'll I take it? In cookies?"

"No, we'll make it like tea and you drink it. We'll have it in the clubhouse and no one will know."

"Okay." And so it was settled. The girls came back armed with a tea pot and a small plastic bag of chopped greenish leaves.

I drank the stuff—and nothing happened. I even ate the pungent "leaves"—and nothing happened. The girls were very disappointed. So was I.

"Oh, well, sometimes it doesn't work the first time." But as far as I was concerned, it would be the last. Alcohol's the caper!

In Manila we went to the Indonesian consulate for visas and permits to call at ports down in the Celebes and West Irian. The consulate officials were cagey and non-cooperative. I guess I was, too, and as no money changed hands we got nowhere. Through the good services of the British Embassy I cabled Djakarta but the days drifted by without even an acknowledgment. I had to make a harsh decision: to refuel at Zamboanga on the southern tip of Mindanao and make a 2000-mile nonstop run through and past Indonesian territory without touching land. This meant that the girls would have to get off the *Whai* and find some other transport into Indonesia. They were pretty glum, but what could I do? I found a yacht short of crew. It was a brand-new boat, all shining with chrome and every mod. con. It was going to Djakarta.

"You'll be happy with these girls," I told the wary skipper. "One is a qualified nurse and they are quite competent on day watches." And as a clincher, "They're good cooks, too—this would leave you free for navigation and maintenance."

Robbie and Monique were enchanted with the glistening galley and the delightful quarters, the curtains and polished woodwork. I didn't let on that the skipper's navigation was by Braille and that it was doubtful if he'd be able to get out of Filipino waters, let alone through the maze of islands of the Indonesian Archipelago. But I had to do something for them, and with Monique's push and luck I couldn't see them being stranded anywhere for long.

We met George Woods again and during a great session we were asked to visit him at Victorias and see the world's largest sugar refinery. We could stay at the company's guesthouse for a few days before sailing down to Zamboanga. Through the Shell agents, arrangements were made for final refuelling in Zamboanga and the extra fuel necessary for the long voyage was to be carried on deck in three 44-gallon drums.

In the club I was approached by a tall blond young man, very neat, almost foppish. He introduced himself as Jorge Meinhart. His two companions were in striking contrast. Herman Dingler was very blond with piercing blue eyes in a squarish face. The third member was scruffy, wore a hippy beard and slouched about with a supercilious manner. I didn't take to him at all, but all three being together he, too, was accepted as crew. They wanted to ship out and were prepared to pay for their passage as well as stand watches and cook. The three new members of our crew meant fewer hours at the wheel and fresh conversation and interests.

"How many of you, did you say?" George Woods asked.

"Well, there were just four of us, but now there are seven. All men—is that O.K.?"

"Waal, there's plenty of room. But who's your hippy friend?"

"Don't really know. He's a Welshman, has a B.Sc. but doesn't believe appearances are important. I think he's harmless."

George grunted non-committally. He described how to find Victorias.

"Go down past Panay. You can get a good anchorage at Maestre de Campo Island and you'll be safe there. Keep an eye out for suspicious-looking boats. Best fire off a few shots into the air if in doubt. And mill around in sight so the crew looks a lot. Come down Guimaras Strait and you'll see the four big smoke-stacks of the refinery. See 'em for miles—the smoke never stops."

Now that the decision to leave was made, regardless of Indo-nesian approval, we completed our provisioning and the three new members moved on board. We squared up our chits, drank what was left on our bar tickets and in a light haze of diesel smoke and alcohol churned out of the basin. On the jetty and from the club verandah our friends waved goodbye. Our twin trumpets burped and gurgled, waterlogged again, so we just shouted our farewells and waved until the sea wall came between us.

CHAPTER TWELVE

Sugar in the Philippines

MANILA faded to a smudge. As we left the big bay we passed *El Fraile* with its concrete gun platforms and rusty naval rifles in twin cupolas pointing towards the sky. Gulls wheeled and screamed over the lonely little fortress. What action had it seen? How long had it withstood attack? If ever there was a last ditch situation for men to be put in, this was it.

The first night out was spent at Puerto Galera, in a pleasant little bay, almost landlocked, with coconut palm-covered hills. Again the water was dark green with minute plant life and useless for spearfishing. A Filipino navy landing-craft lay at anchor like a big grey whale and we circled it slowly so they could see who and what we were. In the shallows a Victorias tug and sugar barge lay side by side. We were given permission to tie up alongside. The skipper had been told to look out for us and to give us any assistance we might need. That evening he radioed his company's headquarters to give our position and E.T.A. for Victorias. It was an easy feeling to lie alongside the barge with a navy boat a few hundred yards away.

Next morning a lot of shouts and feet stamping about. A naval patrol was scurrying all over the tug and barge. The sailors were carrying automatic rifles and torches.

"What's going on?" I asked a tug crewman.

"Inspection," was the laconic answer. I quickly got the boys to cast off. No snap inspection for us!

There was some shouting as we left and I headed directly towards the landing-craft so there'd be no stupid shooting. We slid under the big ship's stern and, waving cheerily to the few sailors left on board, clapped on full revs and turned the point out into the open sea. The tug skipper could do any explaining required.

Around five o'clock we came into the lee of Maestre de Campo Island and, anchoring the *Whai*, slipped into the cooling sea. We swam in the channel between the lonely rocky shore and the coral sands of the mainland.

There were no fish, just little stinging organisms and a few small painted crayfish. Big crinoids clung to the coral outcrops, mostly bright green and yellow—the fronds stuck to my fingers and broke off from the creatures' bodies to cling until peeled off one by one. On the bottom, in a crevice, I spotted a sea urchin new to me. It had black and silver spines radiating out from a very small test (or calcareous body). The spines waved stiffly on their jointed bases and angled towards the tip of my spear as I prized the urchin off the rock to float free. Slipping my hand under it, I let it drift down to rest lightly and be brought to the surface and examined.

A violent pain shot through my hand and then another—and another. The blasted thing was stuck to me and as I tried to shake it off two more bolts of fire were injected into my fingers. The spines were tough and I had difficulty in snapping them. They were actually pushed into me by the urchin's muscular reaction.

"Jeez—look at what the damned thing did to me!"

Five black dots, surrounded by whitish-blue rings, and the whole hand throbbing and aching. I felt sick and had to get out of the water. I tried to work in novacain, which gave some relief, but for a fortnight or more I could barely close my hand. It was as if the muscles were paralyzed, but the nerves were terribly sensitive.

We decided to stay overnight, as the anchorage was good, and I felt too queer to concentrate on navigation. Jorge cleaned the balky .22 automatic and waved it about at the approach of a canoe, which then slunk away.

At about 2 a.m., under a canopy of brilliant stars, we moved off. Heat lightning, almost continuous, played over Tablas Island, flaring and dying and flaring again and again. In the early dawn we entered Tablas Straits. We motored past Carabao Island to port and Borocay to starboard. The island of Panay rose above the sea mists and in the evening we entered the twisty channel leading to the tiny fishing port of Capiz.

As we picked our way up the channel, past rotting piles and broken concrete jetties, the Capiz fishing fleet streamed out heading for the reefs. Trimarans with spidery outriggers and floats surged past. Driven by all manner of ancient engines these craft slid through the gentle swells at an extraordinary pace. We were greeted (in most cases) by their crews, who clung to masts and rigging, waving and calling. But some sliced silently along, and we were eyed coldly and appraised. The "tris" were gaily painted in geometric or floral designs; most had symbolic eyes on their prows. Small cooking fires smouldered on beds of sand on their after platforms, and dried octopus and squid hung in the rigging. We passed at least 50 yet more and more emerged from the harbour, bays and sheltered reaches.

We pulled alongside an old concrete jetty. Quickly there were over 300 people crowding and jostling to look at our strange craft. I didn't care for the attention we were getting. As darkness quickly closed in the crowd thickened until the numbers were quite unnerving. We didn't dare get off the boat. To push through the mob would have been a real problem and having done so, where to go? We settled down to an uneasy night.

At three in the morning we slipped out and, swinging wide off the harbour entrance to miss reefs, headed eastward up the coast. The boats of Capiz were anchored, over a sunken reef, in a huge semicircle of shining lamps to attract fish. I switched off our steaming lights until they were many miles astern. It doesn't pay, in these waters, to advertise your movements.

As we turned south towards Negros Island in early morning we passed a tug lugging sturdily at a string of sugar barges from Victorias. When the sun got hot and the seas glassier we pulled in to the shores of Sicogan Island to spearfish.

There was a fairly stiff current off shore but near the rocks and coral fringes, whirls and eddies ran contra and it was possible to sweep down the deeper trench and then swim shorewards and so make one's way forward and recycle the hunting ground. Several times large fish similar to our kingfish came into view but they were too fast and too wary to be shot. Barracuda and spanish mackerel were seen, and three sharks. But it was hard fishing and nothing worth keeping was killed. As we motored away a light single-engined aircraft buzzed us with the bearded and ruddy face of George Woods peering down. With a laconic wave and a last zoom low overhead they flew off and I followed in their track, checking our compass course again at the chart for confirmation of direction.

On the horizon, against the haze of Negros' hills, four big chimneys stood like sentinels. The water was shallow and green-grey—the charts were confusing in detail as to which was the proper entrance. George had warned me about the shoals and so we kept out about half a mile offshore and cruised slowly, studying the shoreline through binoculars.

"There's someone waving to us from a small boat—over there to the right of the chimneys."

It was George, waving a huge sun hat. He was on a curious little workboat and had come out to show us the way in. We motored closer and, on drawing alongside, he climbed aboard.

Slowly we edged up the narrow channel between steamy mud

banks fringed with stunted mangroves. Rickety bamboo huts were scattered along the edges and canoes were drawn up mud slides to lie like crocodiles bleaching in the sun.

The sprawling sugarmill buildings came into view. A fussy little loco shunted a string of wagons in front of wharf sheds. The docks stood on piles above stinking river water and a fine dust of black cinders drifted from the chimneys.

Dozens of Filipino men working along the wharves paused to watch our approach and George shouted and waved to the foreman of a gang loading a barge.

"Come alongside the *Amihan*—my boatman will keep an eye on the *Whai* for you. There's fresh water and she'll be quite safe."

The humidity was almost tangible. We perspired and our skins stayed wet; there was no drying in the lifeless air. Bubbles of marsh gas rose through the black water to burst in oily rings, and the air smelt of rotten eggs.

"Your chrome-work will go black from the gas but it will clean up O.K. when you leave," remarked George. (It never did and is black to this day.)

We gathered toilet gear, clean and dirty clothes and clambered up the pilings on to shore. As we trudged along the dockside, Filipinos paused to ask where we were from. They were obviously intrigued by our clothes; I don't remember ever seeing a Filipino in shorts, which is extraordinary considering their climate.

"Now, who'll stay with me and who'll live in the guesthouse? There're no kids in the guesthouse—with me you'll have to put up with my young son." Rafe, Jorge, Herman and Taffy plumped for the guesthouse, a mansion with its own servants. Matt, Mike and I shared a room in George's company house. All night the air-conditioner droned as it fought the heat and I heard Matt tossing and turning. Before dawn he dressed and went out for a walk. He was soon back. Company police, four of them, armed with Stirling submachine guns, had rounded him up and escorted him home.

"Yes, we've 40-odd police here. Every year we have threats from extortionists to burn the cane or plant if money's not paid over. The workers, about 4000, live in compounds and have to be policed," explained George.

"Peter, I'm going back to Okinawa. I think this trip is a mistake for me." Matt was most apologetic. "I've worried and thought about it and it's no good. I can fly back from Manila on Wednesday."

We were sorry to see him go; Matt was a very genuine chap and a gentleman in the literal sense.

The Victorias Milling Company is big. They have over 300 miles of narrow-gauge railway to bring in the cane from *haciendas* scattered across the countryside. The cane is cut by peasants who live in *citios*, often built on the vast estates controlled by wealthy families. In a way the system is almost feudal.

Inside the mill three huge machines lay in hot and oily labour. The two older giants with their great spinning governors and clanking chains, had toiled for some 40-odd years, each producing 5000 metric tons of sugar per day. Their younger but bigger companion had spewed out 10,000 metric tons of refined sugar every 24 hours since its installation.

"Yes, it can be dangerous—we've had men slip and fall on to the belts and go through the rollers. There's no time to stop the machine," our guide remarked. I had mad visions of a hastily-summed priest scurrying over the sticky catwalks, trying to catch up to a horrid stain which was being diluted, purified, bagged and weighed.

Outside the noisy buildings, away from the heat and bustle, we stood rapt in the study of a police noticeboard. This was glassed in and carefully sign-written—"Rogues' Gallery." There were photos of all manner of delinquents but it was the captions that amused us; the brief accounts of misdemeanours.

There was the "Phantom Extinguisher Thief" and the unfortunate fat "houseboy" who "lasciviously interfered with a housemaid". The extinguisher thief had specialised in flogging firefighting gear. Another concentrated on non-ferrous metals. It was pathetic and funny at the same time. The photographs showed these miscreants manacled and dejected with the company police, fat and proud beside them, pistols to the fore.

Jean, George's gorgeous wife, turned on a magnificent meal with a 19lb turkey as the *piece de resistance*. She was appalled at the way the food disappeared. She didn't know Mike's mighty appetite and the others, too, were great eaters.

"You don't feed your crew properly, Peter," she admonished.

"That's what we're always telling him!" cried the opportunists. "We're kept short of food 'cos Peter's always trying to skimp and save."

We attended a party in our honour at the company golf club—a magnificent spread of Filipino delicacies. There were some speeches and I was particularly proud of Mike's. Good food in quantity certainly moved him deeply.

A sign on the club notice board interested me:

"Please deposit your firearms to the Caddy master or to our Cashier—By Order."

"Can I have this, George? It'll amuse my wife; she's a keen golfer." George presented me with the novelty.

"Most wealthy Filipinos carry guns," he said. "Sometimes they get a bit carried away if there's been too much to drink." In my mind's eye I could see a golfer being carried away—off Belmont links back home!

The following night we were taken to one of the *haciendas*, and again entertained superbly. As we motored out the gates on our way home, a guard, lounging in the shadows, caught my eye. He had a submachine gun slung around his neck. All evening we'd been under protection. From what? Ransom? It was a queer setup and hard to accept as a very real way of life for wealthy people in these isles. Even George, on occasion and in certain areas, carried a revolver.

The echo-sounder was repaired, all our laundry had been done for us, the huge turkey was gone, and the guesthouse gang had finished all the beer in its freezer. It was time to leave. I'm sure the Woods breathed a sigh of relief as we climbed on board the *Whai*.

I elected for discretion. We sailed up the north-east coast of Negros and then down into the Tanon Straits. The long narrow island of Cebu lay shrouded in cloud with Negros to starboard. I was sorely tempted to put into Calamba, an interesting-looking town on Negros' east coast, but we pushed on and in the dark of early morning passed through the narrows separating Negros from Cebu. Tanjay's lights and the faint glow of Santander marked our exit. We passed by the lonely village of Bacong to head into the Sulu Sea and on towards Mindanao.

We made landfall off Tagolo Point, then crossed a bay to where Liloy sprawled under green hills.

"Let's get in some fishing! This could be a good spot near the islands," suggested Mike. We could see the coral and weed bottom 40 feet below. As we coasted against a fierce rip, several outrigger canoes came into view, strung out in a loose crescent with all the occupants just sitting patiently. There was a bit of a flurry amongst them and some moved off. A deep muffled thud shook our steel hulls and a white fountain of foam shot up from the glassy sea. Dead fish, mostly small, floated on the surface and the fishermen gathered them quickly before they could sink or the stunned ones recover.

Or before sharks could appear to take their share.

"That's buggered the spearfishing," someone muttered. So we moved off half a mile, anchored, and climbed into the water. The fish were scary and impossible to approach. We left empty-handed, cursing the stupidity of blasting fish. Whole areas could be blighted for years—all the delicate ecology of an entire reef destroyed or disrupted, and only time could regenerate the food chain. In Japan it was hard and ruthless fishing but in the Philippines we saw many illegal methods. Simple household and agricultural chemicals are converted into crude explosives and poisons.

We left the Murcielagos Islands to their foolish inhabitants and cruised all night down the peninsula, to round Alimpaya Point at dawn.

> *Oh, the monkeys have no tails in Zamboanga!*
> *The monkeys have no tails, they were bitten*
> *off by whales,*
> *Oh, the monkeys have no tails in Zamboanga!*

And here we were. All I knew of Zamboanga were the remnants of a childish jingle and that Shell had our fuel supplies here.

Zamboanga sprawled on the flat coastal plain. Concrete jetties and wharves shunted out into the sea; big trees shaded the town plaza. Off the coast, a mile or so out, two small islands baked in the sun. We cruised around looking for a berth. There were some naval boats but we could get no sense out of their crews or decisions from their duty officers to lie alongside. Disgusted, we motored along to the Shell wharf, but were waved off by a carbine-carrying guard.

The only thing left seemed to be to anchor among some villainous-looking trimarans with silent, watchful crews.

"Don't like this much," said Herman. "Tough-looking guys."

"Yeah. Let's have something to eat and we'll try that other wharf. We may squeeze in."

A small passenger boat pulled out, crowded with people, chickens, bundles, all jumbled in together. We took its place and a man sauntered over.

"I'm the harbour captain here. Where are you from?"

We tied up and a watchman was appointed to guard the cat day and night.

"Just pay him 4 pesos a day and give him some food," we were instructed. "He'll sleep on board if you like."

This was fine, and for good measure and to make him feel at home, he was issued with the .22 automatic. Everyone else in authority was packing a pistol in his hip pocket, so why not our bodyguard? As dusk crept over the wharves a furtive little man slipped on board. He seemed to know our guard, who looked away.

"Hot! Hot!" he whispered, looking back over his shoulder, at the same time disclosing a small tissue paper packet.

"What've you got there?" I asked, but purely mechanically, because it was expected of me. Years before I'd been nearly caught by one of these tricksters when passing through the Suez Canal. A wog had come on board flashing a large gold signet ring and quickly hiding it again. He demonstrated the genuine properties of the stone by scoring a port-hole glass. The very boldness of his vandalism and the white mark across the glass disc clinched the sale with someone quicker than I. It was not until after he'd long gone that the foolish buyer found it was the artificial stone's own substance which defaced the glass.

Into his grimy hand a dozen "stones" poured to lie softly glowing in the cabin's light. They certainly looked tempting and the Count started bargaining.

"Hold it a minute! I doubt if they're genuine—let's test the bloody things." And grabbing a file I gave one a jolly good rub. The scruffy chap grabbed the defaced gem and was out the cabin door in a flash.

I was sent for by the Customs chief.

"You came here from Manila without a clearance!"

"No, we've come here from Victorias and there's no custom-house there!"

"You are quibbling. You are not the only one. Mr. Fox, the American, was fined for this and I see no reason why you should not be fined, too."

"Fox? What boat did he have?"

"The *Foxtrot*, a yacht," was the interesting reply.

I didn't want to enquire too closely as to how long ago this had been. The last we'd heard, *Foxtrot* was being held in Djarapoura in West Irian by the Indonesians. I cursed Fox and his troubles which were now mine.

"I will telegraph Manila; you must not leave port until we give you clearance."

"Very well; but in the meanwhile can we do our shopping? We need water and food."

It was arranged to report every day, and a man about my own age was detailed off to run me back to the docks. I persuaded him to take me out to the Shell Company to organize the re-fuelling. As he got in his war-time jeep he took out a large .45 automatic because "too uncomfortable to sit on" and later showed me his warrant, a leather folder with a crude enamel shield with the words "Secret Service".

"Secret Service? Why secret service way down here?"

"Much, much smugglers. Five coastguard killed last week. Big fight out in bay."

He confirmed the stories we'd heard so often before. Smugglers try to run cigarettes past the Coastguard and Customs into the Philippines from the Indonesian islands across the Sulu Sea. "Pirates" try to hijack the cargoes and what with the Navy trying to get in on the act, some fierce and desperate actions take place, with fast boats, automatic weaponry, spies and informers, graft and corruption and Secret Service men.

"Be very careful when you leave," he cautioned. "Don't go same day you get clearance and be clear of land by nightfall. Where you go from here?"

"To Wewak in Australian New Guinea," I lied.

"Very far?"

"About 2000 miles."

He stared. "You've got no sails!"

"Oh, we carry fuel for 1500 miles and I'll put on three extra drums of diesel. We can do it, especially if we cruise on one motor."

Back on board Rafe was excited. "The bastard snatched my wallet! Bumped into me, but I belted him and shouted 'Cops! Cops!' He dropped the wallet and had the cheek to say, 'Me no take'!"

The fuel was pumped on board and three drums lashed on the foredeck. I had found out that I could top up with more fuel at a little place called General Santos, down on the southern tip of the island. A Dole pineapple factory was there and that meant Americans and some sort of guarantee of fair play. I hoped.

The Customs chief handed me a letter he'd prepared. The last paragraph worried me:

"State, in writing, any reason why a fine should not be imposed."

"I can't pay a fine! We've got no money until we get to Wewak! We've spent our last on foodstuffs. Even the fuel was paid for before we got here!"

The official stared coldly at me, picked up a 'phone. I heard the name "Arabay" so knew he was on to the Shell agent to confirm my statement. It was a stroke of luck I'd arranged it in

Manila. My friend there had taken the much-prized U.S. dollars
and paid for the fuel himself in pesos by telegraphic transfer.

"I want your reply in writing tomorrow morning!" he insisted. And that was that.

"Be back on board by 10 tonight—sharp! Don't tell anyone
we're off. If you're late you'll be left behind."

The night was dark and still. We shoved off from the wharf,
leaving our watchman confused at the suddenness of his dis-
missal. We didn't put on steaming lights and from 100 yards
distant we were invisible in the soft blackness. To fox any ob-
servers I headed north and when out of earshot, turned the cat
south towards Tictauan and the great Santa Cruz islands and
out into the Moro Gulf. Lankil and Sibago, two bad spots,
showed vaguely on either side. But we were clear, with open
water ahead for the 30-hour voyage to Jarangani Bay.

General Santos is comparatively new, created about 1938,
although, like most small Filipino places, it is hard to tell its age
by appearance, as the heat, lack of paint and general confusion
of new and tumbling-down buildings blurs the image. It was
built at the edge of a magnificent bay on a gently sloping plain
beneath a great arc of high hills.

We found the Dole wharf and made contact with company
men. "Sure, guys. Just moor alongside our fishing boat."

Mike and I greased and tightened everything in sight, changed
filters and engine oils. We topped up fuel and water tanks and
filled three jerry-cans with extra drinking water. It was going to
be a long haul and a dicey one at that.

We hired a jeepnie and all six crushed into the dusty con-
traption for a last trip into town. At the local jail we stopped,
as it was an incredible structure, with wan brown faces pressed
to wooden-barred windows. A sign above the unpainted building read, "House of Correction" and surrounding it and its
sparsely grassed yard was a flimsy wooden pole and barbed-wire
fence about 10 feet high. Mike and I stayed in the taxi and missed
being invited by a couple of guards into the compound and jail
to see the spectacle.

"They were crammed in like sardines," exclaimed Jorge. "Just
wooden cells and bars. Hardly any light and nothing for them to
do."

"The guards told us they'd had a break-out a fortnight ago
and shot five dead, wounded three and five more got away," said
Rafe.

"And the families have to come and feed them or bribe the guards," Herman added.

Tomorrow would be goodbye to the Philippines and back to the island chains of New Guinea and Melanesia. From now on the indigenes would be less comely and intelligent. I enjoyed the Filipinos, rogues and all. They are artistic with their handicrafts and cheerful in their adversity. To make business possible and to unify the people, English is taught as everyone's second language, and public signs are more often than not written in English. I thought of the signs "Guns of Aggression" painted on captured Japanese artillery and "House of Correction" and "Rogues' Gallery". There was a curious slant to the phrasing. A tee shirt's message "I am a Filipino and I love my Country" still sticks in my mind.

We were motoring past a predominantly Moslem stretch of coast near Tinaca Point.

A lawyer we had met in Zamboanga told us how, in earlier days, a man who had reached the end of his tether, one way or another, would visit his religious leader and have his head shaved and his testicles bound up tight. He would don a white robe and sally forth with his kris to kill as many people as he could before being cut down himself. It was a form of suicide, but one which ensured a happy life in the next world.

"They still do it now and again, you know, but they have to inform the police first, so the streets can be cleared. When the chap comes out howling and waving his kris around, he is shot!"

I could appreciate the abysmal unhappiness and desperation of a suicide, and the source of his howling, but not the reason for binding himself in this way.

"The pain makes him ignore minor cuts and wounds," was the explanation.

CHAPTER THIRTEEN

Quick Exit from West Irian

MINDANAO was misty and vague as it slipped below the horizon. It was a lovely day, bright and blue, and the gentle breeze of our passage just enough to cool us. We had passed between Balut and Sarageni Islands and the next territory would be Indonesian. On board we had three and a-half tons of fuel and about half a ton of water. Pineapples galore, big and shiny, were crammed in odd spots and Japanese feather lures flickered in our wake.

The next few days passed in boredom as we crossed open seas and widely skirted islands. A knocking in Big Stinky's engine-room had been worrying me. I was sure it wasn't an engine knock but it certainly was increasing, so I shut it down and when the motor had cooled sufficiently, took the drive covers off and pulled and tugged at the drive shaft, universal joints and jackshaft bearing.

"Start her up, Mike!" And there it was—the jackshaft wobbling and clattering away.

"I think the shaft's broken off near the spigot bearing." Mike agreed.

"Let's strip it down—perhaps there's something we can do. In the meanwhile, we'll just have to carry on."

The rubber coupling was dissembled and the greasy jackshaft withdrawn.

"Thank goodness for that! It's just the ruddy bronze sleeve worn out. And the end of the spigot," Mike pointed out. "We can soon fix it up. All we need is a welding plant and a lathe. The blasted thing must have been out of line. Let's hope the other's O.K."

We checked the port unit and found it sound. We were off the large island of Waigeo right at the tip of New Guinea. That night I decided to put into Manokwari, which had been the Dutch seat of government for all the north-eastern part of Dutch New Guinea.

I tried to radio a tanker which was passing northward low on the horizon, but got no answer. I wanted someone to know where we were and where we were going.

24 September: According to the chart, we were about to cross the Equator and the Equator passed right through a tiny reef between the north coast of Waigeo Island and the small island of Manoeran.

"When I sound the horn we'll be crossing the Equator. In fact, let's actually stop and have a party! I can guarantee the exact position."

So, just as we entered the separating channel, I switched on the echo-sounder and watched the black marking-line shoot up to read 16 feet. I stopped the motors.

"Get ready to drop the pick!"

"Now!" The horns croaked, and the grapnel splashed into the flat calm waters over a delightful reef clearly visible beneath us. We were not just near the Equator, but actually bang on it at longitude 130° 54′ E.

Within minutes we were hunting across the coral fans and guts. A gentle current caused the tiny reef fishes to face against it and scull gently to maintain position near their spiky lairs.

A banded sea snake wriggled to the surface, gulped its minute bubble of air and undulated back to the shelter of the reef. A turtle, rooting in the rubble of broken coral, was oblivious of our approach and we watched as it pushed and shoved to get at a beleaguered crab.

We got pretty merry and bright with our new friend Jim Beam, a smooth fellow, who had lived in his bottle since Okinawa. In fact, I'm sure it was Jim who fired off a smoke float and several red and white star shells to celebrate.

A largish coaster which happened to be passing outside the channel separating the islands, doused all its lights and hared away in the direction we were to take.

"Let's go! We may be reported and this is Indonesian territory." So we pulled up the grapnel and took off.

In the morning a school of big blackfish heaved and plunged while we circled around and over them. Deep below, their fat forms could be tracked quite clearly; it was easy to motor gently above them in anticipation of their surfacing.

False Cape was just ahead and under its rocky cliffs the water beckoned. There was a tiny cove; on the beach, part hidden by a screen of bamboo and banana palms, a simple thatched hut stood on bare brown poles. A solitary native, fishing from a little canoe, pulled in his fibre rope with its stone anchor and paddled frantically ashore. He had a withered leg and hobbled up the beach with the aid of a stick. I pulled down the Indonesian flag and hoisted our miniscule New Zealand affair. Not that it would be recognized, but at least the gesture might mean something even here.

We splashed about for a while—there was good spearfishing but too many sharks, which zoomed up from the deep to flick around us and take our fish.

The native came back and shyly presented a little gift. A few bananas and a handful of green leaves which we later boiled and found excellent. He was a pathetic creature and his wife, too, was disfigured and hid behind the trees. Not so their children, who clambered on board and tasted chocolate and jam for the first time.

We gave our new friend a handful of fish hooks, some matches and toilet paper. Scarcely believing his good fortune, he gathered up his children, scrabbled off the stern and paddled away.

On one motor, at five knots, we crept into Manokwari Bay. It is a pretty place, with great shade trees and winding tarsealed roads. We drew alongside a rusty steel barge which was moored to a wharf. Indonesia's red and white flag hung flaccid in the baking heat and across the wharf, in a grassy park, there stood a bronze statue of an Indonesian soldier, rifle and all.

A crowd of blue-black Melanesians, all shining teeth and fuzzy hair, gathered on the wharf, smiling and chattering. A neatly-uniformed native strode over and attempted to interrogate us. I clambered over the barge and on to the wharf. In silence he led me to a group of offices behind the flagpole. The harbour master sat behind a large desk in a shady room. I was a trifle dubious about our reception, but a gentle smile and firm handshake reassured me. He was my first Indonesian; I don't count the shifty bureaucrats in Manila. Black straight hair, pale copper skin, and slight of build like most Asiatics in hot countries. His English wasn't bad, and slowly, with many a false start, we established an odd sort of friendship in the three days we stayed there. He organized passes for the crew and repairs to the *Whai* with an army major who was in charge of the dockyards and machine shops. Mike and I felt like weeping when we saw the neglect and shortcomings of this magnificent facility taken over from the Dutch.

I gesticulated, embracing the whole scene:

"Poor bloody Dutch!"

The major laughed and slapped his thigh in great glee.

We quickly had Big Stinky's flywheel spinning on a lathe and the worn bush replaced. I insisted on building up the worn spigot bearing myself, and an anxious Indonesian watched every run as I welded happily away.

"How much?" I asked the major.

"Fifty dollars," was the reply. For a moment I felt like asking for a receipt, just to jigger up his graft, but thought better of it.

Mike struggled in the confined engine-room to juggle the 200lb flywheel back on. He muttered away: "Fifty dollars! Fifty bloody dollars!! The thieving bastard!"

John had me called over to his office. He looked worried and embarrassed. He introduced me to a naval officer, immaculate in drill. He in turn introduced me to his wife and two children.

"You can't leave until we have word from Djarapoura, our naval base."

"But we're ready to go. The motors are fixed and the weather's fine."

"I don't think you ought to leave," remarked the naval type casually.

"Are you keeping me here?" I asked John, who squirmed and looked away.

"We should hear in a few days," was all he would say.

I marched back to the cat in a rage. At the gate to the wharf my pass was checked by a soldier in camouflaged coveralls, boots and gaiters. In the corner was propped a Russian sub-machine gun.

We were fed up with Manokwari. There was no cold beer, the food prices shocking and no entertainment whatsoever and the humidity appalling. I wrote a letter to protest to the harbour master, in which I quoted imaginary international law and a promise to call in at Djarapoura. I took it to his office. The naval commander and family had left and John said:

"I'm sorry, Peter. There's nothing I can do."

I told him I was going to invite the guards on board the boat, and start up the engines to charge the batteries. He gave me a note for the guard and soon we were all chummy as could be, with whisky on the table and submachine guns being inspected and admired. We left the engines rumbling away and eventually the soldiers climbed back on the wharf to return to their barracks.

It was midnight and the remaining guard slumped in his watch hut at the end of the wharf. We cast off and ever so gently opened the throttles as the cat drifted away. I hoped the increased noise of the diesels would be compensated for by an ever-widening gap, and soon we were around the back of Mansinam Island and at full bore out to sea.

I knew there were no boats manned and ready to chase us, should the alarm be given, and what there were in port had no radar. That night we headed straight out to sea and about 20 miles off the coast we turned south.

For a long while I had weighed the pros and cons: to stay awaiting instructions from the Indonesian naval base, or to clear out as we'd just done. Future yachts that called in would be more closely watched and perhaps have good cause to curse our escapade. But what the Indonesians were doing was quite contrary to international law. I knew a boat in mechanical trouble or with sickness aboard could call into a foreign port for succour. But the reputation of the Indonesians for holding yachts virtually to ransom was widespread and my duty was firstly to safeguard my own crew. We hoisted the red and white flag of Indonesia and kept going.

"Wake up! There's a boat got its searchlight on us!" Herman shook me roughly. I stumbled past Rafe, who reared up from his bunk. Sure enough a blinding light was glaring full on us, turning night into garish day. A hundred yards away a boat of about 200 tons was steaming parallel. Powerful lights illuminated its foredeck and about a dozen brown-overalled figures milled about on it.

"Turn our light on them!" And after a mad scramble our beam lanced across the waters. It was only a large Jap trawler and we truly sighed with relief. Their light snapped out and our red and white flag, its work done, became a grey blur.

Day after day we cruised off the New Guinea coast. One morning on checking Big Stinky's engine oil, I found the level had risen. At least I thought it had; I couldn't really recall the last reading being abnormal. The next day oil pressure was down a little and I bawled out Jorge for not watching the instruments more closely. I shut off the motor and checked water and oil levels. Sure enough the motor was making, not using, oil. It looked thin and clearer than usual.

Mike and I rubbed it between our fingers, smelt it, and were mystified. "There's no water in it, that's for sure." Mike agreed.

"Must be a diesel leak of some sort thinning the oil."

On starting the motor we could see the drip-drip of pure diesel squeezing past the neoprene oil seals on the injector extensions. "That's bloody lovely, Mike; we haven't any spares." So we tried sealing-tape and gasket goo, but to no avail.

There was only one thing to do—drain and replace the oil and keep the motor on stand-by for emergencies.

And so we set out to cruise almost 700 miles, past islands and reefs along the West Irian coast. At any moment we could start up Big Stinky if we needed it and run for eight or nine hours without trouble, so we weren't worried. Just inconvenienced for the sake of four 10-cent "O" rings.

It was broad daylight when we passed through the Yapen Straits in the Schouten Islands; we got a bit uneasy when a four-engined plane droned over, but it was only an airliner heading for Biak.

Wewak. And Mike in hospital. It was a real blow. He'd stood on a broken bottle at the water's edge and now had a severed ligament in his foot. It was the end of the trip for him, as his foot was in plaster and would be for six weeks. Any complications could permanently ruin it. So we said goodbye, he to fly home and Rafe, Jorge, Taffy and myself to carry on. Herman left us here also; he never got his sea legs and suffered all the time afloat.

"I go Australia and get job. Send for my wife."

Losing Mike was a different matter, as I'd leaned on him and relied on his steady nature and unfailing good temper.

The last I saw of him was a flurry as he tried to grab a giggling black nurse. "Oh! Mister Mike!" she squealed.

"Madang sounds interesting—let's try there. It's only about 180 miles down the coast." So off we went on one motor. A Wewak garage had cabled Brisbane for spares but we'd hung about for four days and an airways strike finally put paid to any hope of an early delivery. The garage promised to forward the pieces to Rabaul. It was only some 500 more miles on one motor, and we'd already done over 1000 on Little Stinky, which was renamed "Little Perfume" as an encouragement.

Madang is lovely. Huge leafy trees and green open spaces. Great aerophytes and lichens hang from thick branches which reach out over water lilies on placid ponds. In the shallows and sedges of the water white herons stalk, and frogs fill the air with their croaking.

There is a dreaming beauty here: the lagoon with its palm-covered islands and native canoes gently paddling across shining blue water. I was tempted to stay and try charter work, but no two Aussie locals could agree on the potential. We exchanged two big barracuda, caught on the troll, for a few dollars and some beer. On the *Whai* was Errol Flynn's book *My Wicked, Wicked Ways;* this was one of his early stamping grounds. "Hell, there's not a man over 60 here who doesn't claim he beat Flynn in a fight," declared one old-timer.

The mosquitoes gave us hell and, nearly driven mad, we headed off across Dampier Strait towards New Britain at a full five knots.

Garove Island. This looked fascinating—the rim of an extinct volcano with part of its lip blown away or eroded to let the sea in. The chart showed it as an almost perfect circle of high ground, perhaps a mile in diameter, enclosing very deep water. I set course to arrive at daybreak. In the early dawn we passed Unea Island with its lonely flashing lighthouse. Curtains of rain blotted out the horizon.

Garove lay green and mysterious—thick jungle sloped steeply to the sea and not until we were within half a mile was the entrance clearly defined. There are no offshore reefs—this is the top of a huge mountain rising from the floor of the ocean—and we motored straight in past coconut palms clinging to the steep faces and bougainvillea flashing cerise against the greenery. Up on the bluff above the entrance to our port, was a tower—the spire of a church hidden behind palm fronds.

"What about the lures?" Jorge asked.

"Leave them out. We might pick up something at the entrance."

And with that we entered the crater lagoon, black and glassy. I decided to cruise around a bit before putting in and making friends with the locals. On the banks above us, excited children hopped and skipped about—a strange boat, any boat, must be a novelty. There is little excitement in these islands of Melanesia— just village life and the occasional visit by medical teams and missionaries.

A horde of screaming children, gay in bright-coloured mumus and lavalavas, burst out of a schoolhouse. We waved and carried on close in to the shoreline, under overhanging cliff faces and past primitive shacks built on stilts over the water's edge. Bare-breasted women stood silently gazing at us and we at them. This place was really unspoiled by tourists. Catamarans are the usual craft for these people—white men build conventional single-hull motor boats—but the *Whai* was really something they appreciated.

A loud splash behind and one of the fishing lines angled off, cutting through the water at incredible speed.

"A strike! A strike!" The fish was big and fast and Rafe cut his hands as the line tore away from him. Down in the depths something flashed silver, and slowly the struggling fish was hauled to the surface—a huge wahoo with pointy white teeth, razor sharp. It must have been all of five feet long and thumped the steel deck with heavy blows of its tail before Jorge killed it with a hammer.

We pulled in alongside the mission's little jetty. A tall white man in an old stained soutane stood quietly under the verandah of the wharf shed.

"Good day! We are on our way to Rabaul and called in to have a look. Is there any good diving around here?"

The priest was German and Jorge had great news.

"There are several sunken Japanese workboats behind an island on the other side of the harbour! In about 20 feet of water!"

"Would you like this fish? It is too big for us." Then we were on our way with a couple of natives as guides. The priest was to follow—on the little island the mission pigs were kept and this day a couple were to be selected for some feast or other. Rain poured down in drumming cloudbursts to clear away with dramatic suddenness. The sun shone and the waters reflected the clouds and crater edge as in a mirror.

We anchored off a shell-encrusted knob which the natives pointed to. It was the cylinder head of a large diesel engine.

"Japan men! Japan men!"

The water was about 30 feet deep quite close inshore. Parrots screamed and flickered from tree to tree. Palms and thick fleshy undergrowth crowded to the water's edge. Apart from the bird cries a deep hush hung over the steamy bush and inland sea. On with flippers, masks and snorkels. Down with the stern ladders and into glorious warm water. Straight away we saw the wreckage.

"Look at the propellers! I've found two!" shouted Rafe.

The native boys were excited by our swimming gear—amazed at the speed and drive given by flippers. We searched on. Not much fish life—the bottom too barren—just sand sloping down steeply into the blackness. Lined up neatly were the wrecks of seven small workboats—wooden craft now reduced to metal bones and engine entrails. From the size of the winches, propellers and engines, they'd probably been about 50 feet long—designed for service as tugs and carriers of small equipment among the garrisons of these islands. They must have been scuttled by their Japanese crews—they weren't destroyed in action.

We spent a happy hour poking about. There were copper fuel tanks and bronze pumps, valves—the big twin-cylinder diesels and heavy winches all exposed and sitting in 20 feet of clear water. Not enough salvage for a special trip, but certainly worthwhile for a larger visitor to work on its way past.

We crept around the coast and into the open sea at dusk. Next port, Rabaul.

There was a strange thump, an exclamation more groan than curse. Jorge lay collapsed across the helmsman's seat, face grey. He was moaning and clutching his left hand which was dripping blood. We sorted him out with a stiff brandy and sleeping pills as tranquillizers. He had slipped while lowering the top hatch. It had fallen, catching his fingers in its steel lips. The wonder was they weren't nipped off.

Next day I saw an outboard motorboat heading towards us. It turned in through a gap in the reef and I followed it to draw alongside a newly-erected jetty thrust out from a slash in the jungle.

"Can you help us?" I called to the boatman. "One of my crew is injured. Is there a road that can get him to hospital from here?"

"No! We're 20 miles from the road. What's wrong with him?"

"I think two fingers are broken; perhaps three. He's had a bump on the head—slight concussion."

"Well, I can buzz him down the coast." Jorge was helped into the runabout and in a cloud of spray was away, bouncing over the sea towards Rabaul. I didn't fancy his juddering ride at speed; I could see him nursing his injured hand. Now we were three, and stood watches of four hours on and eight off.

Late that night we entered Rabaul Bay. I didn't care much for anchoring off the yacht clubhouse at night. While there on the cruise up, a naval salvage team had been diving among the yachts, recovering unexploded shells and bombs dumped during the war. We dropped the pick near a Chinese junk. All night long its single-lunger diesel auxiliary thumped and banged, sometimes missing several beats, only to recover and pick up revs with wheezing effort. A strong smell of rotting fish wafted over us and in the morning we moved nearer the club's jetty, cleaner craft and cold beer.

"I think I'll come on to New Zealand with you." The Welshman speaking.

"I don't think you will," said I. "I told you I'd take you to Rabaul. This is Rabaul and it's as far as you go!"

I'd had enough of the B.Sc. to whom the world owed a living. Had enough of being embarrassed by dirty, wornout jeans, ragged red singlet and unshaven face when boarded by Customs and Police. I disliked being coupled to this slovenly character who insulted the hospitality of strangers by his arrogant disregard for convention.

I was worried about corrosion of the port hull. Where we had scraped on a reef at Lifou the paint had come off in long thin scratches. Our miles of passage had eroded the clean metal, not through electrolysis so much as by cavitation, and I just had to get paint on. Bill and Cobber had tried to work a red plastic sort of paint into the bare places at Beautemps but it had not been a success, and now I could feel the grooves with my fingers. I arranged with a Chinese boatyard to slip the *Whai*, get a team of kanakas and fix it up. The big problem was money and a tentative cable home for $200 was successful in less than 24 hours. Fantastic. Why hadn't I asked for more?

Jorge turned up, released from hospital. No fingers broken after all—he'd been extremely lucky.

"I'll need you guys to get the boat on the slip. After that you may as well look around for a job to earn some dough. We may be here for weeks."

We cruised over to our old friend the *Iberia*, back again with a load of tourists. A strange-looking scow, the *Tomona*, dirty and bedraggled, was grunting along near a wharf and as we passed, a familiar figure caught my attention.

"Dave! You old bastard! What are you doing here? You're supposed to be after abalones in Aussie!"

"Well, if it's not Peter the Pirate! So you got that thing finished! We're anchoring just ahead. Soon as we're in position, come alongside!"

There was a lot of messing about with bow and stern anchors, but eventually Dave had the scow moored to his satisfaction. It was good to see him again—one of the spearfishing greats—a character in his own right and rapidly becoming a legendary figure in the underwater world.

"Barry May and I are in partnership—he's got the *Pacific Seal* and I use this tub. We're going to get up a propeller off a Jap freighter. Would you like to see it?"

And in a trice I was over the side—the water clear and warm. It was hard to make out what was what—great plates of half-inch thick steel were twisted and curled like giant black petals. A heavy ooze formed the bottom and Dave's divers were already stirring it up as they lugged and heaved an airlift tube into place. Dave tugged at my elbow and started in under a plate a few feet above the bottom. Our tanks scraped and bumped noisily and our used air rumbled away. It grew pitch black and, looking back between my legs, I could just make out the green of daylight. This wasn't for me—I should have been briefed on what to expect, so I squeezed Dave's thigh and backed my way out into open water.

The divers had a big propeller down there and had to suck away the harbour mud before blasting it off the shaft. When a black cloud of mud obscured the scene I swam off and surfaced.

Dave explained the valuable find.

"The joker I work with salvaged the spare propeller off this Jap at the end of the war. Everyone thought it was the working propeller and he kept quiet until now when the price of bronze is tops. The port people turned the wreck into a jetty by pouring concrete over the decking. The prop's been down there all along! There's over eight tons of bronze in it!"

We moved off to slip the *Whai*. A dozen laughing, splashing Melanesians fastened wooden blocks in position to secure and support the twin hulls and, black and dripping, the cat was winched ashore. Jorge couldn't help with his injured hand, and Rafe needed money; so I set about the horrid job of wire-brushing square yards of slimy bottom. It took four days of hard work—the less said the better. Native labourers paid at under $1.50 per day were charged out to me at $3 per hour by the slipway proprietors. They were as feckless as children and had to be watched every minute. To see fullgrown men standing dumbly helpless when confronted with an elementary decision gives one a sense of exasperation and futility. The Melanesians and Papuans at first seem incredibly stupid—you have to work with them to fully appreciate the problems ahead for their advancement. There is more to it than lack of education: more to it than environment and opportunity.

They don't have to plan ahead—they don't have to prepare for a rainy day. Food is all around—reach up and there are coconuts: dangle a leaf in the water and you can catch fish. It is not bred in them to be thinkers. Paternalism is the answer—not self-government—not yet. My generation should remember with deep gratitude the selfless heroism and blind faith in their "Mastas" that these people showed when we were overrun by the Japanese. The present-day young "Boss" should think of his educational advantages and be very patient with these simple folk.

CHAPTER FOURTEEN

Divers and Miners

"WE'LL have to do four hours on and eight off—how does that sound to you chaps?" Rafe and Jorge agreed. It was the best arrangement—too short a break between watches and one became tired. After all, there was no real exertion involved at the wheel. I was the one who had the rough time and the worry. My weight had dropped from 12½ stone to under 11 stone and two or three internal bleedings had scared the pants off me. I wanted to get home and see my doctor.

With the 60-odd dollars I'd collected from taking a couple of skindiving parties out, we could move on again. Waving goodbye to the hard cases on the *Tomona* we headed out to sea. Big Stinky was fully operational and we had some spare seals for future replacements. It was some 170 miles to the north end of Bougainville Island and the Buka Passage. We wanted to see Kieta and the huge copper mine being carved from the mountains on the eastern seaboard. Now that we were back in the chain of Solomon Islands and soon to be in the New Hebrides again, I decided to travel down the eastern coast so as to cover fresh ground.

The Buka Passage, scene of many a wild air and naval skirmish during the war, is a strange channel separating Buka Island from the Bougainville mainland. It is deep, about 60ft, and quite narrow, perhaps as little as 150 yards in places. At its western entrance we swam for hours trying to locate a sunken Japanese aircraft we knew to be nearby. But it was siesta time and any locals who knew the exact spot were escaping the heat.

"Teop Island—we'll put in there. Let's hope the daylight lasts. Keep a very accurate track of our progress; mark the charts with the time off each headland."

But it was certain that darkness would catch us with an hour's motoring yet to go, and a fast set was against us. The stars began to twinkle.

"Now we'll have to hang about all night or creep in. Get the lamp up topside and hold it on the shoreline. I'll give it a go."

Reefs slid by, glowing with phosphorescence, as a slow swell covered them. It was pitch black and even 20 yards from the reef's edge the water was over 1000 feet deep. The echo-sounder was almost useless and Jorge stood on the starboard bow while Rafe swept the spotlight's beam from side to side.

The ghostly blur marking the reef-line curved away to starboard; now the odd patch of sand and clumps of bushes came into the spotlight's glare to glide and fade into the darkness.

The chart showed sand shoals ahead and, feeling our way slowly, at last the echo-sounder picked up a gently sloping bottom. First faintly and then with firm black strokes, the electronic echoes marked the shallowing water.

"Put the Danforth down here. We're in about 20 feet of water. It's a sand bottom according to the chart."

The night was completely dark. It was impossible to see skyline, shoreline or even distinguish the actual surface of the water once our eddies had died away. We set about preparing a slap-up dinner—it was marvellous to be safely at rest.

"I'm sure there's someone outside!"

We listened and heard soft voices. Coming out from the bright cabin it took some time to distinguish the shining teeth of two Melanesians in a canoe.

"Hulloa! Do you speak English?"

"Yes, Captain. We came to tell you this dangerous place, no good."

"You speak good English. We can't speak Pidgin."

"Oh, I trained Mission school. My name Samson. These my fella sons."

"Come on board. We are about to eat. Will you join us?"

The big man nimbly climbed aboard, heaving up a small scared kid we had not noticed. The other son was about 16 and smiled nervously while rubbing one horny-soled foot against a shin. We sat Samson down and his great woolly head rubbed the cabin ceiling. His smaller son sat crying silently, clutching his father's massive thigh.

The meal was not a huge success as the elder boy, scared and nervous, suddenly bolted out to vomit over the side.

"He very shy," remarked Samson, helping himself to another huge portion. "Never kai-kai with white fella before."

Our new friend was the native councillor for the northern part of Bougainville. He informed us with a great laugh that his salary was $14 a day—a fortune for a Melanesian. He was chief of the tribe who lived on Teop and we were to let him guide us to a secure safe anchorage for the night. I was doubtful about his ability to do this in the pitch darkness, but he must have had eyes like a cat. We tied the little outrigger to one side and motored slowly ahead, Samson standing on the cabin roof shielding his eyes from the faint glow of the depth-sounder's face.

"You put anchor here," he rumbled and to the shrieks and calls from a hundred excited natives in canoes and on shore, we rested.

Next morning the chatter of dozens of children awoke us. Samson stood up from where he'd been silently waiting, and for the first time we saw him clearly. He'd been well named.

"Are there any old custom goods you people would like to sell? Any sea shells or weapons?" Odds and ends were presented for our inspection. An ancient stone axehead was diffidently proffered and quickly swapped for an old shirt. We gave away lots of the U.S. Army toilet paper, much in demand for rolling cigarettes. We paddled ashore, balanced precariously on the canoes. It was a pleasure to stroll through Samson's village with its neat thatched huts and walkways of swept sand and crushed coral. Bare-breasted women shyly covered themselves from our cameras but not from our interested gaze.

When it was time to go, to much splashing and shouting, a horde of children shoved the *Whai* clear of a sand patch the sterns had drifted on to.

It was but a few hours' pleasant cruise down Bougainville's mountainous coast to Kieta. The mountain backbone was partly hidden in mists, but an active volcano to the north quietly puffed brown fumes. Deep ravines covered in thick green bush and patches of bald rock on ridges and headlands made an impression of wild majesty. Further south, the coast was protected from the open sea by long golden sand beaches and the creaming reefs of offshore islands. About noon we entered Kieta Bay, a deep indent on the rough coast. Jungle covered the hills and it wasn't until we rounded the last headland to starboard that the township came into view.

Kieta is tiny, scattered in an arc around a little bay. As in Madang, trees line the main waterfront road. There is one pub and several stores. It is a boom town, bursting at the seams with new buildings being pushed up helter-skelter. A huge copper company is building a proper port and a company town over the hill, so Kieta may not develop very much more and so be spoilt for ever.

We anchored next to a trimaran off a black sand beach in front of the only hotel. Soon we were buddies with the Australian owner of the *Wanderer II*, who had come to grief on a reef and was forced to put into Kieta for repairs. Here he found he could make $120 each weekend taking bored tradesmen from the mine works down the coast for cruises. He used to specialize in anchoring off Balalae and getting some sleep while his passengers struggled around in the bushes looking for Jap souvenirs.

We met two engineers, service men for some of the mighty earthmoving machinery at the mine. We piled into the back of their station wagon and enjoyed the fantastic ride to Panguna, the mining town, high in the mountains. With giant cuttings and fills, the Australians have literally carved and shaped a 16-mile, $9 million highway over which thousands of tons of equipment will be carried.

"Let's have a feed. You blokes just get in the queue and look as if you work here. If anyone says anything, tell 'em to pull their heads in." And with that we entered the mess hall. After the meals on the *Whai*, this was a tremendous blowout and finishing, we fairly tottered out to the waiting car. Mike would have revelled in it. I had eaten so much my diaphragm was pressed against my heart, and the thumping made me frightened of a heart attack. But it was worth it!

The air was thinner and cooler at the mine workings. It was over 2000 feet above sea level. We were particularly interested in the 41 dump trucks, each of which could carry 100 (short) tons of ore at a loading.

"They're being driven by natives who can't read a ruler, and never saw anything bigger'n a three-ton truck before," our guide informed us. "They've started a special driving school for picked natives—at $221,000 per truck, let's hope they're good!"

At the *Whai* we got a great surprise—the *Pacific Seal* had come in and ex-crewman John Lindsay was alongside in an aluminium work boat. He was having a "mighty" time and thoroughly enjoying life.

"We're off to Buin tomorrow to work on a Jap destroyer. How about coming down before it's all cut up?"

Would we ever! Early, before the rest of the town awoke, the *Seal* pulled out and set off for Buin. A radio message had been intercepted by accident from the *Tomona*. Somehow Dave's crew had "got on" to the destroyer, and Barry suspected they were after the propellers.

We had a breakfast of Alka Selters, and made one more despairing visit to the post office for mail. Then we sailed off in the wake of the *Seal*.

"There she is, over by that low hill. You can see the workboat further down the coast."

Sure enough the *Pacific Seal* was anchored and we tied along-side.

"It's right below us. The other bastards have flogged the props —they were pulling out just as we arrived!"

There was terrific rivalry between the partners and almost anything went.

"Tomorrow we blow the torpedo warheads off. You'd better dive on it today if you want to see her complete. Go down on our hookahs and have a dekko," suggested Barry.

"My turn to go first," I said and buckled on harness. The water was grey green and warm. As I pulled myself hand over hand down the anchor rope, the misty filaments and sediment in the water cleared a little and at 30 feet I could see the destroyer's bridge 20 feet below as a dark shadow.

There was a fair current. By gripping the encrusted and rusty iron projections, I pulled myself down over the bridge super-structure and across the twin-gun turrets to the foredeck. Fish in their hundreds milled about—salmonee, coral trout, caranx and a type of handsome pompano. Large shells with strange lobes and serrated jaws clung in bunches to the edge of the deck where the turbulence was greatest. I wrenched off a couple and worked my way back.

Three turrets of twin quickfiring 5-inch guns pointed towards the long-gone sky and the vanished Hornets which had sunk her. She lay on the bottom complete but for crew, in about 80 feet of water.

Visibility was not good, perhaps 30 feet, and the hulk looked immense. Working past the remains of the smoke stack I sud-denly realized that the rounded object I was fending myself from was one of three torpedoes still in the tubes. A diver from the *Seal* had already wound Cortex around the warheads pre-paratory to the morrow's blasting. Cold shivers ran down my back. There was more than a ton of high explosive and here I was bumping and rattling round the deadly weapons.

It was a curious feeling being anchored immediately over a complete warship with loaded torpedoes and racks of depth charges, full magazines, and all manner of weapons. The *Hatsui-reki* had been sunk by air attack and had gone down with all its guns firing. Dead crewmen were still trapped behind bulkheads yet to be opened.

"You'd better follow us and keep well clear when we blow the heads off," advised Barry. "They may be waterlogged and not explode, as the steel's pretty thin, but you never know. We're going at least a mile away."

With Lord knows how many depth charges and at least nine 24-inch torpedoes, it could be quite a bang. The work boat stayed over the wreck while the *Seal* and *Whai* motored off to safety. John and his offsider set their weird "Mickey Mouse" detonating device going, and through the binoculars we watched them crank up their outboard and tear off as fast as it could go. I edged even further away; I wanted the *Seal* featuring in the movie of the big bang, if and when it eventuated.

The workboat had barely reached the *Seal* when a curious sharp crack was felt, rather than heard. I started filming and caught the immense boil of bubbles and froth as the torpedo tubes split, releasing thousands of pounds of compressed air. The torpedo heads were evidently duds and the depth charges too. We were both relieved and disappointed at the same time. As soon as we saw the *Seal* move towards the mound of white water, I started the cat in chase. There'd be some good movies of the huge quantity of air still escaping and the hundreds of fish floating belly up on the sea's surface. We had a rare scramble with boathooks trying to capture the stunned fish before released bunker oil could spoil them.

"Well, that's that. We'd better be pushing off for Nila again for more photos of the Jap aircraft."

At Nila, we found the sunken planes badly damaged. A Japanese logging concession on the opposite island had been clearing the channel and had knocked over the little floatplane. Also the large wing of the flying boat had collapsed across its fuselage. I was furious with myself for not having taken more photographs of them on the way north.

That night Billy took us crocodile hunting. He sat with his legs draped over the bows of the dinghy. Rafe and Jorge sat in the centre and I handled the motor. As we cruised up the winding mangrove channel, the trees lost their raggedy rooty look and became first grey and then black blurs. The skyline became a fretwork of foliage and a thousand stars sparkled above us.

We cut the motor and Jorge and Rafe rowed quietly. Fruit bats swooped across the sky, silhouetted like huge moths. Queer snapping sounds and plops, furtive scurryings and the odd piercing shriek of something caught kept us on edge. A strange drumming sound throbbed from time to time; the night was alive. Billy swept the beam of the spotlight along one muddy edge of the creek and with a powerful torch Rafe and Jorge took turns on the other. Every now and again Billy would flick the light skyward and then back to the spot where he thought he'd seen something.

It was an eerie performance in deadly earnest and Billy's professionalism kept us on the *qui vive* hour after hour. With slight movements of his free hand he guided us along the gloomy reaches of the creek. He knew where he was in all the miles of meandering waterway. Like Samson, he had incredible eyesight.

We came to a large still pool with overhanging trees. "Hah!" breathed our wrinkled gnome, flicking the light up and then down again, to glance and strike brilliant sparks from something lying in the muddy water. The paddlers froze; Billy signalled them to keep going. Again and again he flicked the light on to the twin diamonds and away again. All the time the dinghy softly slid towards the partly submerged crocodile. And then, without a ripple, it was gone.

Billy's command of English was too rudimentary for him to explain what we'd done wrong.

"He wants us to go faster!" decided Rafe.

"No, go slower! He says slower," argued Jorge.

Twice more, glittering eyes flashed back at us and each time the beasts sank silently and disappeared. By this time Billy was very angry and blurted out "Masta no one tok this fella boy", which could mean we either weren't friends or didn't talk the same language.

Sister Francisca questioned Billy on our behalf.

"He wanted you to paddle like hell towards the eyes when he flicked the light up."

"Told you so!" said Rafe.

"You fella one tok along Masta have spark," said Sister.

"What's that all about?" I asked.

"Well, one tok means that you are friends. One tok means you speak the same language—are of the same tribe and spark is drink. Better give him some beer and tobacco."

But Billy had to be content with some chocolate and tinned meat, as grog was very low and none of us smoked.

We set off for Choiseul and started to thread our way through the islands and reefs to the north and east of Nila. As we neared Balalae we spotted a trimaran anchored close to shore.

"It's John from Kieta with a party."

"He'll get a fright—think the cops have caught him at last!"

But our cheerful Aussie was asleep, surrounded by empty beer cans. He awoke as our motors coughed to a stop. Again we rowed to Balalae's palm-fringed sand and struggled for hours in the hot miasma of its jungle. John had seen the bombers I was so keen to find, but still they eluded us. Hot and sweaty, we staggered out on to the beach to find ten weary passengers, pasty-faced and out of training, lolling in the shade. But they had seen the planes in a clearing—and we hadn't!

We swam out to the *Whai*, started the donkeys and moved off, to get clear of the reefs before darkness caught us. We motored all night.

It was about a third of the way down Choiseul's coast that Pirie and I had sunk the Japanese torpedoboats. This was the spot that had attracted me for so many years and had triggered off the cruise in the *Windswift*. I looked forward to searching for and finding the wrecks. But first I had to locate the correct bay. From the sea's surface with its different perspective of shore and mountain I couldn't orientate at all and I knew the only hope was to question natives who had witnessed the kill, or had heard of it. We stopped at several villages and canoes came out to investigate our craft. They brought shells and sometimes artifacts to barter or sell. But the younger natives knew nothing and the older ones, children or striplings during the war, had mostly been in hiding on the northern coast and well away from the Japanese.

After many false leads the hopelessness of the task made me give up. There were 50 miles of possible coastline and at least a dozen bays. "Let's go. It's impossible with the time we've got. We'll cruise these southern coasts down to Santa Isabel, cross over to Honiara, collect mail and go to the Santa Cruz Islands."

Apart from missionary launches, occasional Government inspection boats and small copra traders, practically no one ever visits these lonely places. Yachties are not very interested.

We called at several lonesome spots and asked the villagers for "old custom" things. They must have thought we were prize bumpkins, and exchanged with glee artifacts very old and strange, for worn clothes due to be discarded on our return to New Zealand. The spearguns fascinated them, but Rafe discovered it was the rubber slings that they coveted. We had scarcely one gun left in working order. Those left by departed crew were stripped bare of shafts, rubbers and nylon in no time.

Jorge proudly showed Rafe and me a white stone disc he'd just traded. Across its polished face a beautiful carving in thin turtleshell was lashed with delicate woven cords of coconut fibre. "Custom" money, smooth rings of heavy white quartz, were offered and exchanged for fish hooks and odds and ends.

The *Whai* looked like a native bazaar with 20 or 30 blue-black natives, men, women and kids, proffering shells and curios. The

boat was being stripped and I had to call a halt, as tinned food
and bits of cordage started to disappear.

We eased into the Honiara Yacht Club basin. Reece Discombe
had asked if he could join us here as he fancied a spell at sea
and the chance to visit Vanikoro Island again. I put a call through
to Port Vila and Jean answered the 'phone. They had just returned from a month in New Zealand and Reece was out. They
hadn't received a letter I had written so he wouldn't be coming.
This was a blow, as I was down to $4 after buying 80 gallons of
fuel and a few groceries. We had some 1500 miles to go to
reach home. My income from the crew amounted to 30 dollars a
week and this had to cover food for three, plus fuel and oil. We
could get to Port Vila, anyhow.

7 November: A lovely hot dry day with a brisk 10-knot wind
from the east. We were away early and as we rounded Lunga
Point I told the others of the time the big ammunition dump
went up near here.

"There was this dump and the Yanks used to stroll around in
it, smoking their fat cigars and flipping matches about. Captured
Jap ammunition was the attraction, for by wrenching the shells
out, the brass cases could be salvaged as souvenirs. Well, one
day it blew up and there was a huge column of smoke, explo-
sions, and shells lobbing all over the place.

"The C.O. called me into his office and said the Americans
were convinced I'd started it off by dynamiting fish. This was
utter nonsense, of course, but it was sticky for a while.

"I used to wait till a landing barge nosed into the beach and
as the shoal fish were concentrated, would throw in a hand gren-
ade. Mills bombs were the best—they had more punch than the
smaller U.S. things. The skippers used to go berko, but I got a
lot of fish."

We put into Kirakira again and met our friend the Scots
doctor who was pleased about Cobber coming right. We had
lunch with the new district commissioner, a tall Welshman who
kept the winged radiator-cap of his Rolls-Royce on the mantle-
piece.

"My car's on blocks in Wales," he remarked. "This reminds
me of home."

We were taken to the little clubhouse, built native-style with
carvings on all the thick pillars supporting its heavy thatched
roof. Some were very strange, one depicting a man clasping a
shark around the body with his legs, and with his mouth pressed
to its anus.

"What's this represent?" I asked.

"Oh, some ancient folk legend," answered our host. "One of their warriors was saved from drowning by breathing that way!"

It was evening when we pulled out. Rough seas slowed us and we switched off one motor as we battled the waves. In the morning of the 9th we entered Utupua's large bay, after an excellent dive in the clear water and deep guts off the western entrance. Out of sheer high spirits I shot a shark and for a few moments had a great tow before the spear pulled out. Normally a powerhead's best, but this day foolish temptation got the better of me.

We slowly cruised Basilisk Harbour and stopped at a village to port as we entered. It was a quaint little place and we made friends with a young man who carried what appeared to be a child's toy bow and arrows. Gesturing for him to demonstrate his skill, we were amazed to see him drop a parrot in flight and hit smaller targets placed on trees 50 yards away.

We entered the tiny church of plaited pandanus leaves and palm fronds. Simple, crudely carved wooden pews lined each side of the hall, and crushed coral formed a clean raked floor. It was evening and the service about to begin. The church was filled, with the entire village attending. A native pastor led the service. His parrot reading of the lesson was almost incomprehensible with its curious pronunciations. The congregation, however, seemed to follow the proceedings and sang the hymns with gusto.

It was still a moving ceremony away out here on the fringe of the mighty Pacific, and we were a subdued trio who climbed into our bunks. We had seen their portable army transmitter and the entire island's medical kit proudly laid out for our admiration. There was something pathetically brave here; it could have been an expedition on the moon. The three basics for modern survival and meaning were the same.

In the morning a smiling native came on board with a bundle of clothes, a flea-covered pup and a trussed pig. Could we take him to Vanikoro, please? He'd been two years away from his village. We tied the scratching pet on to the rear platform, where the pig lay panting in the heat, put the bundle of grubby clothes in the dinghy and shoved off. It was only about 30 miles and soon we were chuffing through the channel. Our passenger was greeted with great enthusiasm. A small baby was shown him which, as far as we could gather, was not only a big surprise but something of an embarrassment. He gave me the impression he'd like to continue the voyage, but we bundled him over the side and moved on.

The Banks Group rose out of the sea. The *Pilot* said syphilis was rife here and we found the natives dull and apathetic at the one island we visited; just sittin' around doin' nuttin'. We sailed on all night and early in the morning of the 13th arrived off Pilot Island on the east coast of Espiritu Santo. The seas were rough and we'd been cruising on one motor. When I turned into Tambo Passage to take advantage of shelter behind Mavia and Aesi Islands, Big Stinky wouldn't start. We dropped anchor in the lee of Aesi and I discovered one of the crazy push-on terminals on the starter motor had become dislodged. Almost immediately we were off again, out through Diamond Passage into Scorff Passage and around into the Segond Channel, to anchor next to the trimaran *Kuokoa* from Honolulu.

We got talking, Jim Stuart, skipper of the *Kuokoa*, his wife and myself. About crews and the problems of confined living.

"We had a navigator—supposed to be hot stuff, or so he told us. Anyway, I got suspicious—we were seven days overdue sighting land and in the end this guy started going queer and I had to lock him in his cabin for three days. One of the kids peeped through the hatch and there he was, trying to eat dry rice. He had a fear we'd run out of food and insisted his share be given to him. We were 1000 miles off course when I took over."

I told some of my hairy stories of human shortcomings and we consoled each other with beer and tales of other Captain Blighs who on occasion fell foul of their crews:

Of the skipper who nearly had his boat confiscated when the "nice young crewman who grew pot plants in his cabin" was found to be cultivating marijuana. And the skipper who marched his crew off at revolver point on to a deserted island, after a mutiny, and reported them weeks later and 1000 miles away.

That night we had a pub crawl and as usual I wandered off and somehow got to one bar before the others. I couldn't get the barman to attend to me. He stood there polishing glasses and gazing at a group of men at the other end of the room. It was a dim and dingy place, with no women in sight. I sent a heavy ash tray zipping along the counter like a curling stone to wake him up, just as Rafe and Jorge arrived.

"I don't like your captain," said the barman, a mincing fellow. "He's a nasty man."

After a couple of rounds Jorge felt like other diversions. "Say, how do you get on for sex around here?"

"You don't have to talk like that! You've only got to ask nicely and I'm sure anyone here would oblige," simpered the barman.

21 November: The boys were too hung over to be of any use on the wheel or dive on the *Coolidge* so, taking first watch, I set off for Vila, which we reached after a choppy cruise down the west side of the group.

There I thoroughly checked over the motors and replaced the injectors. Reece suggested that I might take his garage foreman, George Santos, a Tongan, back to New Zealand, as I needed the cash and George had to leave the Hebrides for a few weeks while his work permit was renewed. I was introduced to George, a cheerful scallywag, and I liked him. A dark saturnine-looking chap came down to the boat and introduced himself. He was another West German. Horst wanted to get to New Caledonia and so he, too, was signed on. After refuelling with the "fares" in hand, we set off for the Loyalties.

CHAPTER FIFTEEN

This was Home . . .

By this time I was so cocky about the *Whai's* seaworthiness that weather forecasts meant only pleasant or unpleasant news and, as I was leaving regardless, they were superfluous. If a hurricane warning was out it would have held me back, but otherwise we just motored off. Sometimes it was almost like being in a submarine, there was so much water flying about, but with everything lashed down and the front seat of heavy plywood tied back over the front ports, we were safe enough.

We had a rough trip to the Loyalties, with head winds all the way. On the 22nd we hove-to off the northern tip of Uvea and went over the side into the magnificently clear waters. This must be one of the world's great spearfishing spots. We found a particularly productive area of deep long guts leading from the depths of the open sea to wind upwards in blue canyons in the coral reef.

Dozens of big brown salmonee hung above the coral lips and silver dots and fat parrotfish flippered along. A whole herd of huge bumpfish, most of them over 80 pounds in weight, cruised back and forth ejecting streams of coral debris from time to time. Sharks, too, patrolled the deeper water and rose to examine us coldly. There didn't appear to be any small fish at all in this happy hunting ground. George and Horst were no swimmers in this type of water and fear of sharks kept them in the dinghy. Horst, an arrogant type, took great exception to being called by one diver or another to "Come here, quick!" as they struggled with a fish before sharks could claim it.

From the depths a large, metallic blue-black fish soared straight towards me. Rafe saw it coming, but it flashed past him, turned and paused right in front of me. A tuna! I slammed a spear into it and the reaction was exactly the same as with a hard-hit kingfish. It stopped still, gasped convulsively with great gill plates distended and its mouth wide open. For a wonderful moment I thought I'd killed it, but suddenly, with a shake and heave, it was off. Off down to the bottom 50 feet below, and towing me behind.

I just had time to lock the reel with my free hand and hold on. At about 30 feet I knew I'd have to pay out line and make for the top for a breath of air. The fish was too powerful. Try as I might I couldn't control his rush for the coral ledges and rocks of the bottom. The braided nylon zipped through my fingers, cutting and burning as I reached the surface, gulped in air and locked the reel again, but scarcely had my weight come on the line before it went slack and I knew the fish had gone.

"That was terrific," shouted Rafe. "He was big! Bored straight down under a ledge and cut the cord."

I was fixing another spear and running slide when Rafe and Jorge came back—several big manta rays had flown up from the deeps flapping their huge wings with ponderous sweeps. And the sharks had become too cheeky and excited. We called it a day and motored past Turtle Island and across the lagoon.

In the morning George and Jorge went walking along a road which lined the magnificent 15-mile beach. Uvea is a typical atoll enclosing a large lagoon. I heard a story that many years ago a fishing party of young Polynesians had killed the un-popular son of their chief. Too frightened to return to their village, they fled across the ocean to land and settle on the northern tip of Uvea. To this day their descendants are quite different from the darker Melanesians scattered over the rest of the Island group.

When Horst had finished taking photos of the great churches of Uvea, he rounded up the others and returned to the *Whai*. There was a pretty fierce wind bending the palms and our craft was gently buffeted by catspaws which streaked across the nar-row strip of water between us and the shore. We secured and checked all the gear. It was going to be a rough night.

We left for New Caledonia about 1.30 p.m. and on clearing the shelter of the lagoon, struck into the heavy breaking seas whipped up by a 35-knot wind. There was nothing to do but cut one motor and slug it out. That night I discovered Horst had no more idea than a gorilla of steering by compass. I had to take him off as diplomatically as possible. As it was, Jorge took Horst's watch and didn't report a flashing light for some square-headed reason, and we nearly came to grief on New Caledonia's outer reef. Again I had cause to thank my sixth sense, which had saved us from disaster so often.

I altered course 10 degrees to port until we were well clear, and then 5 degrees to starboard. Daybreak found us some two hours behind schedule but true on course for the Havannah Passage. We made great time through the Woodin Passage—the tide rip was with us for a change—and so we entered Noumea's big lagoon.

John, the Cercle Nautique's secretary, was on the jetty to greet us. Noumea's water supply had just been turned on for the evening's ration, so we quickly hosed off the glistening cat and filled the tanks.

"Some say a missing person is jammed in the system somewhere—it has happened before," remarked John. But the water tasted fine and, anyway, we were too tired to care. I took a sleeping pill and collapsed for a glorious sleep. George disappeared ashore to see his ex-girlfriend.

25 November: A beautiful clear day and Joe Dreaux and his wife to welcome us. Reece had sent them a letter and here they were to ask us to dinner the next night. George was especially picked out for attention. He was an old friend. He told us how his Wallisian girl had asked him to come along and see her after her B.F. went to work.

"B.F.? George, you mean her Boy Friend?"

"No! Bloody Fool!" George laughed.

Excerpt from the *Whai's* log:

"I'm also sick of being asked when we are leaving Noumea. How in hell do I know? I have $55 for $175 worth of fuel plus $25 worth of groceries. Also Cobber and Bill might fly out to help crew across the Tasman. And what about the weather? Am trying to sell the Kestrel compass, gold watch and gas califont."

I went to the Shell agent and a perfect stranger in his office at the time offered to assist. I was quite flabbergasted. However, an Australian turned up and wanted to come over with us, so my troubles were over. Ray was a great mate and one of the most solid, dependable chaps I've ever met.

Horst left the boat, having got accommodation ashore. He was an odd one; one night I came on board to find three of them lolling back in the cabin in some sort of trance. The lights were out and on the table Horst's small tape deck was softly playing curious Indian sitar music. It was uncanny. I said, "What the hell's going on?" Jorge's eyes were open but they were all deeply unconscious. I switched off the machine and retired to my bunk. In the morning they were still there, but woke quite naturally and made no comment.

Noumea had turned sour for me. My favourite French restaurant had gone downhill and I was tired of exotic food, so the *Asia's* magnificent menu palled. The city was filled with metropolitan French, German technicians and tradesmen come out to build and staff the huge nickel works extensions, and food prices were sky high. Only the spearfishing was the same, but for once in my life I'd had my fill.

On 28 November we motored out from Noumea and set a course for Norfolk Island, almost 500 miles away. We had been watching the Southern Cross growing clearer each night as we headed south, but it wasn't until the 30th that it shone in all its beauty. The seas were still rough and the forecast for strong winds, decreasing, was for once spot on. As we surged and dipped to big ocean swells and pushed aside the breaking crests, I swotted again at my navigation form. I hadn't had reason to take sun shots since leaving Waigeo Island. At Noumea's meteorological station I had re-set my Acutron watch so all that remained was to be careful and follow my own instructions.

The wind died gradually and we were able to increase speed a little. On 1 December several of the pretty little white terns from Norfolk came out to greet us and soon after we dropped anchor at Tablet Bay. It was midday as we rowed ashore, all except Rafe who had seen enough of Norfolk and volunteered to keep watch on the *Whai*.

I had to get the radio fixed, as it was necessary to be in contact with friends at home who would be interested in our E.T.A. I drove out to the aerodrome and the local electronics expert. I needed a fresh weather forecast, too, as the last span of ocean would probably be the most dicey of the trip. I'd had one experience of needing urgent help in those waters when on the *Willomee* and we'd sunk off Whangarei after a storm had sprung the hull timbers.

Next day we set off. The wind had died to about ten knots. Short heavy seas made the going uncomfortable for a time, but they gave way to a long easy swell giving the cat a lazy sleep-inducing motion. George spent most of his time below when he wasn't eating gargantuan meals. For such a skinny chap, he was a marvel. Aussie was enjoying himself. He'd had a pretty strenuous time in Noumea and relished the cruise, even tricks at the wheel which had long since ceased to entertain Jorge, Rafe or myself.

It was early morning on 4 December. The sea had flattened completely during the night and a heavy haze covered the horizon. I was sure of a good landfall because dead ahead a steamer was ploughing through the blue towards us.

"Here's our first New Zealand ship," I called.

But it was a Japanese trawler down to its Plimsoll marks and on its way home.

"Pinching our bloody fish! Wouldn't it rock you! The first ship we see and it has to be one of theirs. I ask you!"

The *Tokyo Maru 41* surged on without a soul on deck to give us a friendly greeting.

5 December, 0645: Land ho! Above a thick haze the high hills of Aotearoa showed in a faint outline.

"I think it's Cape Kari Kari—I meant to hit Cape Brett, but we can check when closer."

The mists cleared and over the sparkling sea the odd shark fin sliced. A sunfish waggled its flabby dorsal and I knew we were home. Gulls rose to fly from our path to circle and ride the air waves above *Whai's* stern. Ashore the hills grew brown and steep.

A small cabin cruiser with big-game outriggers was fishing "on the drift" and I motored over in a broad sweep.

"I know this is New Zealand," I called, "but whereabouts?" My little joke meant nothing to them.

"Whangaroa," a fisherman replied, pointing to the craggy entrance. As we passed across their bows and set the launch rocking, our fantastic cruise became unreal, as if it had never been. This was home and everything matter of fact and orderly.

Cape Brett lighthouse came into view, and Piercy Island.

"There's a hole through Piercy," I remarked. "Used to take my *Tempest* through it just for kicks."

As we drew nearer I could see the narrow gap and steered towards it.

"God! You'll never make it!" Rafe shouted.

"Too late now," I said as a swell lifted us up and the *Whai* almost tobogganed into the tunnel.

"That's the last time I'll do that!" I vowed, shaken by the experience.

George grinned away; Ray laughed. But Jorge said, "You're mad!" and Rafe, "Best part of the trip!"

The radio was on the blink again, giving intermittent signals, crackling with static. This was a blow, as my plans for arrival were now in jeopardy. I wanted Mike to be on hand, and Bill, too. Both had left a lot of gear on board and I didn't even know what they had to declare.

Whangarei was to be my port of entry and as we arrived off Tutukaka in the dark, I shut off the motors and drifted while I studied the situation. We'd get into port about midnight if we continued, and technically it could be awkward hanging around in that crowded basin or trying to moor in the dark. I'd promised Mike and Bill that I'd give them some warning, but how?

"We'll put into Tutukaka so I can use the 'phone. Any of you guys feel sick or anything? Put out your tongues."

They all felt and looked O.K. As we'd been at sea over eight days I felt confident that there would be no problems. The short stop at Norfolk couldn't have mattered, as the hard stuff would have effectively inhibited all normal germs.

"Keep to yourselves and don't get into trouble!" I admonished them as we rowed ashore. We trooped through the soft darkness to the pub whose welcoming lights had attracted us like moths. Through the windows I could see my old mate Fred Cotterill breasting the bar.

"I can't come in. They'll know me. I'll use the 'phone down at the corner. Now watch it and come out just before closing time!"

But the pay-phone was out of order as usual, and I had to enter the hotel and use their desk-phone.

"Haven't I seen you before?" asked the woman who collected the toll charge.

"Probably," I muttered and slunk out. I could see George with a great grin on his brown face downing half a pint. It was lonely out in the night with only the moreporks calling, and the light on the end of the jetty for company.

All the crew were fast asleep when I took the *Whai* down the coast on the last leg of the journey. I wanted to savour this part alone.

Bream Head loomed in front, with the splendid crags of Manaia rearing like the ramparts of some ancient castle. The oil refinery's great flare off Marsden Point sent waves of orange light across the waters to flicker and fade on the hills across the channel.

With red to port and winking green flasher to starboard, the *Whai* purred on. Past Snake Bank, where we had grounded so long ago, past Manganese Point and past the glitter of Onerahi's street lamps. Then we were in the narrow town channel and then the basin of Oram's yard.

I eased the cat in very gently past the sleeping yachts and power boats tethered to floating pontoons. The motors' rumble died. The journey was over.

In the cold light of dawn I wandered along the waterfront looking for a 'phone to use to advise the authorities of our arrival. I had only centavos from the Philippines, and Australian coins, but they wouldn't stuff into the meter. New Hebridean coins were too large, the Noumean too skinny.

In desperation I dialled "o" and explained my fix to the operator. She was a doll and had me connected to the harbour watch office at Marsden—for free.

"I'll tell 'em you've arrived and are at Oram's," the voice said. "They're not open yet, but you stay on your boat until they arrive."

I was too excited to sleep and fussed about, making up a list of items to declare. I hadn't much; Lord only knew what the others had. At seven, I dug them out of bed.

"Come on you blokes, we're home! Let's get the boat washed down and the tanks filled up. After that we'll clean up inside ready for the Customs."

At about 7.30 an official came on board waving a sheaf of papers.

"Skipper, you get your crew to fill these in and we'll pick them up about 6.30 tonight."

"Aw, heck! We've just spent eight days at sea—we're tired and dirty. Can't we go ashore?"

The Customs officer looked me in the eye.

"We've got the *Mariposa* coming into Opua. All our staff will be occupied and we can't fix you up till we get back."

"Well, damn it, this is ridiculous! We've bugger-all to declare. How about letting us off to clean up?"

There was a long pause. The impossibility of policing us was obvious.

"Oh, well, get your medical clearance first. See that all your crew are back on board by 6.30." And with that he was gone.

The port medico asked, "Does everyone feel well? No sickness recently? Let me see your tongues." And five tongues poked out.

And the same to all the doubters, I thought with great satisfaction, who said we'd never do it.

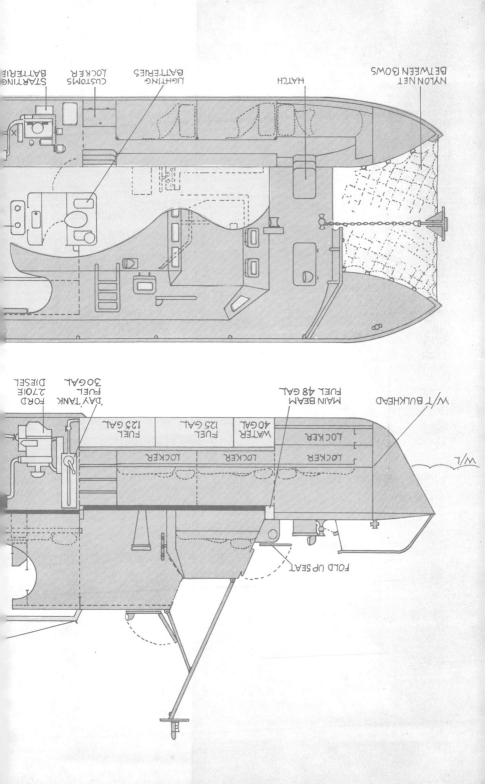